"Mafia? What's the Mafia? There is not a Mafia."

—Joe Colombo

● ● ●

Does the Mafia really exist?
Yes! And this book proves it.

Mafia!

Fred J. Cook

ILLUSTRATED WITH PHOTOGRAPHS

CORONET BOOKS
Hodder Fawcett Ltd., London

Photographs by permission of United Press
International, World-wide Photos, Associated
Press and the New York Daily News
Copyright © 1973 by Fred J. Cook
First published by Fawcett Publications, Inc.,
New York, 1973
Coronet edition 1973

Printed and bound in Great Britain for
Coronet Books,
Hodder Fawcett Ltd,
St. Paul's House, Warwick Lane,
London, EC4P 4AH
by Hazell Watson & Viney Ltd,
Aylesbury, Bucks

ISBN 0 340 17866 3

Contents

Photographs follow page 68 and page 188.

MAFIA!

1.

The Mafia at War

The night of April 6, 1972, was a big one for Joey Gallo, the new gangster idol of chic New York society. It was also a big night in the history of the New York Mafia—a kind of watershed that led to a new carnival of murder, reminiscent of the gory events some forty years earlier in what history calls The Night of the Sicilian Vespers.

For Joey Gallo it was a celebration time. It was his forty-third birthday, and Joey decided it was an occasion to kick up his heels with some élan. His birthday party included: his bride of three weeks, a buxom and beautiful brunette, the former Sina Essery; Sina's daughter, Lisa, 10; Joey's sister, Mrs. Carmella Fiorella; Peter ("Pete the Greek") Diapioulas, 40, who was later to be described as Joey's bodyguard; and Peter's friend, Edith Russo.

Togged out in finery befitting such a celebration—witnesses would later recall especially Diapioulas' blue and white check double-knit suit—the party descended upon the swank Copacabana nightclub, once the favorite watering place of gangster overlord Frank Costello. Comedian Don Rickles was opening at the Copa that night, and Joey Gallo and his party—spotted at a prominent table on the mezzanine—drank, dined, and held court.

Jerry Orbach, the actor who played a gangster role in the film version of Jimmy Breslin's spoof, *The Gang That Couldn't Shoot Straight,* was there. So was his wife, Marta Curro, a writer who had become so enchanted with Joey that she was collaborating with him on his memoirs, built around the theme, "the gangster who went straight." Both went over to chat with Joey and offer birthday felicitations. Columnist Earl Wilson introduced his wife to Joey, who, he later reported, "overwhelmed her with his cordiality and courtesy." By about four o'clock in the morning of April 7, the crowd in the Copa had thinned out so that there was no one left to overwhelm; but this was a big night for Joey Gallo, and he was still going strong.

He left the nightclub with his party and drove down to Manhattan's Lower East Side. There, in the section known as Little Italy, Joey spotted Umberto's Clam House on the northwest corner of Mulberry and Hester Streets. The recently opened restaurant specialized in scungilli, fried shrimps, and other Italian seafood delicacies. Joey's mouth began to water, and he escorted his celebrating party into Umberto's, where they seated themselves in heavy captain's chairs around the butcher block tables that are a feature of the place.

There were only a few patrons at this late hour, and no one paid any attention when one of them quietly paid his bill and slipped out. Joey, after seeing his group comfortably settled, excused himself and went to the men's room. He was gone so long that his sister, Carmella, began to worry, but Diapioulas reassured her.

"I know what I'm doing," he said, a memorable line that was soon to be invested with ironic overtones. . . .

It would be difficult to imagine a less likely candidate for lionization by sophisticated New York society than Joseph ("Crazy Joe") Gallo. He had been the reckless and

savage stormy petrel around whom had swirled one of
the bloodiest gang feuds of the early 1960s—the Gallo–
Profaci war. This had been a conflict in which all the
noblest traditions of the Mafia had been on display. There
had been kidnappings of mob leaders; the exercise of the
Mafia's favorite tactic—the double-cross, a delightful device by which a man's best friend becomes his executioner;
rival armies "going to the mat," holed up in fortress dor-
mitories; and, of course, shootings of the unwary and
murders galore.

Crazy Joe Gallo had swaggered through it all, defy-
ing the laws of probability regarding his longevity. Before
the unpleasantness broke out, he had earned for himself
an awesome reputation as one of the principal enforcers in
the stable of veteran Mafia chieftain, Joseph Profaci,
sometimes called "The Olive Oil King." Crazy Joe in
those brawling years had acquired the kind of police
record that distinguishes the up-and-coming gangster who
has the proper high connections. He had been arrested a
score of times for everything from vagrancy to assault,
rape, and extortion, but he had suffered not a single conviction.

One of the most feared and dreaded hoodlums in the
Brooklyn spawning grounds that had produced Al Capone
and Murder, Inc., Crazy Joe did not have the physique of
a gorilla. He stood only some five feet six or seven. He had
light brown, thinning hair slicked straight back from a
high forehead. His deep-set blue eyes seemed remote,
cold, impersonal. A mole marred his left cheek. His wide
lips, except when he was talking, seemed oddly clamped.
High cheekbones, the dour downward slant of his face, the
hard eyes and the clamped lips typecast him perfectly, had
he been an actor, for the role of Dracula. When those wide
lips broke into a face-splitting smile of overdone joviality,
they exposed a row of strong white teeth that seemed to fit
perfectly with the image of a sinister figure just risen from
the crypt.

Flash and brashness, a breeziness that nothing could
faze, seemed to characterize Joey Gallo. Assistant Chief

Inspector Raymond V. Martin, then in charge of Brooklyn South detectives, recalled his first meeting with the gangster at the outbreak of the Gallo–Profaci war. Crazy Joe jumped to his feet, held out his hand, and said: "It's a real pleasure to meet you, Inspector." Martin wasn't so pleased. He ignored the hand. In the book he later wrote, *Revolt in the Mafia,* the inspector gave this description of Crazy Joe: "He was wearing a black double-breasted suit with white pearl buttons, a black homburg hat, and imported pointed shoes.

"'You look like a salesman,'" Martin told him.

"'Joey Gallo neighed like a horse,'" Martin wrote. "'Not a salesman,' he said, 'but I always thought I would make a good public relations man.'"

He might have been right, for Joe had the knack of coining phrases memorable for their unique twist and pungent humor. But destiny had decreed he was to be a man of violence, not of words. Crime had twisted his psyche like a pretzel, never to be straightened out; and though his standard act was wisecracking and impersonating the likable buffoon, he remained in Inspector Martin's words "a savage."

Both the kibitzer and the savage were on display in those early days of Gallo's career. In 1958 Robert F. Kennedy, then attorney for the McClellan committee of the U.S. Senate, summoned Crazy Joe to Washington, along with his brothers, Larry and Albert, who was also known as Kid Blast. No one who was there ever forgot Crazy Joe's performance.

He waltzed into Kennedy's office and wisecracked: "Nice carpet ya got here, kid. Be good for a crap game." He frisked a visitor to make certain the man wasn't carrying a rod; he explained that this unusual action was just a precaution. In case someone should try to do in the distinguished committee counsel, he said, he didn't want it to happen while he was there and could be blamed for it. Taking a fancy to one of Kennedy's pretty young secretaries, he offered the girl a job with Gallo enterprises—her salary to be as much as she could steal from the till.

On the witness stand, it was another story. The Gallos all claimed the privilege of the Fifth Amendment against possible self-incrimination, and Kennedy, a tough cross-examiner, couldn't get to first base with them. Kennedy grumped later that they were the toughest bunch of hoods he had ever tried to interrogate, and Crazy Joe accepted the verdict like a man who had just been awarded the Congressional Medal of Honor. Bobby Kennedy was so right, he said—a very perceptive man—and he, Joey Gallo, liked him very much.

There was no question about the toughness. Crazy Joe was so inventive he perfected new, unique dimensions of terror. He kept a lioness named Cleo locked in the basement of Gallo headquarters at 49-51 President Street, near the South Brooklyn waterfront. Cleo came in handy whenever Crazy Joe was trying to shake down a victim who was putting up some resistance. On such occasions, Joe would open the cellar door and toss Cleo a hunk of meat. The lioness would roar her appreciation, and it was an obdurate man indeed who failed to get the message.

Some of Crazy Joe's other methods were more personal and more direct. "I knew of one case," Inspector Martin wrote, "where Joey held another man's forearm between his hands and broke the bone over the edge of an office desk, as a way of collecting a debt owed to his combination. The man told the story to one of my detectives but he was too frightened to sign a complaint lest he be killed. He was killed later, anyway."

The Gallo-Profaci war crimped Crazy Joe's style a bit. It was hard for the Gallos to manage a swatch of lucrative rackets when they were cooped up in what became known as The Dormitory on President Street. Even so, even under such circumstances, Joey was irrepressible. He said, in effect, "The hell with it," and rented an apartment for himself and his wife in Manhattan's Greenwich Village. There the couple went nightclubbing, living the gay life so openly that reporters who bumped into them at various bars were amazed. Wasn't Joey afraid of being bumped off? He just laughed and coined one of those spontaneous phrases for which he was noted. "I'm afraid of just one man—that [Russian Premier] Khrushchev, he's nuts blowing off all them atom bombs."

When questioned about his long police record, he was scornful—and picturesque. "The cops say I've been picked up 15 to 17 times—that's junk," he said. "I been picked up maybe 150 times, only they never made a record. I been worked over for nothing until my hat sits on my head like it belongs to a midget."

When Crazy Joe uttered those inspired lines, he was correct, but he was soon to lose his immunity. The pressures of the Profaci feud were strangling the Gallo gang financially, and Joey, who hadn't been nicknamed "Crazy" for nothing, was driven to a dangerous expedient. He decided to cut himself in for a half-interest in a Manhattan café where he had been cavorting. The owner hesitated, understandably, about giving Crazy Joe fifty percent of his going concern just for the honor of being associated with the Gallo name. The café owner tried to stall; and when Crazy Joe came back for his answer, the man still hesitated and asked for more time to think the proposition over.

"Sure," said Crazy Joe, "take three months in the hospital on me."

Unfortunately for him, his intended victim had alerted the office of District Attorney Frank Hogan, and three detectives were sitting at a table within easy earshot. As a result, that little bit of overheard repartee sent Crazy Joe to Attica State Prison to serve a term of seven to fourteen years. . . .

When Joey Gallo came out of prison in 1971 after spending some nine years behind bars, he seemed like a man who had changed his skin. He was, according to the legend New York society bought so wholeheartedly, a totally reformed character. He was now Mr. Joseph Gallo, never Crazy Joe; that odious nickname from his bold, bad past was never mentioned. He sang one invariable refrain: No more rackets for me. Over and over again, he repeated the lines he told Earl Wilson in one interview: "I'll never go back there [meaning the rackets]. I think there is nothing there for me but death."

He announced he was going to write his memoirs with the assistance of Mrs. Orbach, and Viking Press, one of the more prestigious New York publishing houses, was scheduled to give the public this account of how the toughest and most unpredictable bad guy in Brooklyn had discovered conscience in prison and had cultivated his mind with Camus and Sartre.

Joey's entrée into chic New York circles had been gained simply by making a telephone call to the Orbachs. Someone had told him, he said, that Jerry had done such a great job in *The Gang That Couldn't Shoot Straight* that Joey would like to meet the Orbachs.

"We weren't sure what to do at first," Mrs. Orbach said afterwards. "We wanted to meet him—more out of curiosity than anything else."

Nevertheless, so the story goes, the Orbachs checked with a detective who was supposed to know. Was it really true that Joey Gallo had given up the rackets? The detective is said to have assured them that it was indeed so; that all the crooked twists in Gallo's nature had been straightened out by his therapeutic stay in Attica. It was an expert opinion that will never qualify the nameless sleuth for the police department's highest award, the Medal of Honor; but the Orbachs, bolstered by the verdict, had dinner with Mr. Joseph Gallo.

They found him "brilliant" and "charming"—words that were to be repeated ad nauseam in coming months. This was, perhaps, not totally unusual. Society circles, possibly bored with the vapidity of jet-set personages, have a long record of falling in love with gangster chic. There was a time, not so many years ago, when some of the most powerful businessmen and some of the mayors of New York fawned on Frank Costello; and, before that, screen-siren Jean Harlow and half of Hollywood practically worshipped the ruthless, sinister, lethal Bugsy Siegel, who, even while he was being lionized, was busy shaking down everyone who could be shook. Toughness, it seems, creates its own cult, and the Park Avenue swirl into which the Orbachs introduced their new paragon of reformation quickly became enamored of the killer turned intellectual philosopher.

It began that first night. Mr. Gallo asked Mrs. Orbach whether she preferred Camus or Sartre. She was so astonished, as she said later, that "I almost fell into a plate of spaghetti."

Imagine a gangster debating the merits of two French intellectual writers like Camus and Sartre! Just imagine it!

"I said I preferred Camus," Mrs. Orbach recalled. "He said he preferred Sartre. Joey said he thought Camus was suicidal and Joey liked survivors.

"I challenged him on Camus being suicidal. He referred to the auto accident in which Camus was killed and said that anybody who went in a car with somebody driving that fast was suicidal."

After that first dinner meeting, it got to be a habit for Gallo to drop in at the Orbachs' townhouse late at night for a cup of coffee laced with anisette or brandy. The actor and his wife introduced him to a limited number of friends in their circle. He became acquainted with Thomas H. Guinzburg, publisher of Viking, and once dropped spaghetti on Guinzburg's shoes. He played pool with Bruce Jay Friedman's sons. He once called actress Joan Hackett "a broad," and she loved it. It became quite the "in" thing in certain New York circles to go to the Orbachs' regular five o'clock Sunday "brunches" and converse about the higher things of life with Mr. Joseph Gallo.

When the parties were in full swing, Gallo would sometimes sidle over to one of the Orbachs' brocade sofas and engage one of the guests in philosophical discussion. Mrs. John Barry Ryan III—the charming "D.D." of the society columns—recalled an occasion in which Gallo impressed her during one of his long sofa-talks. "He was as bright and interesting as people said," she averred. "He'd done a lot of thinking. It was nice to talk to somebody who'd had time to think." Yes, but what did he say?

"Well, I know it's a cliché," Mrs. Ryan admitted, "but we talked about life. He knew so much about life's value. . . ."

It is perhaps an indication that Joey Gallo, the professional con man, was giving New York society a snow job; for it was remarkable that, afterwards, all those persons who found him so "charming" and "brilliant"—even "shy"—could not remember a single thing he ever said that, put down in cold print, would indicate either charm or brilliance.

Yet the impact of the new Gallo personality was overwhelming, so much so, indeed, that his wedding to Sina Essery became an "in" circle social event. Joey's first marriage had foundered on the rock of his prison sentence, but he had renewed his acquaintance with Sina, a dental assistant whom he had met briefly in his free-wheeling, pre-sentence days. And so, when it came time for Joey to marry again, the ceremony was performed in the Orbachs' townhouse, with Allan Jones singing "The Lord's Prayer." In the days following, there were two small dinner parties at which the newlyweds were guests, one at the Guinzburgs', the other at the Ben Gazzaras'.

Joey Gallo was starring in a new role, the chic gangster of New York society—and then he stopped off at Umberto's Clam House. . . .

The food was good. Joey and his party ordered scungilli, calamari, and mussels, with wine to go with the food. About 5:30 A.M. Joey, relaxed and jovial, ordered a second round of food and drinks. He and his guests were seated at two butcher-block tables at the rear of the restaurant, their backs to an inconspicuous side door. This now burst open, and a stocky man strode in.

Witnesses later described him as about five feet eight, with black hair, balding at the front. He had a .38 caliber revolver in his hand, and he began shooting.

"You son of a bitch!" Joey shouted.

He swept his arms wide on either side, knocking his sister and Diapioulas, of "I know what I am doing" fame, off their chairs and onto the floor out of the line of fire. Other customers dove for the floor in panic; tables and chairs overturned; and spilled ketchup and hot tomato sauce ran out in a red stream, looking like blood.

Gallo, hit and hit again, staggered to his feet and tried to pursue the gunman, who knocked over tables himself as he fled through the front door. The pursuing Joey crashed through the glass, weaved some fifteen feet out into the street and collapsed in the middle of the Hester-Mulberry intersection. He had been struck three times. One shot penetrated his left buttock; a second shattered his left elbow; the third ripped into his left shoulder, angling downward and severing the aorta, the great artery of the heart. By the time he fell to the street, he was dead.

His killer escaped in a waiting car. A small army of police, rushing from headquarters a block away, were soon on the scene and discovered ample evidence that the rub-out had been a team job. Some twenty shots had winged back and forth, and the front of the restaurant and Graziano's funeral home across the street had been pock-marked by the wild-flying slugs. Yet only one other person had been injured—Diapioulas, whose left thigh had been grazed by a bullet.

Joey Gallo's funeral was in subdued style for such underworld affairs. There was no mile-long cortege, no outpouring of gangster legions to honor the departed brother. Mafia chiefs and their underlings pointedly boycotted the obsequies, a mark of disrespect in a society in which it is not unusual for the killers to shed their tears beside members of the bereaved family. The Gallos, of course, said good-bye to Joey in the best style they could muster. He went to his final rest in a $5,000 coffin. And some fifty mourners—members of his family, his mob followers, and a few of his new society friends like the Orbachs—filed slowly past and dropped flowers on his catafalque.

His mother, Mrs. Mary Gallo, hurled herself on the gilded coffin, sobbing: "My baby, my son." Then she was led gently away to her waiting Cadillac.

Joey's sister, Carmella, was even more emotional. Sobbing, half hysterical, she screamed: "The streets are going to run red with blood, Joey."

And she was right.

Within five weeks, ten men were executed in gangland style. And this was not all. The killings continued, keeping pace with time and claiming as the most notable victim Thomas ("Tommy Ryan") Eboli, an old-line Mafioso and part-ruler of one of the five Mafia clans that carve up the rackets of New York and infiltrate legitimate businesses.

It has become a popular fad of late to belittle the importance of the Mafia and even at times to deny that it exists except as a mirage in the minds of some aging dons ruminating on past glories. The ploy plays on a fundamental flaw in the American character—on the simple, blind faith that this is the best of all possible nations and that, therefore, nothing quite so evil or so powerful as the Mafia could possibly have survived for so long in such elysian surroundings. When gang wars break out in murderous refutation of the no-Mafia myth, it is the custom to shrug and dismiss the sanguinary events as matters of little importance. "Who cares if the rats knock each other off?" So goes the standard rationalization used to justify an almost universal apathy.

This apathy, based in part on incredulity, is the best protection the Mafia has. As long as the reality is not believed, the Mafia can go right on operating, handling such fantastic sums of money, wielding such incredible influence, that the average man, whose mind has difficulty grasping the meaning of money running beyond six figures, is tempted to dismiss the whole business as a fairy tale made up by journalists. But it is no fairy tale, and the documented record shows it. Take just a few examples:

● John F. Kennedy International Airport in New York City, the largest air cargo terminal in the world, has been the playground of five Mafia families for years; and the pilferage runs into millions of dollars annually. The same mobs control most of the waterfront of the nation's largest ports, and thefts of cargo by the truckload are not uncommon. A superbly organized underworld fencing system funnels the stolen loot back into the channels of trade; insurance companies, victimized by the rackets, raise their rates; legitimate businesses have to make up their losses by passing the cost on to the consumer who, as a consequence pays millions of dollars more a year for virtually everything he buys from foodstuffs to clothing to television sets.

• One investigation disclosed that more than fifty Mafia figures from twelve organized crime syndicates were involved in the management of some thirty food and food-processing companies, with revenues of more than $400 million annually. From southern New Jersey down through the Middle Atlantic states to Virginia and West Virginia, supermarket customers bought the dairy products produced by these firms. The Mafia supermarket ploy involved more than food. When the Atlantic and Pacific Tea Company refused to handle a mob-produced detergent found substandard by its testing laboratory, A & P supermarkets were burned down at a loss of sixty million dollars; two A & P store managers were murdered, others beaten, and two committed suicide. This was the mob's version of the "hard sell."

• Wall Street has been plundered in recent years through the thefts of securities worth billions of dollars, all of which are funneled through an intricate underworld chain until they can be sold or used as collateral for loans that will never be repaid. Former Attorney General John N. Mitchell told a U.S. Senate Committee in 1971 that, in the previous two years alone, such security losses had amounted to $500 million. Investigators of the McClellan crime committee of the U.S. Senate have concluded after a two-year investigation that a worldwide conspiracy, masterminded by Mafia figures and their allies, has feasted on some *$25 billion* worth of stolen or counterfeit securities. Counterfeit bond and stock certificates have been put up by mob front men as securities for loans from banks and

lending institutions, and some of the lenders, who accepted the spurious paper in good faith, have been ruined.

Summing up such evidence of mob influence, President
Lyndon B. Johnson's Commission on Law Enforcement
and the Aministration of Justice wrote in 1967:

> . . . Organized crime exists by virtue of the power it
> purchases with its money. The millions of dollars it can
> invest in narcotics or use for layoff money give it power
> over the lives of thousands of people and over the quality
> of life in whole neighborhoods. The millions of dollars it
> can throw into the legitimate economic system give it
> power to manipulate the price of shares on the stock
> market, to raise or lower the price of retail merchandise,
> to determine whether entire industries are union or non-
> union, to make it easier or harder for businessmen to
> continue in business.
> The millions of dollars it can spend on corrupting pub-
> lic officials may give it the power to maim or murder
> people inside or outside the organization with impunity,
> to extort money from businessmen, to conduct businesses
> in such fields as liquor, meat, or drugs without regard to
> administrative regulations, to avoid payment of income
> taxes, or to secure public works contracts without com-
> petitive bidding.

The commission's special task force on organized crime
was even more specific. It examined the business activities
of seventy-five identified Mafia leaders who met at the
much-publicized grand council of the clan at Apalachin,
N.Y., in 1957. It reported that "at least nine were in the
coin-operated machine industry, sixteen were in the garment industry, ten owned grocery stores, seventeen owned
bars or restaurants, eleven were in the olive oil and
cheese business, and nine were in the construction business. Others were involved in automobile agencies, coal
companies, entertainment, funeral homes, ownership of
horses and racetracks, linen and laundry enterprises,
trucking, waterfront activities and bakeries.

"Today, the kinds of production and service industries and businesses that organized crime controls or has invested in range from accounting firms to yeast manufacturing. One criminal syndicate alone has real estate interests with an estimated value of $300 million. In a few instances, racketeers control nationwide manufacturing and service industries with known and respected brand names."

Such detailed analyses make clear that the Mafia has infiltrated and exercises a tremendous influence over almost every aspect of American life. How has it gained such power? What are the sources of its seemingly inexhaustible reservoir of cash?

Investigations ever since the Kefauver probe of 1950-51 have all concluded that syndicate crime, dominated by the Mafia, feeds on these principal sources: gambling, narcotics, loan sharking. The Federal Bureau of Investigation has repeatedly estimated the gross take of organized crime from all sources to be in excess of *$20 billion* a year, a figure that is roughly comparable to the wholesale value of all passenger cars produced by the automobile industry, a bellwether of the national economy. The President's Crime Commission in 1967 estimated that the gross profit from gambling rackets alone was between $6 billion and $7 billion annually.

For those who have difficulty comprehending the enormity of one billion dollars, let alone six or seven, the best down-to-earth illustration of the manner in which a buck made here grows into a million there is doubtless the loan-sharking racket. This began as the six-for-five business. "You loan me five dollars this Friday, I'll pay you six dollars next week"—a profit of 20 percent *a week* for the shark. It is easy to understand how a few thousand dollars, returning 20 percent a week, every week of the year, could build in a remarkably short space of time into some mighty fancy cash. The New York State Commission of Investigation in one of its many probes produced this illustration: about 1960 a major Mafia loan shark put $500,000 to work; four years later that half-million had grown into $7.5 million. One of Frank Hogan's assistant district attorneys testified that, in New York City alone, there were "at least ten men comparable to him. A loan shark that we know lent a million dollars in the morning and a million dollars in the afternoon." One loan-sharking combination, a witness testified, had $5 million "on the street" at one time.

One New York builder needed $1 million to finance a large construction project. Unable to raise this amount through legitimate channels, he went to a syndicate shark —and got it. When he began to talk about collateral to guarantee the loan, the shark cut him short.

"Your body is your collateral," he said.

A true and terrifying line. Not many Mafiosi have the ingenuity of Joey Gallo, who kept a roaring lion handy, but they employ a sadism that strikes abject terror into the hearts of potential victims. A borrower never goes into bankruptcy with the Mafia; he pays by surrendering his business, or having his limbs broken one by one, or going in the end to the most horrible death the mind of a fiend can envision. In the movies about the Mafia the killing is always swift and somehow justified; the guys who get it really deserved it in spades. In the real world, however, many who get it don't deserve it at all; in the real world, all too often, murder is to enjoy and horror is escalated.

A classic illustration is a bit of overheard conversation between two "soldiers" in the family of Chicago Mafia boss Sam Giancana. The soldiers—James ("Turk") Torello and Fiore ("Fifi") Buccieri—were telling a friend with obvious relish how they had dispatched one William ("Action") Jackson, who weighed 350 pounds.

> TORELLO: Jackson was hung up on that meat hook. He was so fucking heavy he bent it. He was on that thing three days before he croaked.
> BUCCIERI (*giggling*): Jackie, you shoulda seen the guy. Like an *elephant,* he was, and when Jimmy hit him in the balls with that electric prod. . . .

TORELLO: He was floppin' around on the hook, Jackie. We tossed water on him to give the prod a better charge, and he's screamin'. . . .

No, the Mafia is not composed of nice gentlemen gangsters—and it is decidedly for real. . . .

The reality was borne in upon New Yorkers again, as it had been many times in the past, by the rash of slayings that followed the execution of Joey Gallo. The murder in Umberto's Clam House touched off a chain of events that had the New York underworld writhing in mysterious and bloody convulsions. By mid-August there had been twenty gangland-style slayings. And then on the Friday night of August 11, 1972, there were two more—two that demonstrated it is not just "the rats" who suffer when gangland war breaks out.

On that night four executives in the wholesale meat business took their wives out to dine, as they often did on Friday nights, at the Neapolitan Noodle at 320 East 79th Street. The restaurant was full, and the couples had to wait for a table. They repaired to the bar, which was crowded, too, and husbands and wives became separated. When four men moved away from one section of the bar, the husbands slid into the vacated seats. Some distance away from them, down at the end of the bar, an unobtrusive man, bulky, fiftyish, sat quietly sipping Scotch and water. After a wait of several minutes, the four meat company executives were told that their table was ready, and they rose to leave the bar.

As they did, the Scotch drinker whipped out two .38 caliber revolvers and began firing. He touched off nine shots in rapid-fire succession, then turned, walked out into the street, and vanished.

Behind him on the floor of the Neapolitan Noodle—dead—were Sheldon Epstein, 40, of New Rochelle, and Max Tekelch, 48, of Woodmere, LI. One of their companions—Leon Schneider, 48, of East Meadow, L.I.—had been struck by four bullets and was rushed to a hospital for emergency surgery. The fourth man, Jack Forem, 55, of Brooklyn, had escaped lightly; a bullet had just grazed his leg.

The tragedy, New York police said, was the result of mistaken identity. The gunman's intended victims had been four of the top figures of the Joseph Colombo Mafia family (formerly known as the Profaci family), generally considered the second most powerful of the Mafia families of New York. The four seats at the bar which the meat company executives had had the misfortune to fill had just been abandoned by Alphonse ("Alley Boy") Persico, the older brother of Carmine ("The Snake") Persico, reputedly the top gun of the Colombo mob; The Snake's son, also named Alphonse; Jerry Langella, described as Alley Boy's bodyguard; and a fourth man, who remained unnamed.

Calling the mistaken-identity murders a "terrible, frightening crime," New York Police Commissioner Patrick V. Murphy said that his worst fears had come true— "that innocent people would be caught in a gangland crossfire and be killed or wounded. . . ."

There was plenty of historic precedent for the commissioner's apprehension. Time and again, when gangland has indulged in one of its periodic bloodlettings, it is not just "the rats" who have paid the price, but the innocent—a child, a bystander, a meat company executive, anyone who happens to get in the way of the erratic, indiscriminate bullets.

It has been that way ever since the days of Prohibition, when the Mafia acquired its awesome power; and so it is time—and more than time—to ask the questions: Just what is the Mafia? How is it organized? How has it grown?

2.

Roots of the Mafia

The secret criminal society known as the Mafia has its roots deep in the tortured soil of the Sicily of centuries past. The island in the Mediterranean off the tip of the Italian boot, where American soldiers stormed ashore in World War II, has been almost since the beginning of time the chattel of conquerors. Sicilian slaves made the bread used by Roman armies in the conquests of Gaul and Britain. Invader after invader swarmed over the island—Normans, Germans, Frenchmen, Aragonese, Spaniards, the Bourbons, and finally the black marauders of the Inquisition.

For some two thousand years, native Sicilians were always trampled under some conqueror's heel. Their lands and goods were appropriated; wives and daughters spirited away. Against such injustices, there was no recourse, for law and justice were always the tools of rulers turned legal brigands. The agony of the island's inhabitants probably reached its peak during the seemingly endless three centuries of rape and pillage by the black-cowled familiars of the Inquisition.

The Holy Office, its every deed sanctified by the church, became even more voracious and insatiable than it had been in Spain. Heresy was its weapon, and against this charge there was no defense. To be accused was to be con-

27

victed. Norman Lewis in *The Honored Society,* the best
account of the Sicilian Mafia, has given this description:
". . . Arrests were made on suspicion, often as the result of
anonymous denunciation. The accused was presumed
guilty and the functions of prosecutor and judge were
combined. Women, children, and slaves could be called as
witnesses for the prosecution, but not for the defense. Nor
could the victim be allowed a lawyer to plead his case, as
this would have been tantamount to opposing the Inquisition and, as such, an act of heresy."

Until the dread hand of the Inquisition was lifted in
1787, there were never less than two thousand of "these
psalm-singing marauders, each in command of his own
band of retainers," roaming the devastated land, stripping
the wealthy of their property, the poor of an attractive
wife or daughter. In such circumstances, the Mafia was
born—a secret society of vengeance, the only hope of the
oppressed hungering for retribution. Norman Lewis
writes:

> The poor man's only shield was the Mafia. Justice was
> not to be come by, but the association of "men of re-
> spect"—silent, persistent, inflexible—could at least exact
> a bloody retribution for the loss of a wife or daughter or
> the burning down of a house. It was in the school of the
> vendetta that the traditional character of the *mafioso* was
> formed. As a victim of absolute power, the common man
> had to learn to stomach insult or injury with apparent in-
> difference, delaying vengeance until an opportunity for
> its consummation presented itself. The *mafioso* therefore
> developed a kind of self-control closely resembling the
> quality that the Japanese call *giri.* A true "man of re-
> spect" never weakened his position or armed his enemy
> in advance by outbursts of passion or of fear. When he
> suffered some grave injury, he made a pact with himself
> to be revenged, and thereafter would wait patiently and
> unemotionally for half a lifetime, if necessary—often on
> seemingly excellent terms with the man he proposed to
> destroy—until his moment came. . . .

Unfortunately, it is endemic in the nature of secret so-

cieties that, however justifiable or even praiseworthy the
original purpose, they become perverted in the end by the
selfishness and greed of those who control the machinery
of the organization, protected by its screen of anonymity.
This is what happened to the Sicilian Mafia. Once the Inquisition was removed, once there were no more foreign
demons to fight, the organization, having lost its original
purpose, found a new purpose: Instead of serving as the
shield of the oppressed, it became itself the oppressor.

With the advent of Garibaldi and the creation of the
modern Italian state, the Mafia went covertly into politics
and enhanced its power. Lawyers and doctors, leaders on
every level of society, became bound to it by ties that
could be severed only by death. Mafia support, Mafia
money and intimidation, elected delegates to the Italian
Parliament; and in the immediate pre-Mussolini era in the
1920s, at least two members of the Italian Cabinet were
bound to the Mafia by indissoluble ties. The secret society's power became so awesome and complete that it existed in Sicily as virtually a separate state, an independent
criminal government that exacted tribute from every business, oppressed labor and kept it in subjection, elected
mayors and local officials, and slew police chiefs who had
the bad judgment to become too interested in its activities.

Benito Mussolini, a dictator who would countenance no
rival for power, launched an all-out war against the Mafia
in the late 1920s. The situation at the time in Sicily was
described by the Procurator-General of Palermo in a report dated January 19, 1931. He wrote:

> The Mafia dominated and controlled the whole social
> life, it had leaders and followers, it issued orders and de-
> crees, it was to be found equally in big cities and in small
> centres, in factories and in rural districts, it regulated ag-
> ricultural and urban rents, forced itself into every kind
> of business, and got its way by means of threats and in-
> timidation or of penalties imposed by its leaders and put
> into execution by its officers. Its orders had the force of
> laws and its protection was a legal protection, more ef-
> fective and secure than that which the state offers to its

citizens; so that owners of property and businessmen in-
sured their goods and their persons by submitting to pay
the price of the insurance.

The entire evil conspiracy was protected by the wall of
omertà with which America was to become so familiar.
Omertà was founded on a conception of manliness. Whatever happened—whether one was beaten, robbed, even
fatally wounded—the victim maintained an obdurate silence. In the Sicilian concept, one who was "manly" handled his own problems, took his own revenge; he had
nothing to do with the law, which had been his enemy and
oppressor for centuries. Even if he died, so be it; he died
in "manliness."

When Mussolini began his war against the Mafia in the
late 1920s, he delegated supreme authority to his Prefect
of Police, Cesare Mori. Mori soon discovered that *omertà*
gave the Mafia blanket protection for even the most brutal
and gory misdeeds. It was also a prime element in public
deception. The average Italian outside of Sicily, like many
Americans today, found the concept of a separate, criminal government, operating independent of the machinery
of the State, simply too fantastic for credence. And with
omertà operating, where was the proof? In a book he later
wrote, Mori described his dilemma in this fashion:

> One theory to begin with was simplicity itself. It de-
> nied not only the grave problem of public security, but
> any specifically criminal quality in the Mafia, regarding it
> as indistinguishable from the type of criminal agency
> common to all countries. Some people even went so far
> as to invent the slogan: "The Mafia? . . . Why, Mori in-
> vented it." The conclusion from this total negative was
> that there was nothing to be done, and that the desire to
> do anything was a libel on Sicily. . . .

Mori's principal task was to shatter the protective wall
of *omertà,* and he accomplished this because he was
operating under a dictatorial regime that cared nothing for
civil rights. Mori fought the Mafia the way a general fights

a war. He put hundreds of *carabinieri* into the field, engaged in pitched battles, rounded up suspects by the hundreds, held them incommunicado for days and subjected them to the most remorseless questioning. He theorized that many persons in the upper classes of society belonged to the Mafia only because they had been terrorized and that, once convinced of the power and protection of the state, they would talk and name names. He was right.

Trial after trial was held. The defendants were marched into court, chained to one another, highly polished shoes agleam, eyes fierce above their ferocious moustaches. They were herded, like so many dangerous beasts in a zoo, into great iron cages during mass trials that sometimes lasted for months. The results were dramatic. Twenty-year-old murders were solved; some two thousand Mafiosi were tried, convicted, and sentenced. Mori proclaimed that he had exterminated the evil brotherhood, but he was wrong. Many of the more powerful and more wily Mafiosi had simply changed their spots. They joined the Fascist Party, voluble in their protestations of undying fealty to Il Duce, smoothing their way by disgorging some of their ill-gotten wealth to purchase influence; and then they waited, biding their time until the moment was right to surface again.

Confessions obtained during Mori's drive described the initiation procedures and the internal structure of the Mafia. The remarkable thing about one of these confessions is that it dovetails in almost every respect with the description of the American Mafia given to the McClellan committee in 1963 by the prize informer, Joseph Valachi.

Dr. Melchiorre Allegra, of Castelvetrano in Sicily, was a medical officer in the military hospital in Palermo in 1916 when he was propositioned to join the Mafia. His account, hidden in police files for years, was written in 1937 but did not come to light until 1962. In this, Dr. Allegra described the manner in which he was contacted and taken to a small fruit shop where three sinister Mafia figures gathered around a table and explained the facts of life. He wrote:

They explained to me that they belonged to a very important association, which included people in every rank of society, not excluding the highest. All of them were called "men of respect." The association was what in fact was known to outsiders as the Mafia but was understood by most people only in a very vague way, because only members could be really sure of its existence. . . . Continuing their explanation, they told me that infractions of the association's rules were severely punished. Members were not allowed, for example, to commit thefts, but in certain circumstances homicide was permissible, although always by license of the chiefs. Breaking the rules in this case—that is, by taking the law into one's own hands—was punishable by death. . . .

On the subject of the administrative structure, it was explained to me that the association was split up into "families," each one headed by a chief. Usually, a family was made up of small groups from neighboring towns or villages; if a family became too large for convenient administration, it was split up into units of ten, each with its subordinate chief. In the matter of the relationship between the different provinces, the rule in the main was independence. However, the provincial heads kept in close touch with one another, and in this way an informal working liaison was maintained. The association had powerful overseas offshoots in both North and South America, in Tunisia, and in Marseille. A chief was elected by members of his "family," and he was assisted by a counselor, who could act as his substitute in case of his absence; in matters of high policy, it was absolutely necessary for a chief to consult his counselor before taking action. They then added that in general the association was not interested in politics, but that from time to time a "family" might decide to support the candidacy for Parliament of a politician whose parliamentary influence they could count on.

Dr. Allegra listened with growing apprehension. He could not imagine that, having been made privy to such secrets, he would ever be allowed to leave the little fruit stand alive if he should be so indiscreet as to announce he did *not* wish to join the Mafia. "My one course was not only to accept on the spot but to accept with apparent enthusiasm," he wrote. He then described the ritual of initiation in words almost identical to those of Joseph Valachi in America decades later:

> The tip of my middle finger was pierced by a needle, and blood was squeezed from it to soak a small paper image of a saint. The image was burned, and, holding the ashes in my hand, I was called upon to swear an oath more or less as follows: "I swear to be loyal to my brothers, never to betray them, always to aid them, and if I fail may I burn and be turned to ashes like the ashes of the image."

Such, then, was the secret, evil brotherhood that was imported into the United States along with the first wave of Sicilian immigrants in the late nineteenth century. Some of these newcomers had been members of the Mafia in their homeland; and, once they had settled here, they started up new cells of the criminal organization, and embarked upon a wave of terror and extortion, protected by *omertà*.

New Orleans in 1890 had the first confrontation with the brotherhood. The great Louisiana port had become a major artery for the rapidly expanding fruit trade with Latin America. Fortunes were represented in the produce flowing across its docks, and the Mafia, as it was to do many times in the future in other ports, seized control of the waterfront. No banana freighter could be unloaded without paying tribute to the firm of Antonio and Carlo Matranga, transplants from Palermo. Negro and Italian longshoremen could not work on the docks and would not lay hands on a cargo without the approval of Matranga foremen. Importers, never a militant lot, decided then, as they have many times since in similar circumstances, that it was easier to pay than to fight. They coughed up the tribute demanded—and, naturally, passed the costs on to the American consumer.

It was, seemingly, the most perfect of racket worlds; but then, as always happens in the jungle, some of the beasts got too greedy and war broke out over the loot. Day by day, New Orleans was treated to newspaper accounts about a series of especially sensational murders. One Italian, his throat slashed from ear to ear, was dropped into a canal. Another, his head almost severed from his body, was found partially stuffed into his own roaring fireplace. Shotguns, bombs, daggers—all favorite tools of the Mafia —came into play as murder piled upon murder.

New Orleans at the time had an especially capable and courageous police chief, David Hennessey. He became convinced that there was something different, unique, about this unprecedented wave of violence, and he began to probe beneath the surface for the cause. The instant he did, he ran into *omertà*. Hennessey, of course, had never heard of the term, but he soon discovered, to his own astonishment, that not even the Italian members of his own police force could be trusted. They knew nothing, saw nothing, heard nothing. A similar blanket of silence cloaked the entire Italian community.

Hennessey was stubborn. Unable to rely on anyone except himself, he pressed his own one-man crusade, determined to uncover the secret of the lethal mystery that surrounded him. He was warned to desist; efforts were made to bribe him. He scorned both threats and bribes. Bit by bit, he fitted the pieces together. He learned of the Matranga stranglehold over the New Orleans docks. He got information that brothers named Provenzano, their greed whetted by the sight of the mounting Matranga fortune, had tried to muscle in on the waterfront rackets—and so had precipitated the wave of murders.

With his evidence about ready to present to a grand jury, Chief Hennessey left police headquarters one evening and started to walk toward his home. Four figures suddenly emerged out of the darkness and opened fire with shotguns. Riddled with pellets and mortally wounded, Hennessey still managed to pull of his service revolver. He propped himself on one arm, took aim and kept firing at his fleeing assailants until the gun was empty in his hand.

Hearing the gunfire, a detective in the neighborhood

rushed up. He found the chief alone, sitting on the stoop
of a house to which he had dragged himself. As the detective knelt, the gun clattered to the sidewalk from Hennessey's nerveless fingers; his head pitched forward between
his knees; and he murmured a single word—"Dagoes."

The assassination of Chief Hennessey gave America its
first and one of its most dramatic examples of *omertà* in
action. Lips were sealed as if with cement all over New
Orleans. Even Hennessey's own police department did not
exhibit any zeal to avenge its fallen chief. But the citizens
of the city still had the capacity for outrage, and their demands for action became so vociferous that the slothful
police were compelled to bestir themselves.

The first grand jury investigation only whipped up
greater civic anger. The jury returned no indictments, but
handed up a presentment describing the wall of silence
that had frustrated its efforts. "The existence of a secret
organization known as the Mafia has been established
beyond doubt," the jury declared. It found that the society
was composed of Italians and Sicilians who had fled from
their native land to avoid punishment for their crimes. The
jury, though it had never heard of *omertà,* reported that it
had been "strangely difficult, almost impossible" to secure
witnesses.

Press and public were furious. Demands for more positive action resounded through the city, and the police
were virtually forced to produce. Under the new pressures,
the protective shield of silence began to crack. Some sixty
witnesses were located, including some who had seen and
could identify the four slayers of Chief Hennessey. In the
end, nineteen Sicilians were indicted as principals and
conspirators in the murder of the police chief.

What happened next was what was to happen many
times in the future. The Mafia unfurled its bankroll in a
demonstration that seemed to prove money was superior
to the law. The most eminent defense lawyers in the nation
descended upon New Orleans. Every pressure known to
the Mafia, including bribery and intimidation, was exerted
upon individual members of the trial jury. The result: the

jurors acquitted sixteen of the defendants and reported
they could not decide on the guilt or innocence of the
other three.

Mayor Joseph A. Shakespeare, a reformer, was furious.
In a report to the New Orleans Council, he declared: "A
decent community cannot exist with such a society in its
midst. The society must be destroyed or the community
will perish. The Sicilians who come here must become
American citizens and obey the law of the land, or else
there is no place for them in our country."

The mayor was expressing a popular sentiment. A mass
meeting was called by leading citizens, with the approval
of the mayor and the city's two leading newspapers, the
Picayune and the *Times-Democrat*. The meeting grew into
an unruly mob of thousands. Passions got out of hand, and
an impromptu army marched upon the parish jail, where
the defendants were still being held pending the completion of legal technicalities for their release. Deputy sheriffs
in charge of the jail were brushed aside or simply took to
their heels, and lynch squads found and dragged out the
accused Sicilians.

Two were hanged from lamp posts in front of the prison
and then thoroughly riddled with bullets. Nine more were
lined up in front of a prison wall and mowed down with ri-
fles, pistols, and shotguns. In such fashion was the slaying
of Chief Hennessey avenged; in such fashion did the name
—Mafia—first find its way into American headlines.

3.

The Mafia in New York

New York first became aware that the Mafia was in its midst in the early 1900s. It was then that the dread symbol of the Black Hand made its appearance.

Immigrants from southern Italy and Sicily had flocked into New York's Lower East Side and into slum sections along the Brooklyn waterfront. They herded into overcrowded tenements, battling poverty and trying to learn a new language and adapt to new ways. The honest and industrious gradually improved their station in life—and so became the potential prey of the criminals who had emigrated from their homeland with them.

The campaign of terror and extortion that now began was nurtured by two secret societies, the Camorra of Naples and the Mafia of Sicily. The symbol that these terroristic organizations used was the Black Hand. A prosperous truck farmer on Long Island or a small merchant on the East Side would receive a shakedown note written in the Sicilian dialect, signed with the imprint of a Black Hand. If the victim did not immediately disgorge the money demanded, he received a final warning: a stenciled Black Hand would appear on a fence or the side of his house. The recipient of such a message knew he had only one choice: pay or be killed.

This use of the Black Hand symbol created much confusion. Newpapers began referring to the Black Hand Society. Actually, there was no such society; the hand was simply the decorative trademark adopted by both the Camorra and the Mafia to strike terror into the hearts of those whom they were blackmailing. It was a most effective device.

An elderly Italo-American vegetable grower, who came here from Sicily as a child with his parents, recalled years later for Frederic Sondern Jr. the effect that the final Black Hand warning on a fence post always had. He said:

> Then my father would pay. He would say, "Giuseppe, you see, it is the same here as at home. The Mafia is always with us." Then I would plead with him to go to the police. After all, we were in America. "No, Mother of God, no," he would shout. "The police here cannot do even as much as the police at home. They do not know the Mafia. We get put out of business or killed and no one will know why. They do not understand the Mafia and they never will."

One exceptional New York detective, however, began to understand. Lieutenant Joseph Petrosino had been born in the coastal town of Salerno, near Naples, and as a boy he had heard much from his parents about the Mafia and its terroristic practices. Petrosino was a stocky man, standing five feet eight, with a round head, a slightly pockmarked face and snapping black eyes. As an Italian, he felt that the criminal and bloodthirsty minority among his people were giving the whole race a bad name, and he developed a passionate hatred for the Black Hand practitioners—an emotion that came to rule his life. He persuaded his superiors in the New York Police Department to form a special Italian Squad, and he launched the first determined campaign in this country against the Mafia.

Petrosino appears to have been the first American law enforcement officer to appreciate the full scope of the evil conspiracy he was fighting—the first to recognize the existence of criminal organizations extending their power across city, state, and even national boundaries. Working with a small squad out of the old rambling Metropolitan Police headquarters at 200 Mulberry Street, Petrosino began to identify and compile records on Mafia members, the first thorough dossier of its kind in the nation. He adopted a variety of disguises and mingled personally with the toughest elements in the Italian community, at daily risk to his life. This daring detective work enabled him to identify the principal Mafiosi of his day—the dock czars, the brothelkeepers, the fish and meat market extortionists, the bomb throwers.

The results he achieved were remarkable. In 1900, from information gathered among New Jersey anarchists, he tipped off Italian police to a plot to murder King Humbert. In one year, he personally made seven hundred arrests. Hundreds of Italians, especially Sicilians, who had entered the country illegally, were ferreted out by Petrosino and deported. He became the nemesis of the Mafia; and the Mafia began to hate him with all the venom of which it was capable.

Despite his successes, Petrosino became increasingly frustrated. He knew that he was fighting a huge criminal conspiracy with international ramifications, and he felt balked by his inability to make the public and many officials, including judges, see what he saw so clearly. A second source of frustration was his inability to build viable court cases against the real rulers of the criminal empire. Petrosino had identified the supreme chief of the Camorra as Enrico Alfano, alias Erricone, and the boss of the Mafia as Ignazio Lupo, known as "Lupo the Wolf." Both, however, were so well-protected, so isolated behind the screen of their principal lieutenants—a tactic common in the Mafia to this day—that Petrosino could not pin directly upon them any of the heinous crimes for which he knew they were responsible.

Petrosino, a stubborn and dedicated man, persisted, however, until he finally succeeded in getting Erricone deported to Italy, where he was wanted by Italian law. He was less successful with Lupo the Wolf, who remained so elusive that Petrosino could not lay a hand upon him.

Matters were at this impasse in the summer of 1907 when a new wave of Black Hand violence swept New York. Petrosino located a Harlem saloonkeeper who had been forced to act as broker for the extortionists and an Italian banker who, under threat of death, had been compelled to supply bail for arrested blackmailers, who of course then jumped their bonds, leaving the banker holding the bag. Then, in August, 1907, a plucky Italian merchant, Joseph Trano, came to Petrosino and said he had received a Black Hand letter demanding five hundred dollars upon the pain of death. Petrosino praised Trano for his courage, gave him marked bills and set a trap.

Unsuspecting, Vincenzio Abadezza, one of Lupo the Wolf's principal henchmen, walked into Trano's store to collect the money. Petrosino and his detectives watched the payoff. They then tailed Abadezza to learn the identities of others in the conspiracy. When they finally sprang their trap, Abadezza and eight cohorts were arrested. On one of the suspects, two notebooks were found. One contained a list of some twenty names of members of the secret brotherhood; the other, the names of sixty laborers, scattered throughout the state, who were paying tributes of from one dollar to three dollars a week to the extortionists.

Petrosino's elation over this breakthrough feat turned to despair when the cases came into court. Judges looked down their long noses in sneers of disbelief, just as many do today, at the idea of the existence of a criminal conspiracy so huge it was tantamount to a secret government of the underworld. As a result, Abadezza drew only a two-and-a-half-year prison sentence, and his confederates got off even more lightly, suffering only slap-on-the-wrist penalties of a few days each in jail.

Discouraged by the blindness of the judiciary, Petrosino decided that the only way he could convince such educated skeptics of the reality of the sinister organization he was fighting was to go to Italy and trace there the ties that bound the Mafia abroad to the Mafia in New York. Police Commissioner Theodore Bingham was at first opposed to the idea, but he finally yielded to Petrosino's arguments. Private funds were raised to finance the trip, and in January, 1909, Lieutenant Petrosino sailed for Italy.

Every effort was made to keep Petrosino's mission secret. He sailed under an assumed name, knowing that he was risking his life by going directly into the home lair of the Mafia. As investigations later showed, all of these precautions were futile. Lupo the Wolf evidently had good sources of information, probably inside the New York Police Department itself; and he knew the instant Petrosino departed both his destination and the purpose of his mission. The implication was, though it could never be proved, that Lupo passed the word to Mafiosi abroad that Petrosino was coming.

Traveling incognito, the famous detective contacted Italian officials in Rome and Naples. He was well received by them and obtained the records of more than six hundred desperate criminals known to have emigrated to America. Petrosino was still not satisfied. Wanting more complete, on-the-scene details, he traveled on to Palermo. There, on the evening of March 13, 1909, he dined in a restaurant on Marino Square—then set out to cross the square, walking toward the Hotel di Palma, where he was staying. As Petrosino strolled through the evening crowds, two men came up behind him, whipped out revolvers, and pumped four bullets into his back and head. At the first shot, Petrosino whirled, clutching at his own gun. He managed to get it out, to fire one wild shot—then he crashed down dead on the pavement. The Mafia in Sicily had executed the detective who menaced the Mafia in New York.

Petrosino's murderers walked calmly away from the scene of their bloody deed—and the wall of *omertà* closed in behind them. Though scores of pedestrians had witnessed the assassination, no one had seen a thing; no one would help to identify the killers. Petrosino's body was shipped home. He was given a hero's burial. But the cause to which he had given his life had received a setback from which it never recovered. No one else had either the knowledge or the desire to ferret out all the sinister ties and practices of the Mafia.

In death, it would seem, Lieutenant Petrosino had proved his thesis—the *fact* of an underworld organization so close-knit and far-reaching that it could function across the ocean and strike down a dangerous New York detective on the streets of Palermo in Sicily. Yet even this macabre demonstration made no impact at the time. Lieutenant Petrosino was dead and soon virtually forgotten.

Not until Cesare Mori conducted his relentless drive against the Mafia in the 1920s did additional details leak out about Petrosino's assassination. Mori discovered that Petrosino's murder had been engineered by Don Vito Cascio Ferro, who had been head of the Sicilian Mafia for twenty-five years before Mori jailed him. Don Vito had spent part of his youth in the United States. He had been active in some of the early Black Hand extortions here, and then he returned to his native Sicily where he had risen to command the secret brotherhood. He had been accused of some seventy major crimes, twenty of them homicides; but he had always been acquitted.

Though he was almost completely illiterate, he was a man of peculiar, magnetic force. Norman Lewis in *The Honored Society* wrote that Don Vito

was a favorite of high society and frequented Palermo's most glittering *salons*. He was in demand to open exhibitions of watercolors, he romped with dukes and duchesses in party games, he listened with reverence to famous actors giving poetry readings from Leopardi, he dressed himself fashionably in knickerbockers and Norfolk jacket to shoot thrushes in distinguished company, and he joined aristocratic carriage parties to pelt the children of the poor with cakes and sweets on All Souls' Eve. Women of gentle birth spoke of the strange magnetic force with which a room seemed charged when Don Vito was present, and he once administered a severe admoni-

tion to his barber for selling his hair clippings to a maker
of amulets.

Gangster chic, it would seem, had a snake-eye fascina-
tion for the most exclusive society circles long before Joey
Gallo.

In Don Vito's case, part of his allure lay in the knowledge that he was a man of violence and blood—and yet
one who was so powerful he could defy the entire machinery of the state. The universal fear that he inspired was so
great that he could brag in private, with perfect impunity,
that he had killed Lieutenant Petrosino. Indeed, in his
own version, the second gunman disappeared completely
as Don Vito proudly claimed sole credit for the deed. He
explained that Petrosino's audacity in invading Palermo
had been an affront to his own status that could not be ignored. On the evening of the murder, as Don Vito told the
story, he was dining with a member of Parliament. During
the meal, he suddenly pretended that he had forgotten an
important errand at home and asked if he could borrow
his host's carriage to take care of it. The host was only too
glad to do Don Vito such a favor, and so the Mafia chief
rode to murder in the private carriage of a member of Parliament. Don Vito's information about Petrosino's movements must have been uncannily accurate, for his timing
had been perfect. He came upon Petrosino crossing the
square, fired the fatal shots, climbed back into the waiting
carriage, and returned to the home of his Parliamentary
host in time to enjoy the port. When suspicion later pointed a finger at him, Don Vito had the perfect alibi witness:
a distinguished member of Parliament who was prepared
to swear in court that he had never left the house on the
night of the killing. And so the law was hamstrung; nothing could be done.

Back in New York, the assassination of Petrosino
spurred an all-too-brief campaign against the Mafia. Lupo
the Wolf was finally jailed on a counterfeiting charge, and
some of his hirelings were rounded up. But there the drive
stopped.

The Mafia became more circumspect. It abandoned the crudity of Black Hand letters and refined its techniques of power and persuasion. At the same time—just as it was to do in the 1970s—it promoted a wily propaganda campaign playing on the ethnic sensibilities of New York's large Italian voting population. The effort then, as now, was geared to the lowest common denominator of ethnic pride. It was vicious and unfair, the argument went, to maintain a special Italian Squad in the New York Police Department; the very existence of such a squad was a libel upon the fair name of all Italian-Americans, the hundreds of thousands who had become good, law-abiding American citizens.

The tactic is one that the Mafia had employed time and time again with devastating effect. Mori had found the ethnic-libel argument being used in Sicily to rally public support and to ridicule the very idea that such an organization as the Mafia existed. The same technique was now used to brainwash New Yorkers in the aftermath of Lieutenant Petrosino's murder. And in the early 1970s the hoary device was trotted out again by Joseph Colombo Sr., ruler of the second most powerful Mafia family in New York; and thousands upon thousands of honest but deluded Italian-Americans joined the racket czar in picketing New York FBI headquarters in demonstrations that finally induced even the U.S. Department of Justice to ban the use of the word *Mafia*.

The damage done by such propaganda to honest and courageous law enforcement has been almost incalculable. The loss showed perhaps most clearly in the aftermath of the Petrosino assassination. This great Italian detective, who should have been a martyred hero of his people, was in effect betrayed by them in the outcry whipped up over the ethnic issue. New York politicians, never a notably courageous breed, ran scared at the possibility of losing all those Italian-American votes. The Italian Squad that had been Petrosino's pride was quietly disbanded; and with its liquidation, all of Petrosino's vital information, gathered by such extraordinary effort and at such hazard, was filed away and forgotten. The nation lost its best eyes and ears.

This abandonment of Petrosino's work could not have come at a worse time. The nation was about to embark upon the Prohibition Era and its worst criminal debauch. Gangsters were to become all-powerful millionaires almost overnight; the Mafia was to develop into a national colossus, with tentacles stretching from coast to coast, with a national commission composed of the major dons knitting together the affairs of crime in what was, in effect, an invisible underworld government. And while all this was happening, there was to be no Lieutenant Petrosino or his law enforcement heirs to watch, to trace, to catalogue, to combat this fantastic growth of underworld organization and power.

4.

The Mafia Organizes

The wild and zany Prohibition era of the 1920s created an underworld whose power was capsuled by one of New York's most famous detectives in this pungent line: "The underworld runs the world, only the people don't know it." Even today, decades later, America is still wrestling with the massive problems posed by that all too truthful observation.

Prior to Prohibition, crime had been a relatively minor-league affair. Hoodlums quarreled over the loot that came from waterfront thefts, extortions, gambling dives, prostitution. The more successful entrepreneurs made fortunes and corrupted police; but they had not as yet amassed the staggering bankrolls, running into the hundreds of millions of dollars, necessary to merge the underworld almost inconspicuously into the upper-crust, legitimate life of the nation.

In that simpler world of crime, various ethnic groups staked out individual turfs and operated within fairly well-defined boundaries. The Irish mobs controlled Manhattan's West Side docks; Jewish and Italian gangs, products of the East Side ghettos, claimed the area from the tip of Manhattan up into East Harlem and the Bronx; and, across the East River in Brooklyn, other Jewish and Ital-

47

ian conclaves in the Brownsville and South Brooklyn sections were spawning lethal operators whose names were to become synonymous with crime across the nation for the next thirty years.

This elevation of crime's status, this creation of an underworld that came—just as the Mafia had in Sicily—to dominate for long periods the political life of such great cities as Chicago and New York, resulted from a combination of circumstances. An entire nation, denied the pleasures of tippling, defied the blue-nosed Prohibition Law—and patronized and glorified the thugs who flouted the legal proscription and kept the liquor flowing. Overnight, a veritable Niagara of almost inconceivable wealth poured into the pockets of some of the most ruthless and vicious gangsters the American scene had ever known.

The new Golconda was discovered during those same years that Cesare Mori was making Sicily too hot for many Mafiosi. Thousands fled and headed for America the way the Forty-Niners had responded to the discovery of gold in California. These criminal aliens came filtering across the Mexican and Canadian borders or simply jumped ship at the most convenient American port. Once ashore, they established contacts with "family" members who had preceded them, supplying the Mafia with new muscle for its incipient takeover of the most lucrative American rackets. In fact, Carlo Gambino, today the most powerful Mafioso in New York and perhaps in the nation, arrived by just such a ship-jumping route, scampering off a vessel that docked in Norfolk, Va., just before Christmas in 1921.

The combination of this new army of recruits and the opening up of the vast new world of bootlegging, dovetailing as they did, helped to catapult the Mafia into the saddle. In the beginning, the Mafia was just one of many criminal organizations that sprang up overnight in the wild scramble for bootlegging millions. What distinguished the Mafia from its competitors, however, was its organizational expertise, rooted in experiences centuries old. Individual mob leaders—German, Irish, or Jewish—rose and flourished for a time, cutting vivid swaths across the Prohibition-crazed world; but few, however powerful they were, could survive for the long haul unless they linked up in formal or informal alliances with the secret brotherhood.

"Prohibition really put the Mafia in the saddle," says one veteran, top-level federal narcotics agent. "All of the gangs, of course, went into bootlegging, but the Mafia was the one organization in the underworld that already had a perfected, functioning organization stretching across state lines, across the country. It was the one outfit able to take control."

The logistics of the bootlegging operation gave the New York-based Mafia a decided advantage over competitors and made the city the breeding ground for gang leaders who would go out to dominate the racket worlds of Boston, Chicago, California, Miami, and Las Vegas. The prohibited thirst of a continent could be assuaged only by enormous quantities of smuggled liquor; and, while some of it could be brought in by land across the northern and southern borders, the vast bulk had to be imported by sea, smuggled into East Coast ports, trucked to drops, and then distributed. New York, the hub of legitimate commerce, quickly became just as important a hub of the new, illicit rum-running operation. Not only did the greatest city in the nation suffer from its own colossal thirst, but this city was strategically located to relieve the parched throats of Philadelphia and Washington and of a whole string of cities as far west as Chicago.

Millions of dollars were soon involved in the purchase and manning of the fleet of ships that hovered at sea in the so-called Rum Row just beyond the three-mile limit; in the operation of fleets of swift speedboats that transported the liquor ashore from the heavily laden supply ships; in the arrangements for the clandestine landing and hauling of the cargoes and the intricate fixes needed to insure that neither the Coast Guard at sea nor the police on land would interfere with this bibulous flow. It all required an army of men, the firmest police and political connections, well-established lines of credit.

Since the East Coast mobs were strategically placed to control the neck of the liquor bottle, so to speak, theirs soon became the decisive voice in determining whom they would do business with, what credit they would extend, what arrangements for payment would be made. Inevitably, they preferred to do business with their own, either with brother members of the Mafia or with reliable gang chiefs with whom their Mafia overlords had collaborated on a satisfactory basis. It was, therefore, no accident that the decade of the Roaring Twenties saw gangsters who had received their training on the streets of the Lower East Side or Brooklyn fanning out across the nation to introduce Mafia techniques and build racket empires in other areas. Charles ("King") Solomon emigrated from New York to Boston and became czar of the New England rackets; the Bernsteins went out to form the Purple Gang in Detroit; Johnny Torrio and Scarface Al Capone, products of the Brooklyn breeding ground, went west and subjugated all Chicago; Bugsy Siegel pioneered the fertile field of California and discovered the gambling bonanza of Las Vegas; and his one-time partner in the dreaded Bugs and Meyer mob, Meyer Lansky, opened up the gambling fleshpots of Miami and Cuba and became, as he has remained virtually to the present day, the crime syndicate's financial wizard and prime international "money mover."

To understand how it all happened so suddenly and so swiftly, perhaps the best illustration may be found in the meteoric career of a bootlegging kingpin who was neither Italian nor Sicilian, but Irish—a man who, in less than five years, zoomed his finances from zero into millions, bought his way into society and respectability, and then, perhaps seeing the sign-writing on the wall, moved on and left the rackets to the Mafia to run. . . .

William Vincent Dwyer was known as "Big Bill," not for his physical size but for the heft of his bankroll and the reach of his influence. He was a chunky man, heavy jawed, with a tough James Cagney way of talking out of one corner of his mouth. He had grown up in one of the toughest sections of New York's West Side, the area around 10th Avenue and 23rd Street, where a gang known as the Gophers ruled. Dwyer never became a Gopher; but, instead, in his teens, he ushered in the old opera house in West 23rd Street that robber baron Jim Fiske had built for the greater glory of his beautiful concubine, Josie Mansfield. When Prohibition closed the saloons in 1920, young Dwyer was developing his muscles as a stevedore on the Chelsea docks, and the percentages seemed to say he would probably remain a dock walloper the rest of his life.

Then the Volstead Act came along and radically altered his prospects. Dwyer knew George J. Shevlin, owner of a string of saloons, and Shevlin, like many others, had no intention of going out of business through respect for a law that defied all the instincts of nature. He and some of his associates formed a syndicate to get liquor, and Bill Dwyer was taken into the combine as a handy man who knew his way around the West Side dock area.

In anticipation of dire dry days, the liquor industry had built up enormous reserves, which were stored in bonded warehouses under government supervision. These supplies of the bubbly were supposed to be released only upon the presentation of official permits and only for "medicinal purposes." But such permits could be forged; or deals could be made with the custodians of the warehouses; or, failing all else, the places could simply be raided at gunpoint. Dwyer, as Shevlin's aide, became active in all such activities, hiring trucks, leasing garages to be used as "drops" for the illicitly obtained liquor, and arranging for its sale and distribution.

The profits were so enormous that the racket soon ceased to be a gentleman's pastime. Guns came into play as one gang hijacked another's liquor trucks and left corpses strewn around the streets in the process. This rough business was more than many of Shevlin's associates had bargained for, and they got out of the traffic while their persons were still intact. But not Bill Dwyer. He was tough. He stayed.

His future fortune was probably founded upon widespread recognition of one simple fact: he was a man who, when he paid a bribe, would never squeal. This invaluable reputation was based on an incident that happened to May 28, 1921. Shevlin had given Dwyer $2,500 for use in case of "emergencies," and on that day Dwyer and a New York City patrolman were riding shotgun on a load of Shevlin liquor that was to be delivered to a West Side client. They had gone only a few blocks when a couple of nosy New York detectives halted them. One thing led to another, and before the misunderstanding was resolved, Dwyer had parted with Shevlin's $2,500.

A novice at the time in the art of bribery, Dwyer began to worry whether his boss would think he had been too generous; and so he scurried around, contacting politicos who might help to recover the $2,500. He soon learned another fact of life: a bribe once paid is irretrievably gone; the bribed official has no more intention of giving up the money than he has of giving up his life. The fuss Dwyer raised, however, caused some rumbles in the police department, and the two detectives were brought up on departmental charges. When the case came to trial, Dwyer refused to admit anything. He wouldn't concede he had been riding on a truck loaded with liquor; he refused to say he had paid the detectives $2,500. And so the case was dismissed.

This was, events would indicate, the launching pad for the career of Big Bill Dwyer, for no rocket ever zoomed more swiftly into the stratosphere than did Big Bill's status from that moment. Two short years saw him rolling in millions—and this was just the beginning. The federal government subsequently charged that, as early as 1922, the one-time stevedore had shortchanged it $100,000 on income taxes. The following year, according to Uncle Sam, Big Bill chiseled it for $800,000. And in 1924 he capped all his previous performances by overlooking payment of $1,200,000. This figure, it must be remembered, represented *taxes alone, not income*.

Big Bill's business and life styles during those few brief years indicated that the government must have been right. By 1923, he had a two-room suite of offices in Loew's State Theatre building on Broadway at Times Square; he had other offices over the East River National Bank at Broadway and 41st Street. He had a fine new home in Belle Harbor, L.I.; he maintained a marine garage for his fleet of rum-running speedboats on the East River in the shadow of Hell Gate; and he owned some half-dozen mother ships anchored in the off-coast, Rum Row fleet.

This meteoric success story—stevedore to millionaire in one easy leap—was built upon just one technique: wholesale corruption. Big Bill firmly believed that the man didn't exist who couldn't be bought, and it must be acknowledged that he pretty well proved his point. No one will ever know how many New York policemen or Coast Guardsmen were on Big Bill's payroll, but all the evidence indicates there must have been legions. The grapevine carried the word to these so-called guardians of the law that, whenever there was unanticipated trouble, a telephone tip to Big Bill's Loew office would always bring a satisfactory reward. As a result, when some overzealous official happened to seize one of Big Bill's liquor-laden boats, he invariably found Big Bill's lawyers and bondsmen already waiting at dockside when he brought in the seized vessel.

The extent of Big Bill's corruption of Coast Guard and police was demonstrated by one exploit so flamboyant that it became a prize tale of the Prohibition Era. A Coast Guardsman by the name of Paul Lewis Crim had been recommended to Dwyer as a willing prospect. He came to Dwyer's offices in the Loew building attired in full uniform. Big Bill took one look at him and remarked: "That is a bad outfit for things like this. Here's $100—go and buy some decent clothes."

Crim departed, a happy man, but his joy faded when, after several weeks, no more $100 handouts were forthcoming. When he protested, Dwyer told him: "If you want any more money, you'll have to land some liquor."

Crim was a member of the crew of Coast Guard cutter 203, and he began sounding out his mates about whether they would be willing to run a cargo of liquor for Big Bill. He reported back that a couple of the men were incurably honest, but the rest were willing—and so the incorruptibles could be ignored.

Big Bill then issued his orders: take 203 out to Rum Row and pick up seven hundred cases of liquor from his supply ship, the *Ellis B*. Off steamed the Coast Guard cutter, ploughing through a slightly choppy sea. Up and down the Rum Row fleet, the cutter ranged, inquiring for the *Ellis B*. None of the skippers would give the desired information; for, not unnaturally, it passed their comprehension that a Coast Guard cutter could have been turned into a rum-runner. Finally, after a diligent search that became the talk of the Rum Row fleet and of waterfront bars forever after, the 203 located the *Ellis B*. Now a final contretemps added the perfectly ludicrous note to the whole affair: there was another Coast Guard cutter standing by, watching the *Ellis B*. The 203, having located her quarry after such infinite difficulties, had to stand off to sea and wander around until, with night falling, the crew of the other cutter got tired and headed home. Then the 203 loaded up Dwyer's seven hundred cases of liquor and brought the cargo into a West Side dock near Canal Street. There, under the watching and benign presence of local police, the men in uniform loaded Big Bill's whiskey into waiting trucks.

Crim and his coworkers each got $700 for their day's work, and Crim was so delighted that he quit government service and became Big Bill's chauffeur.

The saga of the 203 had important side-effects: it demonstrated in the most graphic fashion the far reach of Big Bill's protective arrangements. This point made, Big Bill introduced a new caper into the action. He passed the word to his Coast Guard hirelings that, not only were they to protect his shipments, they were to harass his rivals.

And so it came about that other rum-runners began coming to Big Bill for insurance. These were always one-shot deals, covering a single shipment or a single truckload; each time there was a new cargo, there had to be a new deal. But it was worth it. Big Bill guaranteed satisfaction—complete protection both afloat and ashore.

Such flamboyance, such prominence carries with it its own risks. Inevitably, even in the almost totally corrupted atmosphere of the day, Big Bill became a marked man. The federal government decided to prosecute him for income-tax evasion. When Big Bill appeared in court for trial in July, 1926, it was evident at a glance that prosperity had transformed the ex-stevedore. He wore a diamond stickpin in his tie, and on one finger was a dazzling ring fashioned in the shape of a swastika, with a ruby in the center and diamonds sparkling on the four bent arms. Big Bill was in some physical difficulty at the time. His chauffeur, Crim, had crashed his car, and Big Bill's fleshy jaw had been broken. It had been imperfectly mended, so that his mouth sagged off at one side while he tried, from lifelong habit, to tough-talk out of the other.

Though his words came out twisted in the utterance, Big Bill put up the front of a legitimate businessman. He was, he said, just a racetrack owner. He had the sole interest in the Coney Island track in Cincinnati, and he was a half-partner in the Mount Royal track in Montreal. The government's evidence, however, was overwhelming; and Big Bill was convicted and sentenced to serve two years in the Atlanta Penitentiary.

With time off for good behavior, he came out after serving only some thirteen months. Released in August, 1928, he returned to New York, where his principal partners, Owney Madden and Waxey Gordon, had looked after his bootlegging interests while he was in prison. Both were tough and powerful men. Madden, in fact, had been so brash that, early in the game, he had hijacked some of Big Bill's liquor trucks; but Big Bill, instead of having him executed, had liked his nerve and made a partner of him. Backed by such redoubtable figures, Big Bill, it would seem, could have taken up right where he left off. But he didn't. Perhaps he was sensitive enough to sniff the winds of change. New forces like those represented by his one-time disciple, Frank Costello, had grown ever more powerful during the years of his entanglement with the law; and so Big Bill decided to retire into the background and become legitimate.

He did this so successfully that he introduced the sport of hockey to New York and made dapper Mayor James J. Walker his partner. Next, he became a principal stockholder in the new Rockingham Park racetrack in Salem, N.H. And finally, after disposing of his interests in the Cincinnati and Montreal tracks, he capped his career by founding the famous Tropical Park racetrack near Miami. With this last coup, he crashed society circles in a big way.

By March, 1936, the society columns of *The New York Times* were reporting straight-faced the news that William Vincent Dwyer of New York, "managing director of the Gables Racing Association" (no mention, naturally, of those Chelsea Dock and bootlegging origins) had entertained at a buffet luncheon a distinguished list of society guests, headed by "Sir Graeme Sinclair-Lockhart, Bart., and Lady Lockhart. . . ."

The racket wars on which William Vincent Dwyer turned his back to embark on his new career as racetrack impresario and host to titled visitors were later described in vivid terms by two *New York Times* reporters, Craig Thompson and Allen Raymond. In their book, *Gang Rule in New York,* they wrote:

> More than a thousand gangsters died in New York in the bootleg liquor wars of the 1920's and the murder of a minor bootlegger became so ordinary an event as to be worth not more than a paragaph or two on the inside page of a newspaper. The conviction of a gang slayer was a rarity.
>
> Rum runners and hijackers were pistoled and machine gunned. They were taken for rides on the front seat of sedans and their brains blown out from behind by fellow

mobsters they thought were their pals. They were lined up in pairs in front of warehouse walls in lonely alleys and shot down by firing squads. They were slugged into unconsciousness and placed in burlap sacks with their hands, feet and necks so roped that they would strangle themselves as they writhed. Charred bodies were found in burned automobiles.

Bootleggers and their molls were pinioned with wire and dropped alive into the East River. They were encased in cement and tossed overboard from rum boats in the harbor. Life was cheap and murder was easy in the bootleg industry, and those men of ambition who fought their way to the top were endowed with savagery, shrewdness and luck. . . .

They were endowed, too, as time was to make clear, with the power of organization behind them. The savage, untamed maverick who muscled his way to headline prominence and sometimes to gaudy wealth was playing a game of Russian roulette in a world in which the loosely knit Mafia organizations and their allies began to concentrate power in a mutual benefit society known as the Combination. Their aim was to turn the disorganized, racketing world of crime into a business cartel under the czarlike rule of "family" heads; and those who stood in their way, who did not belong to the family, stood not a chance. Big Bill Dwyer had been wise when he took himself off to Tropical Park. Equally astute, his partner, Owney Madden, as tough as they came, hied himself away to Little Rock, Arkansas, where he established his own resort-gambling preserve and for years impersonated the role of retired, lovable, cracker-barrel philosopher. The third partner in Dwyer's combine, Waxey Gordon, was not so perceptive —and, in the end, paid the inevitable penalty.

What was happening depended in great degree upon the swatch of crime lords spawned in that hatchery of underworld leadership—Brooklyn, the Borough of Churches. There in an area of stews, saloons, and loathsome tenements hard by the waterfront was the depraved, crime-ridden Barbary Coast of the East. The section was known as "the eighth of the eighth"—a phrase meaning the Eighth Election District of the Eighth Assembly District—and it was a saying that came to have a dark significance in Brooklyn; for it is doubtful that any other slum, anywhere, ever graduated so many crime lords whose names would make headlines across the land. Even today, the mere calling of the roll revives images of the dominance the underworld achieved over much of the legitimate life of the nation. There were such names as these: Johnny Torrio, the first to unite the warring gangs of Chicago and the first businessman of crime; Alphonse ("Scarface Al") Capone, his heir, who in effect ruled the Chicago police and the Chicago municipal government; Frankie Yale, national head of the Unione Siciliano; Salvatore Luciana, to be better known as Charles ("Charlie Lucky") Luciano, the eventual mastermind of the American Mafia and architect of the international narcotics traffic; Albert ("Big Al") Anastasia, commander of the goon squads of Murder Inc., enforcers for allied syndicates across the country; and Joseph Doto, better known as Joe Adonis, soon to become the gangster-political boss of Brooklyn and the powerful partner of Frank Costello.

The elder statesman of this group, a man who was to be valued for his sage advice even after he had surrendered power, was Johnny Torrio. Torrio had been born in Naples in 1882. He was a small man, slightly built, with small hands and feet. He didn't drink, smoke, curse, gamble, or chase after loose women. He stayed home nights and played pinochle with his wife or listened to good music, and Mrs. Ann Torrio always vowed she had the most marvelous husband in the world—even though he was the same man who ran a whole string of the most gaudy whorehouses Chicago or the nation has ever known. A bundle of human contradictions that would have fascinated a psychiatrist, Johnny Torrio shrank from physical violence and claimed he had never pulled a trigger in his life—but he could order executions to be carried out by his henchmen without batting his little, dark, watchful eyes. His small stature led some to dub him "Little John";

his deeds earned him a more appropriate sobriquet—
"Terrible John."

Torrio in the early 1900s operated in the vicinity of
Navy Street, hard by the Brooklyn Navy Yard. Here he
came to know a large and powerfully built boy named Al
Capone, who had been born on January 17, 1899, in the
tenement area near Sands and Navy Streets. One of young
Capone's first schoolmates in P.S. 7—one with whom he
was to establish a lifelong friendship—was the boy who
was to become known as Lucky Luciano.

Capone was swarthy-featured, an overgrown hulk of a
lad, with powerful fists and a volcanic temper that would
erupt on the least provocation. He shook the dust of the
schoolroom from his feet when he was fourteen after an
altercation in which he struck his teacher and was in turn
thrashed by his principal. Torrio, who operated a so-called
"social club," The John Torrio Association, always had a
sharp eye out for likely young recruits and quickly recognized the potential in the unruly, quick-tempered Al Capone. It was probably through his influence that Capone
and Luciano both became members of the Five Points
gang in Lower Manhattan. This was one of the toughest
mobs ever to terrorize New York, and it operated in an
area bounded by the Bowery and Broadway from 14th
Street south to City Hall. As a Five-Pointer, Capone was
arrested three times, once for disorderly conduct, twice on
suspicion of homicide. But the police could not make any
of the charges stick.

As a teen-ager who had already scored in such brutal
fashion, Capone had much to recommend him to the Sicilian Frank Uale, better known as Frankie Yale, who, at
25, was coming to dominate the Brooklyn rackets. Yale
owned a dive known as the Harvard Inn on the Coney Island waterfront; he commanded a squad of goons who
were for hire by either side in labor-management disputes;
he managed prizefighters and owned racehorses, nightclubs, a funeral parlor. He was also the national head of
the Unione Siciliano, a fraternal organization that had
some legitimate charitable objectives but one that was rid-

dled with gangsters and whose chief was always a Mafioso. Frankie Yale certainly wasn't interested in the fraternal side of Unione. He had, above all else, one specialty—
murder. "I'm an undertaker," he said brashly.

The "undertaker" had uses for a rising young punk like
Al Capone. Yale hired Al as a bartender and bouncer for
his Harvard Inn; and Al with his huge, pile-driving fists
bounced most efficiently. It was, however, a risky profession; and one night, when Capone made an offensive remark to the sister of a small-time thug, Frank Galluccio,
Galluccio surprised him by pulling a knife with which he
carved up Al's face in remarkable fashion. Al was left with
a four-inch scar across his left cheek and smaller scars on
his left jaw and neck, disfigurements that later would lead
newsmen to tag him with the nickname he hated, Scarface
Al.

While Al Capone was bouncing obstreperous customers
and acquiring his scars, Johnny Torrio was becoming a
racket power in Chicago. He had been called west in 1909
by his uncle, James ("Big Jim") Colosimo, the whoremas-
ter and nightclub impresario of that most depraved city.
Big Jim was a huge, fleshy, bearlike man, jovial and mous-
tachioed. He had started his career by becoming a pimp at
eighteen and had laid the foundation for his fortune by
marrying a madam some years his senior. An enterprising
man as such stepping-stones to affluence show, Big Jim
had then developed a whole string of bawdy houses and
had masterminded the activities of a white slave ring that
lured attractive, unsuspecting girls into the city on the
promise of jobs; imprisoned them, had them "broken in"
by professional rapists, then used them as human mer-
chandise in the bagnios of Chicago's infamous red-light
district.

This traffic, it was estimated, gave Big Jim a gross annual income of some $600,000, a flow of cash that al-
lowed him to indulge loftier aspirations. These took the
form of Colosimo's Café, founded in 1910, which soon
became the most famous nightspot in Chicago, the "in"
place where celebrities from all walks of life cavorted. Big

Jim was a jovial, popular host. A sartorial fashionplate literally dripping with diamonds, he would make his way among the tables, fawning on the famous, flattered by them, frequently springing for champagne and cigars on the house.

Such ostentatious prosperity, however, had its perils. The Black Hand was still active in Chicago; and, even before Big Jim opened his famous club, he had become a prime target for shakedowns. At first, he paid; but the Black Hand's demands became ever more exorbitant, and Big Jim saw that there would have to be an end to paying. In this emergency, he appealed to his nephew, "Terrible John" Torrio.

Torrio went out to Chicago and quickly lived up to his nickname. There was a sudden rash of violence; police kept finding Italians whose bodies had been turned into sieves by shotgun pellets. The police were baffled, naturally; but the underworld understood. The word rapidly spread that it was no longer safe to try to pluck Big Jim Colosimo, and Big Jim bestrode Chicago's red-light Levee district, a more powerful presence than ever.

He was naturally grateful to Terrible John, who had accomplished this miracle, and he gradually delegated to his nephew the tedious chores involved in the daily management of his string of saloons, gambling dens, and whorehouses. Torrio proved a most efficient, farsighted and ruthless manager, and profits piled up in larger mounds than ever. Given an ever freer hand, Torrio began to build his own organization within unsuspecting Big Jim's organization; and in 1919 he sent a call to Brooklyn for Al Capone to come west and help him.

Two events now conspired to change the face of the Chicago underworld. The first was the coming of Prohibition; the second, a bad case of love. Big Jim's fabulous nightclub had become his one real interest in life, and it was there that he fell hopelessly in love with a young singer, Dale Winter, who had been discovered in a church choir. Big Jim made her the singing star of his nightclub act, and he paid the madam who had been his wife all

these years $50,000 to give him a divorce. When he told
Terrible John about his new matrimonial aspirations, Torrio replied: "It's your funeral." A most prophetic remark.

Torrio had been trying to get Big Jim interested in the
astronomical fortunes to be made in the new bootlegging
racket, but Big Jim wasn't lured. The money was rolling in
from his nightclub, his gambling casinos, and his whorehouses. Who needed more? Besides, he was in love.

He and Dale were married and went off on their honey-
moon. The word began to get around the Chicago underworld that Big Jim had "gone soft," and there were reports that he was being shaken down again for fancy
amounts of cash—and that now, afraid his young bride
might be harmed, he was paying the extortionists. In any
event, the newlyweds had just returned to Chicago when,
on the afternoon of May 11, 1920, Big Jim received a
telephone call from his nephew, Terrible John. Torrio told
him that he would have to be at his club at four P.M. to
accept the delivery of two truckloads of illegal whiskey.
Get it, Big Jim? Be sure to be there at four; Torrio was
quite emphatic about it.

A homburg on his head and a rose in his buttonhole,
Big Jim had his chauffeur drive him to the café, promising
Dale to send the car back so that she could go shopping.
At the club he conferred with a couple of members of his
staff and seemed annoyed that no one had appeared, no
one had phoned. About 4:25 P.M. he started to walk
alone through the deserted vestibule. A few seconds later
the staff members with whom he had been conferring
heard two sharp reports. Backfires? No, they didn't sound
quite like backfires. The employees went to investigate,
and there on the porcelain tiles of the vestibule, they
found Big Jim lying face down, dead, blood streaming
from a bullet hole behind his right ear.

Subsequent investigations, though they never could establish a case that would stand up in court, didn't leave
much room for doubt about what had happened. Chicago
police caught up with Frankie Yale, the Brooklyn "undertaker," as he was about to hop an eastbound train. He ex-

plained that he had been just visiting in Chicago for the past week, and police, having nothing on him, had to let him go. Later, the underworld grapevine reported that Terrible John had paid the "undertaker" $10,000 to do the job on Big Jim, dearly beloved uncle and benefactor. It couldn't really have been true, could it? When Chicago police quizzed Terrible John, his eyes filled with tears. "Big Jim and me were like brothers," he said. And when Big Jim went to his final rest in the gaudiest gangster funeral Chicago had ever seen, two of the most elaborate floral tributes bore cards saying "From Johnny" and "From Al."

Almost from the instant of Big Jim's sudden and unfortunate demise, grieving Johnny Torrio became the ganglord of Chicago. Johnny didn't like violence—not if it could be helped, that is—and he went to all the greedy, cutthroat gang bosses with a businesslike proposition. In effect, he said this: Let's stop blowing each other's brains out; let's organize so that each man has his own territory, we respect each other's turf, we work together. There are enough millions for everyone.

Johnny Torrio was a good salesman, his mutual-interest pact was negotiated, and for three years relative peace came to the Chicago underworld. Torrio had Al Capone to back him up, and the two of them bribed just about every policeman and politician who mattered. They enjoyed a perfect immunity from the law and were soon rolling in more millions than Big Jim Colosimo had ever envisioned.

But, as so often happens in gangdom, mere millions are not enough. There is always some insatiably greedy bastard who can't be content with a fortune; he wants the whole hog. And so it was now. Dion O'Banion, head of the Irish gang, began to act up; he broke the Torrio-Capone pact and touched off a new underworld war.

O'Banion operated his rackets from an innocent-looking front, a flower shop. He was in this shop trimming some chrysanthemums just before noon on November 10, 1924 when his porter saw a sedan stop in front and three men get out. One was tall and wore a brown fedora; the other two were short and stocky. O'Banion greeted them as if they were old friends and told his porter to leave them alone and shut the door to the back room.

The man had hardly obeyed his boss when the most fearful racket broke out. As police later reconstructed the event, the tall man had held out his hand to shake with O'Banion, then had gripped the flower shop proprietor, jerking him forward and pinioning his arms while the two thugs with him pumped six bullets into O'Banion's body. By the time the porter got back to the front of the shop, the murder squad had vanished and O'Banion was dead, his blood staining a blanket of white peonies.

Police investigations once more indicated that the deed was the work of the "undertaker" from Brooklyn. It was really a remarkable coincidence the way Frankie Yale always just happened to be visiting old friends in Chicago when sudden bursts of lead poisoning struck down their enemies. . . .

The murder of Dion O'Banion ripped it. Guns began to blaze all over the streets of Chicago, and the day that didn't have its new corpse, or corpses, was an unusual day indeed. The blood bath reached such proportions—some five hundred gangsters were slaughtered before it was over —that even Lucky Luciano was appalled. On a visit to the Windy City, he called Chicago "a real goddamn crazy place. Nobody's safe in the streets."

One of the first persons to find the streets unsafe was Terrible John Torrio. Only some two and a half months after the O'Banion unpleasantness, on the afternoon of January 24, 1925, Torrio, his wife, and their chauffeur were carrying some packages from their car into their apartment house. A Cadillac limousine with four men inside pulled up at the curb. Two of the men leaped out, guns blazing. Torrio caught the full blast. He was blown down to the pavement, his jaw shattered and his chest, right arm, and groin pincushioned with bullets. As the gunmen sped away, he managed to crawl along the sidewalk to his wife, who dragged him inside the apartment house. Later, in the hospital, with his jaw wired up, Torrio adhered to the code of *omertà*.

"Sure, I know all four men," he muttered, "but I'll never tell their names."

As a man who shunned violence except by remote control, Johnny Torrio now discovered that violence had become much too personal. Recovered from his wounds, he announced that he was retiring from the rackets; he and Ann were going for a visit to the old country; and he was turning over all of his Chicago interests, free of charge, to Al Capone.

Scarface Al assumed command in a very parlous time. With Johnny Torrio's peace pacts gunned into discard, the Polish, Irish, and Jewish mobs of Chicago were uniting with O'Banion's followers in a war of supremacy. Though Capone was of Neapolitan descent—a fact of considerable importance in an age of clannish prejudice in which Mafiosi looked with suspicion on any gangster who could not trace his roots back to Sicily—the struggle for survival drove the Italian and Sicilian factions of Chicago into Capone's army. And Capone quickly demonstrated that he was one of the most ruthless and efficient commanders the underworld had ever known.

Some of his deeds were so bloody and so savage that they stand out with unique distinction in the sanguinary annals of a savage time. Once, learning that three Sicilian leaders were planning to double-cross him, he invited them to a banquet at his Hawthorne Inn in Cicero, the Chicago suburb he had turned into a mob haven. When the three had been wined and dined to repletion, Capone sprang the trap. His henchmen bound them to their chairs, and Scarface Al, a baseball bat in his powerful hands, methodically bashed them one by one until, when their corpses were found, there was hardly an unbroken bone in their bodies.

Equally memorable in the sagas of crime was the St. Valentine's Day Massacre of 1929. George ("Bugs") Moran had taken over the O'Banion mob and had been so indiscreet as to renew the warfare with Capone. Scarface Al, not liking the sub-zero chill of Chicago, had taken himself off to sunny Florida; but he had arranged a little caper. Seven of Moran's henchmen were lured to a warehouse where they were supposed to receive a shipment of liquor. As they were waiting, a black Cadillac roared up, and five men sprang out, two wearing policemen's uniforms. The seven Moran henchmen were lined up against the warehouse wall and cut to pieces with machine-gun fire. Moran, who had been approaching the warehouse at the time of this bloody coup, managed to escape the fate that had been arranged for him; and, with the racketing of Capone's guns in his ears, he recognized the futility of further battle.

By such methods, Capone decimated the rival mobs of Chicago and grabbed for himself supreme power. Some 70 percent of the Chicago rackets were in his hands, and it was estimated that, in 1928, when he was only 29, he was reaping a gross income of some $105 million a year.

His was a headline name in newspapers from coast to coast, and his power spread nearly as fast as the headlines. On the East Coast he had his deputy—Frankie Yale, the "undertaker," the Mafia boss of Brooklyn. Yale's principal responsibility was to protect Capone's liquor trucks, to see that nothing untoward happened to them as they rumbled westward with their high-proof cargos from Rum Row. For a time, all went well; but then the greed endemic in the mob, where enough is never enough, began to addle the brain of Frankie Yale.

Scarface Al's liquor trucks began to be hijacked just like anybody else's liquor trucks. Capone, whom no one ever accused of being stupid, soon deduced that such disasters couldn't happen—and keep right on happening—without the connivance of his deputy. Suspecting a double-cross, Capone sent an undercover agent to Brooklyn to investigate, but the event quickly demonstrated that Yale had good sources of information, too. The undercover man didn't last long; he was murdered. And Capone declared war.

Yale was a loud, brash, swaggering hood, as his boast about being an undertaker showed. He fancied tailormade suits and diamond-studded belts; and about three o'clock on July 1, 1928, a quiet Sunday afternoon, he arrayed himself in his most resplendent finery, his belt buckle ablaze with brilliants, and went out for a relaxing ride. Behind the wheel of his powerful new sedan, bulletproof windows down to let in the air, he tooled along Brooklyn's 44th Street, a quiet residential area. He was so at peace with the world that he paid no attention to another sedan, going a little faster, coming up from behind and pulling out to pass. Right alongside, the strange sedan seemed to accommodate its speed to Frankie Yale's, and at that instant, the most frightful rat-tat-tat shattered the silence of the Brooklyn street. It sounded as if all the automobiles in Brooklyn had started backfiring at the same instant, but Frankie Yale never heard the unseemly Sunday uproar.

A machine gun held on the level of his head only a few feet away pumped its bullets unerringly, and Frankie sagged forward over the steering wheel, dead. His car, out of control, leaped the sidewalk, crashed through a low hedge, hit the stone steps of a nearby house—and dumped Frankie Yale's suddenly unlovely body into the midst of a Sunday afternoon garden party.

The sensational extinction of Frankie Yale, amid the screams of hysterical women, was one of the more dramatic events of a series demonstrating to a sage new breed of gangsters that matters were getting a bit out of hand. There was all that never-ending bloodletting in Chicago. In New York, the pathological killer, Jack ("Legs") Diamond, and the beer baron and numbers king of the Bronx, Arthur ("Dutch Schultz") Flegenheimer, were blasting away at each other. It was all giving the bootlegging business a bad name, and something should be done to stop it. Such was the rationale behind the first conclaves of crime —sessions that were to become known as Grand Council meetings of the Mafia.

The first of these of which law enforcement officials became aware took place in Cleveland on the night of December 5, 1928. Patrolman Frank Osowski spotted a group of men entering Cleveland's Hotel Statler at an unusually late hour. "They looked both ways and pulled their hats down as they entered the hotel," Osowski later testified, explaining the reason for his suspicions.

Acting on his hunch, Cleveland police raided the hotel and rounded up twenty-three Mafiosi. All of them were well supplied with folding money, and thirteen had guns. Several, like the powerful Joseph Profaci, of Brooklyn, who was soon to become head of one of the five Mafia families of New York, were to turn up nearly thirty years later at the much more highly publicized Mafia conclave at Apalachin.

Little is known about the purposes of this first grand council session, probably because the police broke it up before discussions could get under way; but the second crime conference just a few months later was probably the most important ever held in America. It perfected the framework for the nationally functioning criminal organization that was to be known through the years by various names—the Combination, the Syndicate, the Mafia and, finally, the Cosa Nostra.

The meeting was held in the President Hotel on the Atlantic City, N.J., boardwalk from May 13 to 16, 1929. Delegates came from New York, Chicago, Detroit, Philadelphia, Boston, and other cities. They represented, not just the Sicilian Mafia, but gangsters of various ethnic origins who had acquired such power that their cooperation was needed.

According to reports, Enoch J. ("Nucky") Johnson, then the unrivaled political boss of Atlantic City and himself a numbers racketeer, welcomed the brethren. From Chicago came Al Capone, accompanied by his bodyguard, Frank Cline, and his leading henchmen, Frank ("The Enforcer") Nitti and Jake ("Greasy Thumb") Guzik. Philadelphia was represented by Max ("Boo Boo") Hoff, Sam Lazar and Charles Schwartz; New York, by Dutch Schultz, Frank Costello, Lucky Luciano, and Joe Adonis.

Don Vitone Genovese rose from pimp to multi-millionaire and Boss of Bosses, or the Kingmaker. The era of Genovese was marked by a carnival of murder. WIDE WORLD PHOTOS

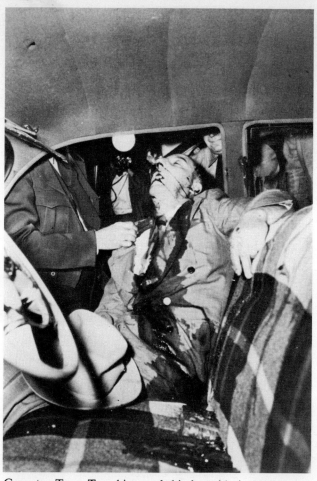

Gangster Tony Trombino took his last ride in Hollywood and turned up looking like this. Police believe he and his companion were shot by someone sitting in the back seat.

UPI

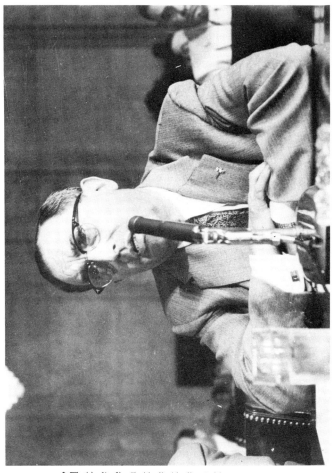

Joseph Profaci, another survivor, died of natural causes at 65. Known as the Olive Oil King, the veteran Brooklyn Mafioso always had at his command some of the deadliest torpedoes in the underworld. UPI

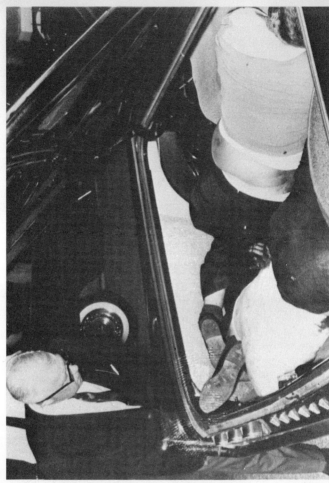

In Chicago, these two bodies were found crammed into the trunk of an automobile. The men, reported missing a month before, had earlier been involved in a loan company holdup. The police assume they were silenced because they knew too much. UPI

Larry Gallo, button man for Joe Profaci; he and his goon squad took credit for Anastasia's murder.   UPI

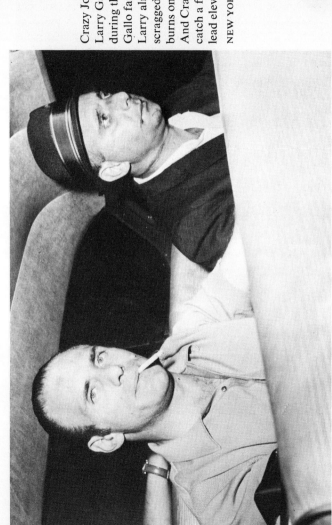

Crazy Joe (*left*) and Larry Gallo in 1961, during the Profaci–Gallo family war. Larry almost got scragged; note the rope burns on his neck. And Crazy Joe was to catch a fatal dose of lead eleven years later. NEW YORK DAILY NEWS

An innocent man, whose claim to fame was that he could identify the murderer in a barroom slaying, was killed in what police call "the gangland style." He was taken for a ride and dumped from a moving car into an empty New York street, the sash cord knotted around his neck.   UPI

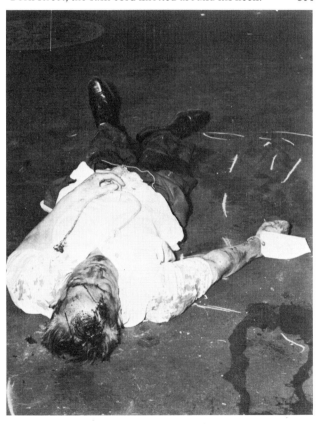

Famed underword informer Joseph Valachi blew the lid off
Mafia operations before the Senate Investigations subcommittee. At one time, Valachi had been a cellmate of Genovese in Atlanta.

Joe Colombo Sr., arrested as alleged multi-million-dollar policy boss in 1971. When he assumed command of the Profaci family in 1964, he was only 41, the youngest Mafia boss in the nation. WIDE WORLD PHOTOS

Joe Colombo (in fur parka) went public when he started the Italian–American Civil Rights League and picketed the New York office of the F.B.I. He had always denied that he had any connections with the Mafia, and even that the Mafia existed at all.

UPI

Joe Colombo lies critically wounded while in the background his attacker is being shot by one of Colombo's bodyguards, 1971.   UPI

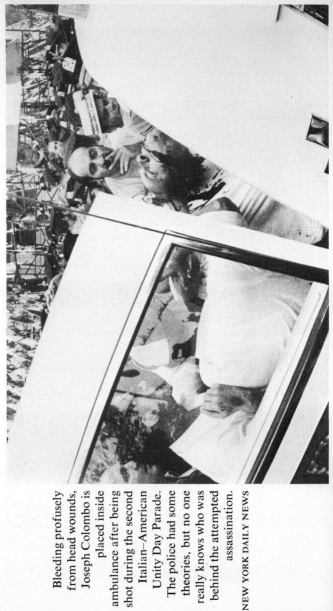

Bleeding profusely from head wounds, Joseph Colombo is placed inside ambulance after being shot during the second Italian–American Unity Day Parade. The police had some theories, but no one really knows who was behind the attempted assassination.

NEW YORK DAILY NEWS

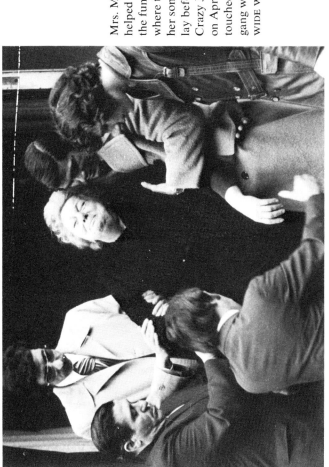

Mrs. Mary Gallo is helped as she leaves the funeral home where the body of her son, Joe Gallo, lay before burial. Crazy Joe's murder on April 7, 1972, touched off a bloody gang war.
WIDE WORLD PHOTOS

World-famous singer Frank Sinatra was called by a House Select Committee on Crime for questioning on alleged mobster connections with a New England racetrack. It's also been alleged that Sinatra had ties with some ten of the best-known gangsters in the country during the '50s and '60s.   WIDE WORLD PHOTOS

Thomas ("Tommy Ryan") Eboli, a major power in the Genovese family, was killed July 16, 1972, possibly as a result of revolt within the ranks of that family.

Carlo Gambino (*center*) flanked by two F.B.I. agents, was charged with conspiracy in connection with a planned $6 million armored-truck robbery. Free today, Gambino is reputed to be the chairman of the Syndicate's national commission and is the most powerful Mafia boss in the nation.

WIDE WORLD PHOTOS

Johnny Torrio, returned from Italy and now in the position of an elder statesman of the rackets, was also there.

Costello is generally believed to have been the brains behind this epochal session. He was then a third-echelon figure—the *consigliere,* or counselor, of the New York Mafia family of Joe ("The Boss") Masseria, whose right-hand man was Lucky Luciano. Costello, however, already had acquired considerable stature. He was widely respected for his wiliness and wisdom, and he had compiled a millionaire's fortune as one of the kingpins of the East Coast rum-running cartel known as the Big Seven. Like Torrio and Capone, who had tried unsuccessfully to revive Torrio's peace-pact among the Chicago gangs, Costello was convinced that gang wars in the streets, in which innocent bystanders and even children were sometimes killed or wounded, were doing infinite harm to the profession. He argued that the self-interests of all the mobs and their leaders would be served by a businesslike administration of the affairs of crime.

The result was a series of key decisions. The Federal Bureau of Narcotics, over the years the best federal source on the activities of organized crime, has concluded after careful checking and cross-checking of the accounts of a number of informers that the Atlantic City conference arrived at four major decisions. They were:

1. It established the basis for the organization of a national crime syndicate. Delegates reportedly took a map of the United States and carved the nation up into specific territories. Gang bosses, regardless of ethnic background, who had established their rule and demonstrated their efficiency were confirmed in their control of specified areas and special rackets. The most important were named to a national board or, as it was to become known, the national commission of crime.

2. The hierarchy was to be protected. No top-level boss could be executed unless the national commission judged him guilty of unpardonable offenses against the organization. Lowly button men (or soldiers) were protected, too; they were not to be killed without a hearing before the un-

derboss or lieutenant in their particular family. In effect, a
system of kangaroo courts was established, providing
gangland with its own judicial system.

3. Emissaries were appointed to deal with politicians
and police on a national basis. According to some informants, arrangements were made to establish a multi-million-
dollar slush fund to bribe law-enforcement officials and to
insure the election of complaisant politicians to important
offices.

4. Another slush fund, an "educational fund," was to
be established to further the development of promising
young gang members and to guarantee them the education
and give them the proper veneer to serve the organization
as innocent-appearing front men or future executives.

Such was the sweeping program outlined at Atlantic
City. To implement it, the conferees relied upon that master advocate of the crime pact, Johnny Torrio. He was to
serve, at least temporarily, as senior adviser and adminis-
trator to get the machinery of the new organization running.

The course that had been charted for organized crime
was no less than revolutionary. The inbred, stubborn clannishness of Italian immigrants had led them to trust only
their own; the Mafia historically had been willing to accept
into its ranks only those gangsters of Sicilian background.
The idea of collaborating with Neapolitans was anathema;
and the new concept that the national combination should
include other ethnic gangsters like the Irish and the Jews
was heresy of the worst order.

The old-line Mafia leadership, the "Greasers" or the
"Moustache Petes," as they were called, would never accept such a radical departure from orthodoxy; and so they
precipitated the bloodiest underworld coup in gangland
history—the event that was to be given the grandiloquent
title, The Night of the Sicilian Vespers.

5.

The Changing of the Guard

Giuseppe ("Joe the Boss") Masseria was the prototype of the old order. Short, chunky, vain, and suspicious, he trusted only Sicilians—and his own limited brand of Sicilians, at that. He had risen to power in the early 1920s; he had dueled rivals in the very shadow of New York Police Headquarters; and he had escaped assassination so many times that the legend grew he could run faster and dodge quicker than any bullet could fly. Like most legends, this one strayed from the truth. As events were to show, agile Joe the Boss could duck only the bullets of his enemies, not those of his friends.

Joe the Boss began his climb to power in 1920 by gunning down a rival bootlegger named Salvatore Mauro in a pitched battle in the middle of Chrystie Street. For some years afterwards, he was engaged in running warfare, first to establish his power, then to keep it. His principal rival was a gangster named Umberto Valenti, and the protracted struggle between the two created the legend of Joe the Boss's invulnerability.

The curtain on the first act was raised almost under the windows of the Police Commissioner. In their brash contempt of the law, the bootleggers had practically ringed

71

headquarters with what became known as "the curb exchange." This was the underworld's version of the stock exchange. If, for example, a bootlegger became overburdened with bourbon just at the moment when his customers developed an exclusive thirst for scotch, it became necessary for him to swap the liquor he had for the liquor he needed. To make such a deal, he had to contact fellow bootleggers at their favorite rendezvous, the curbside exchange they had established along Kenmare, Broome, Grand, and Elizabeth Streets, virtually encircling the headquarters of New York's finest.

Joe the Boss, feeling certain that Umberto Valenti would be visiting the curb exchange, set a trap early in the evening of May 8, 1922. He stationed himself and two henchmen in the doorway of 194 Grand Street, only a short distance from the southern end of headquarters. Valenti and a hired gun, Silva Tagliagamba, appeared almost on schedule, and Joe the Boss and his two torpedoes popped out into the street, the guns in their hands going off like firecrackers. Valenti and Tagliagamba fired back, and bullets from the fusillade, zinging along the street, wounded four passersby, two women and two men. Valenti and Tagliagamba fled.

With the gunfire almost splitting the eardrums of detectives in headquarters, the law made an appearance on the run; and Masseria and his helpers took to their heels. Joe the Boss churned around the corner of Mulberry Street into Broome, where his agents were transacting the day's business. The boys ducked into doorways when they saw The Boss charging by with two detectives on his heels. Joe the Boss lightened his load by tossing a .38 caliber revolver into the gutter. One of the pursuing detectives stopped to pick it up, and Joe the Boss dashed on toward Kenmare Street. Here he ran into Edward Tracey, a detective sergeant on his way to headquarters. Tracey swerved his car directly into The Boss's path, leaped out and clunked Joe the Boss over the head with a nightstick.

When the stunned boss was taken to headquarters, detectives frisked him and found a most curious document—

a gun permit signed by Supreme Court Justice Selah B. Strong permitting him to carry a gun anywhere he went in the state. Since it was hardly the duty of the courts to legitimize the possession of murder weapons by notorious criminals, this discovery touched off a twenty-four-hour scandal. But the shock lasted no longer than that; in those days, in New York as in other sections of the country, a lot of strange things were happening.

The aftermath of this affray, like a one-two punch in the prize ring, gave a further demonstration of Joe the Boss's ability to mesmerize the law. Valenti's henchman, Tagliagamba, wounded in the gun battle, held on to life until late June, then succumbed. The law went through the motions of charging Joe the Boss with murder; but then, in an act of almost unheard-of generosity, it permitted him liberty on bail. A further indication of Joe the Boss's stature in the eyes of guardians of law and justice was to be found in the fact that the murder case against him was never brought to trial. Postponement followed postponement, and Joe the Boss continued to do business as usual almost under the windows of headquarters.

Umberto Valenti became impatient. He had waited, hoping the electric chair might do his work for him; but when it became evident the law had no intention of plunking Joe the Boss in the seat-of-no-return in Sing Sing, Valenti decided to give justice a hand. For this high-minded mission, he picked four torpedoes who were supposed to know their business.

At the time, Joe the Boss lived with his wife and two children at 80 Second Avenue, just a few doors from the corner of Fifth Street. Shortly after noon on the hot summer day of August 9, 1922, he left his apartment, sporting a new straw hat, and turned north toward Fifth Street. Two of Valenti's torpedoes were waiting in a black limousine parked down the street, and two others were in a nearby coffee house, watching from a window. This pair, the instant they saw Joe the Boss leave his home, dropped their coffee cups and ran out, one dashing behind him, the other racing ahead to cut him off.

The man in front was too eager; he opened fire too soon and Joe the Boss, alerted to his danger, sprinted into Heiney's Millinery Shop at 82 Second Avenue. The gunman followed. Fritz Heiney, the proprietor, stood petrified at the scene that now took place before his eyes.

"The man with the revolver came close to the other fellow and aimed," he said. "Just as he fired the man jumped to one side. The bullet smashed the window of my store. Then the man fired again and the fellow he aimed at ducked his head forward. The third shot made a second hole in my window."

The frustrated torpedo clicked the revolver a couple of more times at Joe the Boss's bobbing head; then, out of bullets, he dashed from the shop and ran with his companion to the getaway car. The car swung the corner into Fifth Street, which was swarming at the time with members of the International Ladies' Garment Workers' Union coming from a meeting in Beethoven Hall, half a block away. Some of the workers tried to stop the speeding car, but the thugs who hadn't been able to hit Joe the Boss proved equal to the task of picking off targets in this massed, unarmed crowd. Their shots felled five workers, and two others were knocked down by the speeding car. One man subsequently died of his wounds.

Arriving belatedly at the scene of this latest shootout, detectives tracked Joe the Boss to his home. There they found him sitting on the side of his bed, his feet, aching from his latest marathon with death, immersed in a pan of hot water. On his head he still wore his new straw hat—with two bullet holes in its crown. Thus was born the legend that Joe the Boss could outrun and outdodge bullets.

No legend could settle the feud with Umberto Valenti, however; and Joe the Boss, considering the problem, decided to put his trust in a favorite Mafia tactic—the sophisticated double-cross. He let it be known that he was tired of dodging bullets, and he suggested to Valenti, through an emissary, that the time had come to live and let live. The deluded Valenti agreed to drink the wine of peace, and he and Joe the Boss, each with just one retainer by his side, dined in a spaghetti house on East Twelfth Street near Second Avenue on August 11, 1922.

The love feast finished, the fraternal foursome, who had demonstrated their good will by coming unarmed, took a leisurely stroll along Twelfth Street in the direction of Second Avenue. What Valenti didn't know was that Masseria had stationed two extra hands at the corner. At a signal from Joe the Boss, his waiting gunmen whipped out their barkers and blazed away.

Valenti, trying to emulate Joe the Boss's agile footwork, fled diagonally across the intersection toward a waiting taxicab. One of Masseria's gun-toters followed him out into the intersection, stopped, and touched off a full clip of bullets. Valenti managed to reach the taxicab and jerk open the door. Then he pitched over backwards from the effect of the final and fatal shot.

In such fashion did Giuseppe Masseria pull off his coup. Valenti had been eliminated, and Masseria became, in reality, Joe the Boss. True, he had another murder charge hanging over his head, the second that had been brought against him in three months. But potential witnesses, aware of the sinister power of the Mafia, suddenly lost all recollection of events; and the law, for whatever mysterious reasons of its own, seemed possessed of no overwhelming passion to prosecute. So Joe the Boss went on his way, running the affairs of crime.

Joe the Boss now ruled a family that was to produce over the next decades a succession of the most powerful Mafia chiefs in the nation. Directly under him as underboss was Lucky Luciano; and next to Luciano, Vito Genovese. Frank Costello followed in the pecking order; and then came Joe Adonis, Albert Anastasia, Carlo Gambino and Willie Moretti. It was a combination that should have overawed all rivals and, indeed, might have except for the flaws of its leader. Joe the Boss was not a modern man; he belonged to the generation of "the Greasers," with the purblind clannishness that leads to vendetta bred into the marrow of his bones.

After the gunning down of Valenti, Joe the Boss ruled for a few years with some discretion. He retired into the background and spread the story that he had given up the rackets and was living on his accumulated hoard. He was, of course, doing nothing of the kind. He was simply letting his chief lieutenant, Lucky Luciano, run the rackets for him while he maintained all of his alliances with other bosses in the underworld power structure. In the Bronx he remained, as always, the close ally of Ciro Terranova, the Artichoke King. In Brooklyn, Frankie Yale was his deputy as well as Capone's; and after Yale took his last Sunday afternoon ride, Joe the Boss had an equally satisfactory understanding with his successor, Anthony ("Little Augie") Pisano.

Everything would seem to indicate either that Joe the Boss did not know about the master plan for underworld organization drafted at the Atlantic City conference in 1929 or, more probably, that he was simply contemptuous of the whole idea and determined to go his own way. For, in 1930, he touched off a new war of the underworld.

Joe the Boss's purpose, according to the swan song sung by Joseph Valachi before the McClellan committee in 1963, was to exterminate Sicilian gangsters who had come from the area of Castellammare del Golfo. Valachi never could explain why Masseria developed such a sudden blood-thirst for the Castellammarese; but he declared that Joseph Profaci had assured him it was a fact—that Masseria planned to eliminate the Castellammarese wherever his gunmen found them; in New York, Buffalo, Chicago, anywhere in the United States. The signal for the purge was given on February 26, 1930, when Joe the Boss had his triggermen gun down Tommy Reina, head of a Castellammarese crime family. He then attempted to impose one of his own henchmen on the family as the new boss, and the war was on.

The Castellammarese lined up behind a tough Mafioso, Salvatore Maranzano. He, too, gathered about him Mafiosi who were to become powerful as bosses of their own crime families. They included: Joe Profaci, Thomas ("Three-Finger Brown") Lucchese, Joseph ("Joe Bananas") Bonanno, and Stefano Maggadino. Valachi himself was a lower echelon button man in the Maranzano army.

Forces on both sides "went to the mat" in Valachi's phrase—meaning that they holed up in rented hideaways, sleeping on the floor on mattresses—and there was much "sneaking" of victims, first by one side, then by the other. In this war of attrition, the Masseria forces began to be whittled down, and Maranzano's army grew until he had six hundred troops, with more "coming over" to the winning side regularly.

This continuous blasting made little sense to Joe the Boss's most powerful aides, Lucky Luciano, Vito Genovese and Frank Costello. Not only had the feud been touched off by the whim of one power-mad boss, contrary to the spirit of the Atlantic City convention, but it was bad for business. It was difficult to run complicated rackets when the strongarms of the underworld were huddled in their private fortresses, intent on slaughtering each other. There was only one way to end the bloody disaster—Joe the Boss would have to go.

Secretly, according to Valachi—and other sources agree—Luciano and Maranzano reached an understanding. Charlie Lucky would arrange for the slaying of his own boss. This would re-establish peace in the brotherhood. It would also, naturally, create a vacuum at the top of the Masseria family, and Charlie Lucky, the heir apparent, did not appear to be distraught at the prospect.

Lucky Luciano had one of the wiliest brains the American underworld has ever produced, and in time virtually all of the crime lords would come to consider him as the master. He was small, spruce, dapper, with a scar from a knife wound running along his right cheek from the corner of his eye to his chin. This gave the nearly knifed eye a permanent droop and added a sinister cast to his otherwise chubby, wide-lipped, wiseacre countenance. The misadventure that had given him the scar and the sinister eye had also bestowed upon him the nickname by which he was to be known forever after—Charlie Lucky.

After his boyhood adventures with Al Capone in the Five Points mob, Luciano had gone into narcotics peddling, a traffic that was always to remain his special thing. He afterwards explained that he had not wanted to be a "crumb"; he had only contempt for "crumbs" who grubbed out their lives holding down seven-dollar-a-week jobs. And so, as a way to climb up out of "crumb-hood," he began peddling heroin and morphine—and, by the time he was eighteen, he was caught and committed to six months in a reformatory.

Released—unreformed, of course—he continued to peddle narcotics, but he branched out into other activities as a gambler and gunman. He served for a time as a hired gun for the Diamond brothers, Legs and Eddie. In his journey up through the rackets, he made invaluable contacts with rising East Side hoods who were to become powers in their own right: Louis ("Lepke") Buchalter and his partner, Jacob ("Gurrah") Shapiro, soon to be known as the most savage industrial extortionists of their time; and an East Side band whose specialty was murder —the Bugs and Meyer mob, headed by Benjamin ("Bugsy") Siegel and Meyer Lansky.

Luciano, having forged such connections, was becoming an ever-larger figure in the crime world when he was taken for a ride from which he was not expected to return. Annals of the time assign various motivations for the deed. One has it that Luciano had raped a young Italian girl, and her male relatives were out for revenge; another, that a bunch of young gangsters, looking for narcotics, kidnaped Luciano and hoped to make him talk. In any event, he was spirited away to a lonely spot in Staten Island. There he was hung up by his thumbs; the soles of his feet were burned with cigarettes; his cheek was slashed with a knife, and his body perforated with a number of icepick holes. He was left for dead, but he survived—and became the legendary Charlie Lucky.

By the time of the Masseria-Maranzano war, he had become the underboss of the Masseria family; and Joe the Boss had come to depend upon him, to rely on him almost totally. While the boss had been carrying out the charade that he was no longer interested in the rackets, Lucky Luciano had handled all the intricate details of his crime family and handled them well. Besides, Charlie Lucky had an old-world flair for living and a way of ingratiating himself that Joe the Boss had found irresistible. Their relationship had flowered to the point where Joe the Boss regarded Charlie Lucky as more than his indispensable right-hand man; he looked upon him almost like a son.

Not being a mind reader, Joe the Boss therefore had no suspicion when his almost-son suggested they should go off for a pleasant luncheon at Scarpato's Restaurant in Coney Island on the afternoon of April 15, 1931. They would have a good dinner, play some cards, get away from it all—so Charlie Lucky proposed. And Joe the Boss welcomed the idea.

Others welcomed it, too, and strange things began to happen. Samuel S. Leibowitz, later a judge in Brooklyn's Kings County Court, was then a young lawyer with a growing reputation for his skill in criminal trials. He had represented some of the mobsters and was well known and well liked by them. On the morning of April 15, 1931, he was trying a case in court and his secretary was in his office at 66 Court Street when the door opened and in walked Albert Anastasia, the man who in the not too distant future would be known as the Lord High Executioner of Murder Inc.

"What time is it?" Anastasia asked Leibowitz's secretary.

She pointed to a big clock on the wall.

"There it is," she said. "Look for yourself."

"That says twelve o'clock," Albert A. responded, a bit doubtfully. "Are you sure that's the right time?"

The girl, glancing up at the clock, began to get annoyed.

"Sure," she said, "it's twelve o'clock. If you don't believe it, look out the window at the clock on Borough Hall."

Anastasia looked, pretended to be convinced.

"Is the law man in?" he asked, referring to Leibowitz.

"No, he's in court. He won't be back until one o'clock."

"I'll wait," said Albert A., apparently happy at the prospect.

He settled himself in a chair and sat there patiently, establishing for himself an ironclad alibi should anyone ever want to question him about the events that were soon to take place in Scarpato's Restaurant.

Charlie Lucky and Joe the Boss were already seated at the table there. They had an excellent and leisurely meal, relishing Scarpato's excellent clam sauce, the succulent lobster, and the chianti wine. When the dishes were cleared away, Charlie Lucky proposed a game of cards. Joe the Boss, mellow by now, was perfectly agreeable.

"Good," he grunted, "just for an hour or so; then I must go."

Lucky called for a deck from the house, and they played and chatted companionably for about forty-five minutes. It was by now a little after 3:30 P.M. The restaurant had cleared. Just Joe the Boss and Charlie Lucky, his almost-son, sat there at the table in Scarpato's playing cards. It was at this point that Charlie Lucky politely excused himself and made a trip to the men's room.

He was hardly out of sight when four crude characters wandered in from the street. The underworld grapevine later reported that they were led by that artist in murder, Bugsy Siegel. They walked right up behind Joe the Boss, sitting there bemused by food and wine, and before he could turn his head, they whipped out guns and began blasting away. Some twenty shots were sprayed around the premises. Six of them plowed into Joe the Boss's head and body, all from the back. He had no chance to turn, to dodge and weave this time. He pitched forward across the sparkling white tablecloth, his right arm extended as if it had been his play at cards, in his death-frozen grip the ace of diamonds.

Back in the men's room, Charlie Lucky heard the unholy racket.

"As soon as I finished drying my hands, I hurried out and walked back to see what it was about," he told investigating officers.

All he found, of course, was his dear, beloved patron dead. Those who had done the deed had left.

Joe the Boss, who had managed to outrun and outdodge the bullets of his enemies, hadn't been able to elude those of his friends. He had made gangland's cardinal mistake of trusting completely the man closest to him, and this error of judgment wrought profound changes in the underworld. Charlie Lucky succeeded to his power and perquisites. And Salvatore Maranzano ruled supreme as the boss of bosses. At least for the time being. . . .

It seemed at first as if Don Salvatore Maranzano would be the perfect man to bridge the generation gap between the illiterate "Moustache Petes" of the old order and the new generation of businessmen-gangsters symbolized by Luciano, Costello, and Adonis. Maranzano had been born in Sicily, where he had received a good education and had studied for the priesthood. Valachi, who stood in respectful awe of him, later reported that he could speak seven languages and added: "Gee, he looked just like a banker. You'd never guess in a million years that he was a racketeer."

There was one Maranzano trait that was not so obvious but was just the same all important. He was "a nut about Julius Caesar," as Valachi put it; and just like his Roman hero, he had the soul and mind of a dictator, thirsting for supreme power, unable to brook the slightest opposition.

According to Valachi, Maranzano summoned the mob to a huge, days-long rally during the course of which he told them all, like an emperor speaking from his throne, just how matters were to be arranged in the future. The meeting was held in a big rented hall on Washington Avenue in the Bronx, and some five hundred of the faithful attended. Maranzano began by describing the evils for which Masseria had been responsible—the unjustified shootings, the murder of Tom Reina, the Castellammarese war.

"Now it is going to be different," he said. "We are going to have—first we have the boss of all the bosses, which is myself."

After this modest beginning, Maranzano described in detail the organizational structure which henceforth would govern the affairs of crime. Each Mafia family was to have its own boss. Next in rank would be an underboss, and below him a *caporegima*, or commander of the troops. "Now, if a soldier wants to talk to a boss," Valachi explained in his testimony, "he should not take the privilege for him to try to go direct to the boss. He must speak first to the caporegima; if it is required and if it is important enough, the caporegima will make an appointment for the soldier. . . . This is what I called second government."

Maranzano also imposed upon the New York Mafia the family structure that has endured to this day. He created five major Mafia families. His own army he divided into two wings, one under Joe Profaci, the other under Joe Bonanno. The original Reina family was to be governed by Tom Gagliano, with Three-Finger Brown Lucchese as his underboss. Lucky Luciano was confirmed as ruler of the Masseria family, with Vito Genovese as his underboss. Control of the Brooklyn family that had been ruled by Frankie Yale was less clear-cut. Philip and Vincent Mangano were declared the bosses by Maranzano, according to Valachi; but the power in Brooklyn was soon to be concentrated in the hands of Joe Adonis, with Albert Anastasia as his grim enforcer.

Having issued these decrees Maranzano decided it was time he held a coronation party for himself. According to Valachi, the banquet lasted for five days. Every evening the mob gathered and held high revelry until three or four the next morning; and each mobster who attended, as proof of his fealty, was expected to toss a heavy donation into Maranzano's waiting pot. Valachi "understood" that the five-day celebration netted Maranzano some

$115,000. Maranzano, he said, sent a thousand tickets to Al Capone and Capone sent back $6,000. Another thousand tickets went to Buffalo, and the Maggadino family there contributed $6,000. Charlie Lucky sent another $6,000. "Them were the big amounts I know," Valachi told the McClellan committee.

The "button men" like Valachi had expected to be rewarded for their services in the recent war, but it soon became apparent they were to get nothing. Maranzano kept all the money for himself. As he later explained to Valachi, he needed it for a "war chest," for as far as he was concerned the war was not over. Valachi described how he received a summons to come to Maranzano's home one night and found the "boss of bosses" bandaging a cut on his son's foot. After finishing this fatherly task, Maranzano gave Valachi a peep into the future.

"We have to go to the mattress again," he said.

Maranzano explained that he couldn't get along with Lucky Luciano and Vito Genovese. "We have to get rid of these people," he added, handing Valachi a list. To Valachi's amazement, the list contained some sixty names. As he later recalled it: ". . . On the list was, I will try to remember as I go along: Al Capone, Frank Costello, Charlie Lucky, Vito Genovese, Joe Adonis, Dutch Schultz. These were all important names at the time." And many, Valachi might have added, were still to be important decades later.

Valachi was understandably worried. Knocking off any one of the sixty ganglords on Maranzano's death list would certainly raise bloody hell—but executing sixty of them! Valachi figuratively shuddered at the thought. He was also worried, in the circumstances, by a strange new development at Maranzano's headquarters. The boss had recently instructed his guards not to come to work lugging lethal hardware under their coats because he had heard a rumor the police might raid the place. Valachi didn't like being left so naked and helpless. "I'm afraid they are trying to prepare us to be without guns," he had said to his friends at the time. "I just don't like it."

Now, having been made privy to Maranzano's grandiose plans, he liked it even less. The boss told him that he had scheduled a last conference with Charlie Lucky and Vito Genovese. Valachi protested and urged Maranzano to let a deputy sit in for him. But the boss was obdurate. "No, I got to go," he said.

He was to meet Charlie Lucky and Vito Genovese at two o'clock the following afternoon, September 10, 1931, in his own suite of offices, Rooms 925 and 926, at 230 Park Avenue. Shortly before the appointed hour, four men, all Jewish, walked through the entrance door. They identified themselves to Maranzano's headquarters staff as city detectives. Hearing the discussion, the boss poked his head out of his inner office and invited them in. After all, he had been expecting a call by police.

The door had hardly closed behind the visitors when Maranzano sensed that something was fatally wrong. He lunged for a gun kept in his desk, but the "detectives" had the drop on him. They pounced upon him, stabbing him with knives and blasting away with their guns. In seconds, it was over. The "boss of bosses" was dead with six stab wounds in his abdomen and four bullets in his body.

The "detectives"—all specialists in murder supplied by Luciano's friend and close ally, Meyer Lansky—fled from the scene of their coup. As they ran, they encountered face-to-face one of the most ferocious killers-for-hire of the day, Vincent ("Mad Dog") Coll. The Mad Dog had been hired by Maranzano to take care of Lucky Luciano and Vito Genovese in a planned Maranzano double-cross. Only Luciano had double-crossed the double-crosser first and with finality. Lansky's torpedoes, in the fraternity of murder, simply waved to the Mad Dog to get lost; his employer was dead and the cops were coming.

The execution of the "boss of bosses" touched off a nationwide purge—a sweeping and historic and bloody changing of the guard that has become known as The Night of the Sicilian Vespers. Lucky Luciano was determined to bring a new orderliness to the American underworld, and he did it in just twenty-four hours, eliminating the old "Moustache Petes" in a cross-continent carnival of murder.

One of the first to go was Gerardo Scarpato, proprietor of the Coney Island restaurant where Joe the Boss had been eliminated. Scarpato had insisted to the cops that he had been out for a walk, that he knew nothing about the identity of the gunmen who had blasted Joe the Boss. But he knew that others knew that he knew—and he had lived in terror. "Take my fingerprints," he had told police. "Take 'em for your books. I may be next."

He was not next, but he was right. He was on Luciano's purge list. On September 11, his body was found in the trunk of a parked car in the Prospect Park section of Brooklyn. He had been knocked unconscious by a blow on the head and thrust into a burlap bag, trussed up in such fashion, with his knees drawn up under his chin, that he had strangled himself when he tried to straighten his legs.

Scarpato was not alone. Across the nation, in precisely timed executions, some forty of the old "Moustache Pete" contingent were murdered. It was a purge made possible only by the executive genius of Lucky Luciano, and it was carried out with an efficiency and ruthlessness that would have done credit to a Stalin or a Hitler.

The face of the American underworld had been changed, literally overnight. The Mafia had been Americanized, and the underworld government envisioned in Atlantic City had been established.

6.

Rule of the New Breed

Charles ("Lucky") Luciano imposed the new system of underworld government upon the affairs of crime at a moment in history when events were moving at lightning speed. The Great Depression, which had hit Wall Street in 1929, had deepened into a nationwide disaster that saw banks everywhere closing their doors in 1932. The bad times had brought upheavals in the political structure and customs of the nation. Franklin D. Roosevelt was about to bring the Democratic New Deal to Washington. And anyone with half an eye open could see that public revulsion would soon doom Prohibition and make liquor legal again. The mob's most lucrative racket would be taken away, and substitutes would have to be found to keep gangdom rolling in the millions to which it had become accustomed.

All of these considerations led to a series of grand council meetings of the Mafia and its affiliated mobsters. The first was held in Chicago, with Al Capone as host, shortly after The Night of the Sicilian Vespers. The major item on the agenda was the ratification of Lucky Luciano's deeds and suzerainty. He had had no authority other than his own will for the sweeping purge he had conducted, a deed that violated cardinal tenets in the Atlantic City compact of 1929; and if the system tentatively agreed upon there was to be implemented, if order was to be imposed on the unruly mobs, Luciano and Vito Genovese needed to justify their actions.

According to Joe Valachi, who had a ringside seat at the maneuvers that now began, the first basis of justification was laid in a campaign of innuendo against the character of his departed boss, Salvatore Maranzano. The technique was the same that Nikita Khrushchev would later employ in discussing the sins of Josef Stalin; the same that Vito Genovese would use again some twenty years later in undermining the rule of Frank Costello. Did Valachi know, Genovese asked, that Maranzano had been hijacking Charlie Lucky's liquor trucks? Valachi protested that he had never heard of such a thing. Genovese was scornful. Didn't Valachi know, he asked, that Maranzano had also hijacked trucks carrying piece goods from Tommy Lucchese's garment factories? Valachi hadn't heard of this either. But Genovese assured him that Maranzano had performed such unforgivable deeds, that he had been a traitor to the brotherhood—and so had deserved what he got.

This tarnishing of the memory of his old boss saddened Valachi, but he confessed that Maranzano had showed him the list of fellow chieftains whom he had intended to eliminate. This evidence fitted perfectly into the need of Luciano and Genovese for self-justification. It was suggested that Valachi should go to Chicago and tell the assembled dons his story; but Valachi, out of old loyalty, was reluctant. It made no difference. A fellow mobster, Bobby Doyle, to whom he had told the details, went to the big meet and relayed the information. Since Al Capone's name had headed the prospective murder list, the ratification of Luciano's purge and his rule was almost automatic. . . .

Only a few months later, in April, 1932, the powers of gangdom were meeting again in the Congress Hotel in Chicago. This time, they were called together to consider what action should be taken in the light of an unprece-

dented event. The untouchable, all-powerful Al Capone—
the ganglord who had dominated the Chicago police department and collected politicians as easily as he collected
millions—had fallen. The Internal Revenue Bureau had
nailed him for income tax evasion, and he had been sentenced to spend the next eleven years of his life in federal
prisons. His power had been broken, and control of the
Chicago mobs was up for grabs.

Luciano and other sophisticates of the new breed, shud-
dering at the prospect of another wholesale bloodletting
that would give their business a bad name, went to Chicago, hoping to reach an accommodation. Their task was
difficult. Frank ("The Enforcer") Nitti, considering the
lethal services he had performed for Al Capone, staked a
claim to the throne and wanted to be crowned immediately. Luciano and Meyer Lansky, who had accompanied
him to the parley, preferred the more tactful Paul ("The
Waiter") Ricca. There was heated debate about the rights
of various claimants, but Ricca wound up with the bless-
ing of the powerful Eastern wing of the syndicate. Only
partial pacification had been achieved, however; the quar-
relsome Chicago mobs, as events were to show, would go
right on quarreling in their own bloody fashion.

Conference followed conference in the next few years as
Luciano, with the retiring figures of Johnny Torrio and
Meyer Lansky behind him, gradually put into effect the
more orderly underworld government that had been envisioned in Atlantic City. His conduct of affairs would have
horrified the old Moustache Petes, so completely did it
break with the clannishness and exclusivity of Sicilian traditions; for Luciano and the new national commission of
crime under his aegis dealt impartially with racketeers of
various ethnic backgrounds. Moe Dalitz and his Jewish
Cleveland syndicate were confirmed in control of their
fief; Abner ("Longie") Zwillman, another Jew, one of the
largest bootleggers of the Prohibition Era, was recognized
as the boss of all New Jersey; Dutch Schultz, the German
beer baron from the Bronx, ranked as a full-fledged associate. Mafia membership was still exclusively Italian, and

Mafia crime families still formed the backbone of the organization, giving it their centuries-old expertise. But this
made less difference than formerly because, under the new
regime, the premium was placed upon an amicable, working–business relationship in the affairs of crime.

The new structure had a twofold base. Established
bosses were confirmed in their rule of specific rackets and
given localities. Within these boundaries, they could conduct their own affairs without interference from the national organization; but if they ran counter to overall syndicate policy (if, for example, one major boss wanted to
eliminate another) or if they wanted to branch out in
rackets beyond their assigned territorial limits, they had to
have the approval of the national commission. As an example of the manner in which the spoils were divided,
Lucky Luciano appropriated for himself the prostitution
and narcotics rackets of New York; Dutch Schultz was
confirmed in his hold upon the numbers, or policy, racket
which he had pioneered and made into a multi-million-
dollar gold mine; Bugsy Siegel was sent out to California
to bring that backward state into the world of crime;
Meyer Lansky became the syndicate expert on gambling
at Saratoga, in Miami, and eventually in Cuba and the Ba-
hamas, a role that made him the financial wizard of the
mob, indispensable to bosses of every stripe because he
made them so much money. Despite such specific assignments and allocations, the system was flexible. There were
certain "open" territories like Miami and Las Vegas where
there were no exclusive franchises, where mobs from different sections of the nation merged their activities, receiving their assigned share of major rackets.

With the death of Prohibition imminent, Luciano and
his conferees devoted their attention to the cultivation of
new sources of revenue. Corporations were formed to put
the mob into the legitimate liquor industry the moment repeal became effective. New rackets were promoted. The
decision was made to concentrate heavily on gambling,
both the bookmaking of horse races and the daily numbers
play that had returned such a cascade of dollars to Dutch

Schultz. Industrial extortion and narcotics, ever the favorite of Luciano, were to come in for a big play.

In charting this future course of crime, the new underworld rulers did not overlook the emphasis on politics that had been so strongly recommended in the deliberations at Atlantic City. Their aim was the increasing domination of the political system of the nation. The increasingly close ties between the rackets and politics were especially observable at the 1932 Democratic National Convention at which Roosevelt was nominated. James J. ("Jimmy") Hines, the powerful Democratic boss from the West Side of Manhattan—a power broker who was soon to go to prison because he had dealt with Dutch Schultz not wisely and too well—went to Chicago accompanied by the gangster who was soon to swallow Tammany Hall: Frank Costello. Hines' rival, Tammany leader Albert C. Marinelli, was pledged to support Alfred E. Smith; and Marinelli's entourage was graced by none other than Lucky Luciano. In addition, Meyer Lansky floated around, hobnobbing with politicos from Huey Long's Louisiana machine and James Curley's Boston organization.

The merger of the underworld and politics was eventually to be achieved in many sections of the country, but not before it had suffered some severe initial setbacks. The New York leadership was especially hard-hit. Fiorello H. LaGuardia was an independent, fiery, principled Italian who considered the Mafia an affront to his race; and one of his first acts, when he became mayor of New York on January 1, 1934, was to denounce Lucky Luciano as Public Enemy No. 1. In a followup stroke at the mob, he personally took ax in hand and demolished the slot machines installed in practically every corner candy store by Frank Costello and his partner in gambling, Dandy Phil Kastel.

Even more personal disasters came swiftly. Vito Genovese, Luciano's ruthless underboss, committed a cardinal indiscretion. He both murdered Ferdinand ("The Shadow") Boccia and left an eye-witness alive to tell about it. The suddenly revived law in New York, under the prodding of a special rackets-buster named Thomas E. Dewey, began to build a case against Don Vito, and Genovese hastily departed for the healthier clime of his native Italy. He reportedly took some $750,000 in hard cash with him; and with this kind of talking testament to virtue, he quickly became, irony of ironies, a popular figure at the court of Il Duce, the dictator who had sworn the death of the Mafia.

While Genovese was being chased overseas, his peerless leader, Lucky Luciano, was living a very fashionable life as the immaculately groomed, fastidious Charles Ross of the Waldorf-Astoria Hotel. But not for long. Thomas E. Dewey penetrated his disguise, proclaimed Luciano the city's overlord of vice, and charged him with living high on the proceeds of a $10-million-a-year prostitution ring, with more than two hundred madams and a thousand working girls paying him tribute. Dewey, with his awesome reputation of always getting the man he went after, persuaded some of the prostitutes to talk; and in 1936 Luciano was convicted and sentenced to spend the next thirty to fifty years of his life in New York state prisons.

The underworld was stunned by the conviction and sentence, but there was not now, as there most certainly would have been in the era of the Moustache Petes, a sanguinary battle for supremacy. The new system functioned smoothly, and Frank Costello stepped quietly into the boss's empty shoes. And over in Brooklyn there was a new power, Costello's close ally, Joe Adonis.

When the late Senator Estes Kefauver conducted his probe of the American underworld in 1951, he found one gangster who, more than any other, typified the whole range of mob activity and influence. In his book, *Crime in America*, he wrote that Joe Adonis "was the evil personification of modern criminality. This man with bloodstained hands [who] for years set himself up as bigger than the law . . . had achieved pre-eminence in all three fields that have become an unholy trinity in areas of the United States—crime, politics and business."

Joe Adonis, born Giuseppe Antonio Doto, in a small Italian town about thirty miles south of Naples on November 22, 1903, was known as "the gentleman of the mob." When he spoke, his voice was soft and low; he ordered in whispers. He had even cultivated the novel habit, not of snarling, but of whispering out of one corner of his mouth. Yet the effect on minions who knew his power was more electric than any shout or snarl.

Stockily built, he was swarthily handsome, with black hair and dark brown eyes. The eyes were perhaps the key to the inner man. They were coldly, inhumanly hard, and they were set in a face of unblemished stone, unwrinkled, unrelieved by any traces of past laughter.

Joe A. was one of four sons of Michele and Maria de Vito Doto, and he grew up in the Gowanus section of South Brooklyn, hard by the waterfront. He never got beyond the elementary grades in school, but in later life he refined his speech so that he could converse like the gentleman he impersonated. Only in moments of extreme stress would he lapse into the patois of the Brooklyn streets, the idiom of dese, dose, and, dem.

He began his career as a lowly punk, and his rise was as meteoric and his power far more lasting than Big Bill Dwyer's. At twenty-two, he was just a lowly "soldier" in the mob; at twenty-six, he was a millionaire and one of the bootlegging powers of the Eastern Seaboard.

In his first brushes with the law, he used a variety of aliases—Joe Arosa, James Arosa, and Joe DeMio. He was arrested for robbery and grand larceny; he was involved in hijackings. But the only blemish on his record was a $25 fine for disorderly conduct.

His persuasive way with the courts was traceable to his Mafia connections. On the day of his first courtroom appearance, Frankie Yale swaggered in at the head of a glowering bodyguard troop. Frankie was as resplendent as a walking jewelry store, two huge diamonds on his fingers, another glowing from his stickpin, and some seventy-five brilliants studding his belt. Justice was literally blinded by this splendor; and Joe Adonis, though he had been caught red-handed in a stolen car loaded with guns, walked out of court spotless in the eyes of the law.

By the time Frankie Yale was bumped off in 1928, young Joseph Doto had acquired the name by which he was to be forever known and had climbed to such a position in the rackets that he inherited a portion of his fallen chief's preserves. The origin of the name that stuck to him is misted in underworld legend. One version has it that a Broadway cutie—Joe A., like all rising young gangsters, collected the species the way Frankie Yale did diamonds —took one look at his sturdy handsomeness and gurgled, "That guy looks like a real Adonis." Another version is that a pimply-faced Brooklyn hoodlum, having stumbled upon the name of the beautiful youth of Greek mythology, tagged young Joseph A. Doto with it.

Joe Adonis, he remained; and in an astonishingly few years, he was the *de facto* political boss of Brooklyn. He ruled from a speakeasy that he established at 260-62 Fourth Avenue, at the corner of Carroll Street in Brooklyn. Joe's Italian Kitchen, it was called, and it soon became the favorite rendezvous for the most eminent politicians in Borough Hall. This was not because Joe A.'s tavern was so convenient. On the contrary, the Kitchen was located five long blocks away from Borough Hall in the same slum neighborhood in which Joe A. had been reared —"one of the poorest and toughest in the country," as a witness later called it.

Some attempted to explain the irresistible allure of the Kitchen for politicians on the ground that Joe A. served the best Italian food in town and such pure, undiluted liquor. Few were so naïve as to believe such rationalizations. Years later, some cynical diners would ascribe Joe A.'s popularity to a different cause. They recalled that it was not unusual to see a waiter sidle up to a VIP and slip a little white envelope half under his plate. The politico never opened the missive in public, but simply tucked it away carefully in the inside pocket of his jacket—a suspicious maneuver that led the evil-minded to suspect such envelopes contained some of Uncle Sam's favorite folding green. Whatever the truth of such suspicions, one fact was undeniable: the Italian Kitchen ran throughout the Prohibition years undisturbed by the law and, when repeal came, it had no difficulty in getting a liquor license, despite the notorious racket ties of its proprietor.

Names were named in the Kefauver probe, making abundantly clear the far reach of Adonis's political influence. Francis J. Quayle, then sheriff and later Brooklyn postmaster and Fire Commissioner of New York, was identified as a faithful patron of the Kitchen. So was his undersheriff, James G. Ambro—and so were Magistrate David I. Malbin; James V. Mangano, later sheriff of Kings County; and Patrick J. Diamond, the Democratic district leader in Adonis's own Eighth Assembly District.

Ambro, who had a long career as a State Assemblyman and Deputy Attorney General, added some important names to this list when he testified before the Kefauver committee. He declared that William O'Dwyer, who was to become the prosecutor of Murder Inc. and the mayor of New York, frequented Adonis's restaurant, and that he saw Irwin Steingut, subsequently Democratic minority leader in the State Assembly, there "sometimes, many times."

"You could meet anyone that was anybody in Brooklyn in his restaurant, in his place of business. . . ." Ambro told the Kefauver committee. "Most everybody and anybody. . . ."

Ticking off the names of Democratic party leaders in all twenty-three Brooklyn districts, Ambro identified about two-thirds of them as among the Kitchen's clientele, and with at least one-third the relationship to Adonis seemed to be especially close. Joe A., Ambro said, would always circulate among the tables, the gracious host. "He would come to a table and sit down and say 'Hello' and talk," Ambro testified. The talk would almost always be of politics, and many a public career, most notably that of William O'Dwyer, was furthered by arrangements made right there at Joe Adonis's tables.

Ambro recalled how he helped give O'Dwyer his first vital leg-up on the political ladder. They were both dining in the Kitchen one day when O'Dwyer approached Ambro. O'Dwyer had been serving under temporary appointment as a city magistrate, and he asked Ambro to say a word on his behalf to Kenneth Sutherland, one of the most powerful Democratic leaders in Brooklyn and a friend of Adonis. Ambro said the word, O'Dwyer became a full-fledged magistrate, and the career that was to lead to City Hall was launched.

The Kefauver testimony did not exaggerate. Years later, one of the best-known public figures in Brooklyn described for me how Adonis had the power to make or break a candidate for District Attorney.

The District Attorney's office is, of course, vital to a racketeer. If he controls the man who is supposed to prosecute crime, he doesn't have to worry about being prosecuted. In this particular election, the man with the well-known name was seeking the Democratic nomination against a party hack who was rumored to have close ties to the mob. The independent needed all the help he could get, and so he was instantly interested one day when he received a telephone call from a man who was a power in Brooklyn politics.

"I have a man here who has seven district leaders in his pocket," the caller said. "He would like to talk to you."

"Who is he?"

"I can't tell you, but can you meet him here at two o'clock?"

The hard-pressed candidate naturally could. At the appointed hour, he went to the rendezvous and was ushered into a small back room that served as emergency living quarters. There at a table sat Joe Adonis. He wasted no time beating about the bush. He controlled, he said bluntly, seven district leaders; they would do what he said. His support could be had on certain, very specific conditions. He started to name them.

At this point, the candidate interrupted.

"If I'm elected," he said, "my first order of business will be—*you!*"

He stalked out.

Naturally, he was snowed under when the votes were counted. The party hack was nominated and elected—and went on to preside over one of the blacker administrations of the District Attorney's office in all of Brooklyn's seamy history. . . .

The mid-1930s marked the heyday of Joe A.'s power in Brooklyn—the halcyon period when it seemed that nothing could go wrong, when all threads tied together, when political influence made him secure in his rackets and his rackets made him secure in business. Every source of income watered and supported another source, and all grew like the prophet's gourd.

Bankrolled by an illicit fortune of millions of dollars, Joe Adonis, racketeer, became Joe Adonis, businessman. Directly across the street from his Italian Kitchen, he established the White Auto Sales Co., an agency for Ford cars. In the rear of the auto agency building, in July, 1934, he also set up the Kings County Cigarette Service. This venture achieved instantaneous success. Joe A.'s strongarms were probably the most persuasive salesmen in New York; and so, practically at the blink of an eyelash, some ten thousand of his cigarette-vending machines were installed in bars, hotels and restaurants all over Brooklyn. Business was so flourishing that one vending-machine company couldn't handle it all, and so in 1936 Joe A. organized the Shamrock Cigarette Service in a building adjoining his White Auto Agency.

There now occurred a coincidence that seems remarkable to this day. During those very years from 1934 through 1937 in which Joe A.'s vending-machine companies were doing such a roaring business, there was an unprecedented wave of cigarette-truck hijackings at gunpoint. Police estimated that, in a little less than four years, some $6 million worth of cigarettes were stolen.

Trucks carrying cigarettes to retail outlets in Brooklyn

and parts of adjacent Queens County were generally loaded in the Bush Terminal on the South Brooklyn waterfront, in the heart of Adonis's territory. The narrow,
clogged streets were ideal for ambush. The instant a truck
had to slow down, strange men jumped it, jammed guns
against the driver's side, gagged and bound him and tossed
him into the rear of his own truck. One of the hijackers
would then get behind the wheel and drive off to a drop
where the cargo would be unloaded. The truck would then
be driven to some lonely, outlying section where it would
be abandoned with its trussed-up driver still inside it.

This wave of cigarette-truck hijackings reached such
proportions that unusual protective measures were adopted. Detectives were assigned to ride shotgun on the cigarette trucks. Cabs were bulletproofed and locks designed
so that the doors could be opened only from the inside.
Sirens were installed to wail instant alarm, and the sides of
trucks were plastered with huge letters so that patrolling
police could spot them instantly even in the worst traffic
jams. Such extreme remedies finally ended the hijackings,
but not before Joe A.'s vending-machine companies enjoyed years of unrivaled prosperity. As one detective remarked: "Hijacked cigarettes can be sold at one hundred
percent profit, and that's a lot better than the legitimate
competition can do."

With profits pyramiding, power increasing, Joe Adonis
expanded both his racket and legitimate interests. He
opened a new and swankier restaurant. He had two other
automobile agencies besides White Auto Sales. He had a
hidden partnership in two large liquor-distributing companies. And finally, in his most important business coup, he
acquired a controlling stock interest in the Automotive
Conveying Company, of Cliffside Park, N.J.—a firm
whose trailer trucks had a monopoly on the delivery of
new Ford cars assembled at the Edgewater, N.J., plant to
agencies throughout New Jersey, New York, Rhode Island, Massachusetts, Connecticut, Pennsylvania, Dela-
ware, the District of Columbia, Virginia and Vermont. In

the eight years from 1932 to 1940, Ford paid this Adonis-controlled company a cool $8 million.

The Adonis tie to Automotive Conveying was exposed by the *New York Post* in 1940, but eleven years later, when the Kefauver committee investigated, it found that the same firm was still controlled by Adonis—and was still enjoying an exclusive contract with Ford to handle all deliveries from the Edgewater plant. Joe Adonis, it would seem, was as invaluable to big business as he was to the rackets.

There was no question about his stature in the underworld. From the moment in 1933 when Little Augie Pisano took himself off to Miami to manage a hotel he had purchased there, Joe Adonis was king of the roost in Brooklyn. He was backed by Albert Anastasia and the squad of sadistic killers who later became known as Murder Inc. His power was such that he didn't hesitate to muscle even the dreaded and lethal Louis ("Lepke") Buchalter.

The citadel from which he ran the Brooklyn rackets was the same one, Joe's Italian Kitchen, where his blandishments, of whatever sort, had proved so irresistible to the political leaders of the Borough of Churches. The Kitchen was a schizophrenic establishment. Out front there was the public dining room for distinguished guests—and in the rear a private, padded and more sinister chamber, isolated from the public, that became known to the underworld as "The Slaughterhouse."

This private headquarters from which Joe Adonis ran the rackets of Brooklyn had its own private, rear entrance. A sliding panel and an "icebox door"—the kind of heavy, soundproof and almost indestructible barrier that gamblers favor in their establishments—separated this extremely private caucus chamber from the Kitchen that the world saw. To this control room, Joe Adonis summoned his minions for conference—or, in case of misdeeds, for punishment. The underworld grapevine had it that, on more than one occasion, unfortunates who had incurred the boss's displeasure suffered amazing losses of consciousness in the private chamber, and their inert bodies were dragged out and disposed of without disturbing the hilarity of the guests out front. Hence the name—"The Slaughterhouse."

Operating with such power in both the upper world and the underworld, Joe Adonis levied tribute on every racket in Brooklyn. Huge floating crap games with stakes that sometimes ran as high as $25,000 were his special preserve. When various gangs began to quarrel bloodily over the linen supply business to hotels and restaurants, Joe A. called a conference, laid down the law, and saw to it that Lepke Buchalter's extortionists were given control. Anastasia's Murder Inc. goons and other hirelings ran the lucrative loan-sharking racket. Hijacking was remunerative. So was narcotics.

Memoranda in the old files of the Federal Bureau of Narcotics contain much information about the powerful secret role Joe A. played in the narcotics traffic. In 1935, according to one of the bureau's informants, Joe A.'s thugs hijacked $20,000 worth of opium that had been brought into a Bay Ridge pier by another mob. From that time on, Brooklyn narcotics importers were compelled to purchase their supplies from Adonis "or pay Adonis a percentage of all the narcotics" they smuggled across docks in his territory. In a report in October, 1939, one of the bureau's crack agents noted that, while Lepke Buchalter's mob had formerly been the big importers of dope in Brooklyn, they had finally been squeezed out by the Mafia musclemen of Joe Adonis. No racket that would turn a profit was too picayune for Joe A.'s attention. There was even the shadow of old Black Hand days. . . .

In the mid-1930s a certain Brooklyn businessman decided that he had prospered sufficiently to be able to afford a Cadillac. He had made his money legitimately, he had no connection with the mob; but as a businessman who got around, he was well aware of the terrible power wielded by the gangs in Brooklyn. He began to quake, therefore, when he received a telephone call a few days after he had purchased his Cadillac. A man spoke to him in a deep, gruff voice.

"We want $8,000," he said. "We mean business. We know you've got the dough or you wouldn't be buying a new Caddy. You'll be hearing from us again."

With that, the telephone line went dead.

A few days later the businessman got another call. This time he was told it was time to sit down for a personal discussion of his problem. He was warned: if he notified the police, he would be killed.

"We know you got two kids who go to school," the caller added in a threatening sign-off.

The Cadillac owner now began to worry, not just for himself, but for his family. Seeking help, he went to a friend who was so astonished that such things could be happening a quarter-century after the Black Hand was supposed to be dead that he has never forgotten the details.

"Go to the police," he urged. "They'll take care of it. Nobody can get away with something like this."

But the Cadillac owner, like Frederic Sondern's Italian farmer a quarter-century earlier, feared the Mafia more than he trusted the police.

"I can't do that," he said. "They told me they'd kill me if I go to the police, and they mean business. If I don't pay, they'll kidnap my kids."

He decided to try to bargain for a more reasonable shakedown. A meeting was set up on Manhattan's Lower East Side, and for the first time a name crept into the negotiations, a dreaded one—that of Lepke Buchalter. After much wrangling, the extortionists agreed to reduce their demands to $5,000. The Cadillac owner protested that this was still too high, and he went to Philadelphia and contacted a mob boss who, he was told, had influence with Lepke. Finally, a price was agreed upon—$3,500. And the place for the payoff—Joe's Italian Kitchen.

"It all had to be in cash," the victim's friend recalled years later. "On the day that had been set to close the deal, the guy came to me and asked me to hold half the money—some $1,750—for him while he went to Manhattan to raise the rest. He didn't want to run the risk of carrying that much money around the streets with him and perhaps being robbed. So I'm left holding the $1,750, and he goes off to Manhattan, and in a little while he comes back with the rest of it. Then, since Joe A.'s place was in a tough neighborhood, he begged me to go with him and see him to the door at least, to make certain that nothing happened to him or his money."

The pair set off for the Kitchen. When they got there, the escort left the extortion victim by the circular entrance at the corner of Fourth Avenue and walked on down Carroll Street. It was a hot day, and the side door on Carroll Street was open. As the friend passed the door, he happened to glance inside; and there, sitting at a table, was Joe Adonis himself. His heavy face was stolid, impassive; his fathomless brown eyes alert. But what astonished the Cadillac man's friend even more than the sight of the boss was the sight of Joe A.'s companion. He was a police captain.

"I almost fell through the sidewalk," the man who relates this tale remembers. "I thought to myself, 'My God, here I've been urging him to go to the cops with his story, and there's Joe A. sitting in the rear of the place, with a *captain* no less, right while the payoff's being made up front.'"

Sometimes in Brooklyn during the reign of Joe Adonis it wasn't safe for a man even to buy a Cadillac.

7.

The Law Rides High—
But Briefly

The few years immediately prior to World War II were a trying period for the Mafia, and the decade of the 1940s was a time of such prosperity and power that even the bonanza days of Prohibition could be recalled without regret. The threatening days for big-league crime—a storm that was to pass in the night leaving only a few sacrificial limbs torn from the tree—were caused by upheavals in the political structure that, for a brief and exciting moment, seemed to suggest that a lackadaisical law might actually be prodded into enforcing the law against the rulers of the underworld.

Peppery Fiorello LaGuardia was responsible for much of the trouble. Figuratively hopping up and down, the mayor screeched in his shrill voice over the radio: "I have driven the tin-horns out of New York, and they've fled across the bridge to New Jersey."

"Tin-horn" in LaGuardia's vocabulary was a term of contempt, but it was not very accurate when applied, as he applied it, to multi-millionaire lords of the underworld like Joe Adonis. Yet, regardless of the misconceptions that might result from picturing a czar as a guttersnipe, the La-

Guardia Administration did succeed in making the streets
of New York too hot for many of the top powers of crime.

This happened, not from LaGuardia's efforts alone, but
because the years of post-depression and recession were
geared to the passions of reform. The public, having suffered the worst debacle in the nation's history, wanted
change in many areas, and the mood was right for the
emergence of the pure knight riding his white charger
against the blackguards of crime. Thomas E. Dewey was
the first to cry, "To horse!"—and he rode in the lists so
well that he sent Jimmy Hines and Lucky Luciano to prison and Lepke Buchalter to the electric chair in Sing Sing.

Observing the performance that was to make Dewey
governor of New York and a two-time Presidential candidate of the Republican Party, an ambitious politician in
Brooklyn mounted his own charger—one that turned out,
unfortunately, to be a dappled gray instead of pure white
—and became the ringmaster of his own tournament. William O'Dwyer certainly had furthered his own career by
the contacts he had made in Joe's Italian Kitchen, and it is
a certainty that he knew both Joe Adonis and Frank Costello far more intimately than a pure crusader should have.
But at the moment this did not matter. There were political chips to be collected by charging against the evil brotherhood à la Dewey; and the result was the exposure of that
band of sadistic executioners known as Murder Inc. . . .

Abe Reles was a squat, repulsive thug. He had thick,
powerful fingers, ideal for scragging the necks of his victims, an art that he delighted to practice and that had
given him his underworld nickname—Kid Twist. His expertise in removing objectionable citizens from the realm
of the living had made him the field commander of a
Brownsville troop engaged in the nationwide marketing of
murder under the top-level guidance of Albert Anastasia
and Joe Adonis.

In 1940 Abe Reles and his murder goons, who had
committed an estimated one thousand killings from coast

to coast as the enforcing arm of the Combination, encountered a prosecutor who was unique in their experience. He was incorruptible and dedicated to the novel proposition that the hired killers of the underworld belonged in the electric chair at Sing Sing instead of in political clubhouses in Brooklyn.

Burton B. Turkus, a political independent, had been chosen by William O'Dwyer to be his chief assistant in the Kings County District Attorney's office in Brooklyn. Turkus was suave, intelligent, a courtroom magician. In his private practice of criminal law, he had defended seventeen men accused of first-degree murder, and not one of them had suffered the ultimate penalty. His courtroom skill made him invaluable to O'Dwyer—up to a point.

When Turkus began to pore over the criminal records he had inherited from his predecessors, he discovered that there had been in recent years a wave of some two hundred unsolved murders in the Brownsville, East New York, and Ocean Hill sections of Brooklyn. They had all the earmarks of planned, skillfully executed gangland slayings; and Turkus, with willing William O'Dwyer behind him, began to hunt for the key to this macabre mystery.

His technique was as old as the history of criminal prosecutions. It was simply this: build an ironclad case against some lowly stumblebum, convince him that his life is forfeit unless he talks—then he will talk. His disclosures will inevitably involve others slightly above him in the hierarchy; and a good prosecutor, if he is lucky, repeats the process as he follows the trail up the ladder to the top. Turkus was not entirely lucky, but his success in sending seven killers to the chair illustrates a truth that law enforcement, for whatever reasons, has all too frequently ignored: despite *omertà,* despite the underworld code of silence, a killer can be persuaded to talk because the very thug who has no regard for anyone else's life has an infinite and tender concern for his own.

Turkus's appreciation of this basic fact of life—that a bum so devoid of conscience he will kill for hire is also so devoid of conscience he will betray anyone to save himself

—broke open the Murder Inc. case. The energetic and determined prosecutor followed a trail of little squeals until he got the big squeal when Abe ("Kid Twist") Reles decided to talk to save his own scabrous person.

Reles was an invaluable informer. He had a photographic mind and the faculty of total recall. When he began to spout, he wore out stenographers in relays. He recalled the minutest details and was able to recite in its entirety the menu he had enjoyed years previously while dining with a prospective victim at his unsuspecting last supper. Checking such details wherever possible, Turkus always found that Kid Twist had been a model of accuracy. He was so accurate and so unshakable, in fact, that his testimony stood up in a whole series of murder trials despite the relentless battering in cross-examination by the cleverest trial lawyers mob money could buy.

Reles's account covered some eighty-five Brooklyn murders of which he had personal knowledge. He told of other executions carried out across the country all the way to California. His Murder Inc. squad was so efficient, he said proudly, that its members became the elite enforcers for the Syndicate or, as it was often called, the Combination. Even mob bosses who had their own lethal "troops" frequently imported Murder Inc. goons for especially sensitive jobs in which it was necessary to divert suspicion from themselves. Even the master extortionist, Lepke Buchalter, who had his own band of experts, paid Murder Inc. a special annual retainer of $12,000 to handle certain "contracts" for him, Reles said.

Because he had been strategically placed in his murder command post, Reles had had important contacts with the ruling powers above him, and he had much important inside knowledge about the mechanics of underworld organization. He gave Turkus what was probably the first authoritative description of the 1929 Atlantic City planning session and of the subsequent grand council meetings that had established crime's functioning underworld government. He described the system of kangaroo courts and the manner in which important bosses sat on the board of the national commission.

Reles left no doubt about the internal structure of Murder Inc. His direct superior was Albert Anastasia, he said; but above Anastasia, both in the local pyramid of murder and the broad structure of national crime, was Joe Adonis. According to Reles, Adonis was one of the powers on the national board of the Syndicate, and he was the Syndicate's coordinator and mediator in intergang disputes. Other songbirds of Murder Inc. agreed. Blue Jaw Magoon put it this way: "He [Joe A.] is a part of the national Combination. In other words, if he got crossed, the guy who crossed him would have the whole Combination on his back." Testing such testimonials, Turkus became convinced of their veracity by observing the reaction of every mobster to whom he mentioned the name of Joe Adonis. He later wrote that a "tone of profound reverence . . . comes into the voice of any hoodlum, anywhere, whenever he mentions Mr. A."

With all his knowledge, however, Reles never got close enough to build a legal case against Joe Adonis. But the same was not true of Anastasia. Anastasia had been Adonis's protective buffer in the murder chain, and he had also been Reles's immediate superior. One of the first bits of information that Reles dropped when he began to talk involved a garment district murder directly involving Anastasia. O'Dwyer proclaimed at the time that he had "the perfect" murder case against Anastasia, and there was a much-publicized manhunt for the Lord High Executioner of Murder Inc.

Headline fervor was one thing; prosecutorial zeal another. Though Abe Reles lived for nineteen months after he began to talk, it was curious that crusading Bill O'Dwyer never took him before a grand jury to testify about Anastasia, never tried to get a murder indictment against Anastasia. As time went on and Reles was used to send lower-level killers to the chair, he began to worry about the seeming lack of enthusiasm where the major crime figures were concerned.

He knew that his life wouldn't be worth a nickel unless the murder probe was pressed all the way to the top of the Syndicate. He commented to Turkus that there wasn't any place in the world where he could be safe from "those bastards." He ticked off their names: Albert Anastasia, Longie Zwillman, Willie Moretti, Meyer Lansky, Bugsy Siegel, Joe Adonis.

This was the ambivalent situation when Abe Reles— "the canary who could sing but couldn't fly"—plunged to his death from his bedroom window in the special squealers' suite on the sixth floor of Coney Island's Half Moon Hotel. It happened in the early morning of November 12, 1941; and in all the years since, despite hearings and investigations, there has never been a satisfactory explanation.

The suite where Reles and other informers were holed up was guarded by a special detail of policemen; yet, so far as is known, no one had any suspicion that Abe Reles wasn't peacefully sleeping in bed until his body was found at daybreak. Around him fluttered a couple of twisted sheets that could have been used as an improvised rope to let him lower himself to the window of an unoccupied room directly below his own. A length of wire apparently had been used to attach this sheet-rope to the radiator in Reles's room, and the wire had parted. The immediate official assumption was that Reles had climbed out his window all by himself and had fallen to his death when the wire failed to hold, but there was one bit of evidence that seemed to conflict with this comfortable rationalization. His body was found, not directly under his window as would have been the case in a straight drop, but some fifteen feet out from the wall.

This telltale circumstance led many to believe that Reles had not fallen but had been deliberately pitched to his death. In mob circles, there was no doubt. Joseph Valachi twenty-three years later told the McClellan committee what the underworld thought. "They threw him out," Valachi said. He could not, of course, identify the "they."

William O'Dwyer and his closest associates had a difficult time forever after in trying to explain Reles's possible motivation and their own reaction to this sudden and tragic loss of their invaluable canary. Captain Frank Bals, an O'Dwyer favorite who was in charge of the police detail that had been supposed to protect Reles's life, insulted the intelligence of the Kefauver committee in 1951 by advancing the theory that Reles had been just playing a little game. What he had intended to do, Bals said, was to lower himself to the fifth floor window directly below his own, then return to the squealers' suite and cry "peek-a-boo" to his shocked guardians. The late Senator Charles W. Tobey, the Bible-pounding Republican from Vermont, was so incensed at this fairy tale that he almost had apoplexy.

Even O'Dwyer, who was fulsome in his praise of Bals, couldn't go along with Bals's theory. O'Dwyer told the Kefauver group that he thought Reles had been trying to give his guards the slip and escape. But why would Reles do this when he recognized, as he had told Turkus, that his only chance of living was to remain in protective custody until the Murder Inc. probe reached the top levels of the Syndicate? Neither O'Dwyer nor anyone else could answer that question.

Even more peculiar was the manner in which O'Dwyer had reacted to the loss of his star witness. Here was the man whose testimony was vital for "the perfect murder case" against Albert Anastasia—and for a number of other cases, including an important Syndicate murder in California. Here was that man suddenly and mysteriously dead. One would have thought that crusading Bill O'Dwyer would have been so shocked that he would have launched an investigation that would have torn half of Brooklyn apart. But he did not. O'Dwyer's investigation into Reles's death was perfunctory; it was closed out by noon on the same day. And Burton Turkus, who was in court at the time, didn't even know that his star witness had died until a newspaper reporter let him in on the secret. As Turkus later commented cryptically, this "was not, by a considerable margin, the only peculiarity which had developed" in the Murder Inc. probe.

He was, of course, right. Abe Reles's death touched off a weird chain of events. O'Dwyer asked Turkus to review "the perfect murder case" against Anastasia in view of the fact that "the perfect witness" was no longer available. Turkus's subsequent report was based entirely upon the investigative information furnished him by Captain Bals, who concluded that the Anastasia case had gone out the window with Reles. Turkus refused to accept this view. In a confidential memorandum to O'Dwyer dated April 8, 1942, he declared in the strongest possible language that "should Anastasia frustrate justice, it would be a calamity to society. Somewhere, somehow, corroborative evidence must be available." He urged "redoubled effort" to overcome the loss of Reles and build a strong case.

What happened next was instructive. Just twenty-six days after Turkus called for "redoubled effort," the slate against Albert Anastasia and some of his top killers was wiped clean. The "wanted cards" that showed they were being hunted for murder were spirited right out of police files!

A Brooklyn grand jury investigation in 1945 and the Kefauver probe in 1951 established the manner in which this magic had been performed. O'Dwyer throughout his long public career was served most faithfully by a large, hulking individual named James J. Moran—O'Dwyer's Man Friday, as Senator Tobey called him. It was Moran, subsequently sent to prison for running a $500,000-a-year extortion racket in the New York Fire Department, who ordered the wanted cards against Anastasia and two of his ace killers, Dandy Jack Parisi and Tony Romeo, removed from police files and destroyed. Police Sergeant Elwood J. Divers testified: "Moran came in and gave me a list of the cards he wanted taken out of the file, and he told me to destroy them all." O'Dwyer denied to the Kefauver committee that he had ever ordered such an action. Moran attempted to deny it too at first, but he finally admitted that it was just possible he had done the deed.

The effect was to kill "the perfect murder case" for all time. There was no record in the New York Police Department that Albert Anastasia was wanted for anything. With the death of Reles, with the removal of the "wanted cards" out of police files, the top-level rulers of the Combination had ridden out the storm and had triumphed, in effect, over the most ballyhooed investigation of the day. The net result of the Murder Inc. probe was a disaster for law enforcement on several levels. The fate of Abe Reles served as a graphic deterrent for informers who might be tempted to talk in the future; what it said was, in effect, "The law cannot protect you even in a guarded squealers' suite; death awaits the turncoat." And Albert Anastasia had been freed to continue the practice of his vocation, murder—a result that would cost many other lives, including several who tried to help the law, in the long, long years ahead. . . .

When LaGuardia, Dewey, and Turkus made the pavements of New York too hot for comfort, the Mafia and its cohorts had at hand the ideal antidote. They resorted to a tactic that the Mafia had employed time and time again. When the ironclad protective arrangements in Chicago became so notorious that they were an embarrassment to the protectors, Al Capone simply moved across the municipal boundary line and established an ideal sanctuary in Cicero. Confronted with a similar dilemma in New Orleans, Mafia boss Carlos Marcello transferred his most flourishing gambling operations into neighboring parishes. And so when adversity came to the mob in New York, dethroning Joe Adonis and company, there just across the Hudson River was New Jersey, waiting like a lady of easy virtue to be had.

The Garden State, as it is called, is a jigsaw bit of geography squeezed in between two mighty neighbors, and so an ideal playground for the corruptions of both. James Madison, the Father of the Constitution, had likened it even in his day to a wine keg tapped at both ends, on the north by New York, on the south by Philadelphia. Its history in the nineteenth century was redolent with accounts of how the robber barons of Wall Street packed up their money bags and fled one hop ahead of the sheriff as they boarded ferries to carry them to their refuge across the river. Emulating their artistry, the mightiest powers of the New York Mafia simply removed themselves, as LaGuardia said, "across the bridge to New Jersey," and there established what was probably the most remarkable capital of crime ever to flourish in America.

Those words "capital of crime" are no exaggeration; they are literally true. Joe Adonis, Albert Anastasia and their allies practically took over Bergen County just beyond the western edge of the George Washington Bridge. There they corrupted police departments and politicians on a massive scale; and there they established a headquarters that functioned as a daily operating capital of crime, running multi-million-dollar businesses, both legitimate and illegitimate, and serving as a focal point for mob rulers across the nation.

This perfect oasis of crime was pioneered for the underworld by one of the slickest fixers the Mafia ever produced —Willie Moretti, alias Willie Moore. Willie was born on June 4, 1894, in the heart of the East Harlem section that later became known as the preserve of the 107th Street mob of narcotics peddlers and killers. He was short, only 5 feet 4, slim in youth when he had a brief whirl as a small club prizefighter; stocky in age as prosperity and good cuisine added weight to his frame. His was a wiseacre's face if there ever was one, with sparkling bright eyes and lips that broke readily into the wide, knowing, and half-mocking smile of the precocious street urchin; the whole radiating a sharp intelligence and a gift for repartee that earned him a reputation as the wisecracker of the mob.

To hear Willie Moretti tell his life's story as he did before the Kefauver committee, he had always been a much-maligned man. His record showed that he had been arrested for the attempted robbery of a neighborhood barber when he was nineteen; and, after that, almost every time Willie turned around, he found the law hitting him with some ridiculous charge or other. Streetwise, Willie found a way to stop such harassments. He located a well-connected lawyer, a gentleman who later became a New York Supreme Court Justice, and this eminent representative, who remained a lifelong friend, called at the District Attorney's office to plead the cause of poor, innocent Willie. It was remarkable how swiftly, after this visit, that the law lost interest in Willie Moretti.

The Kefauver committee tried to pin down Willie's connections with the hierarchy of the underworld, but Willie was so nimble with his answers that he outfoxed his inquisitors. It was a virtuoso performance, entirely at variance with the false impression later created and disseminated so widely by Vito Genovese in the bloody drive for power that was to make Willie Moretti the human hinge for a mighty convulsion of the underworld in the mid 1950s. Willie, it is true, admitted to the Kefauver probers that he knew practically everyone worth knowing, but to hear him tell it they were all just fine, sporting gentlemen. Typical was his description of his relations with Al Capone. They met at a racetrack, Willie said, and they liked each other immediately because—he actually used this phrase—they were both such "well-charactered" men.

When Willie transferred his operations to New Jersey at the start of the 1930s, the law held no mysteries for him. The stature of a Mafioso may be judged by the degree of his immunity; and when a Mafioso is so powerful he can laugh at a clear-cut case of murder, he has demonstrated in a most convincing way that he is a very big man indeed. Willie Moretti performed this supreme feat in 1931 after he and some aides gunned down a Hackensack taxicab operator named William Brady, whom they suspected of having given detectives information about a Waxey Gordon still.

Brady was well-ventilated by twenty-three buckshot pellets fired at him from close range; but unfortunately for Moretti, the effect, though final, wasn't immediate. In four separate statements, the dying Brady identified his killers as Willie and Solly Moretti, aided by Chicago Fat and Kid Steech. Such statements by a dying man, however convincing they may be, are admissible in court later only if it can be demonstrated that they were made in full awareness of the imminent end. Even this loophole had been buttoned up in this case; Brady's final deathbed statement had been made to an assistant prosecutor after a priest had administered the final rites of the Catholic Church.

There was only one flaw. This vital statement, which might have sent Willie Moretti to the electric chair, performed a disappearing act as remarkable as the one that had seen Albert Anastasia's wanted cards whisked out of the New York Police Department files. Twenty years later, in the early 1950s, when rackets buster Nelson F. Stamler charged into Bergen County, he found faithfully preserved in the records of the prosecutor's office all of the reports of detectives containing Brady's dying information. Just one document was missing—that deathbed statement Brady had made to Assistant Prosecutor Charles Schmidt.

Schmidt, when Stamler questioned him about it, was still indignant at the manner in which Moretti had been permitted to walk out of court a free man, the murder charges against him dropped because the statement Schmidt had taken was mysteriously "gone." Another witness who backed up Schmidt was a former federal agent, Joseph Aloysius Frayne, who had been in the hospital room and had heard everything Brady told Schmidt.

Frayne had been curious, he told Stamler in a sworn statement, about the manner in which Willie Moretti had performed his magic. And so over the years he had bandied the question back and forth with the cocky, wisecracking little hood whenever they happened to meet. Moretti enjoyed the game and would tantalize Frayne with little hints here and there, without really telling him anything of value. This went on for some time until finally, one day, Willie boasted about the manner in which he had beaten the rap in that old William J. Brady murder case.

"You thought you had me where the hair was short," he remarked to Frayne, practically laughing in the agent's face. "Well, I took care of that. It cost me twenty-five grand, but I got the deathbed statement right out of the files."

The Garden State where such feats of *legerdemain* could be performed was obviously a fertile field to till when investigations upset the cozy status quo in New York. . . .

Bergen County soon became like a feudal barony, with Mafia chiefs its lords and masters. The heart of their empire was the capital of crime that they established in Duke's Restaurant at 783 Palisades Avenue, Cliffside Park, directly across the street from the entrance of the large and popular Palisades Amusement Park. Duke's had a drab-looking front, discouraging to a visitor, but in its appointments it was virtually a replica of Joe's Italian Kitchen. Inside, it had a long bar on the right, booths on the left. Like the Kitchen, it served good food and liquor; and, like the Kitchen, it had at the rear a separate council room well padded for sound and well protected against public intrusion, with its own separate side entrance. The casual diner could eat, drink and depart with no conception of the real purpose of Duke's. In 1953 when I described the restaurant to a federal grand jury as a camouflaged headquarters of crime, one obviously intelligent and much concerned member of the panel was almost incredulous; he had dined there many times and had enjoyed the fine food.

Yet the real purpose of Duke's as a capital of crime is documented beyond dispute. The true facts are established in the records of two unimpeachable sources, the files of the old Federal Bureau of Narcotics and of District Attorney Frank S. Hogan's office in New York. In one report dated March 31, 1941, the narcotics bureau emphasized the importance of Duke's and listed the names of a whole coterie of mobsters whom watching agents had found congregating there.

Here are some of those named in the 1941 memorandum:

Thomas ("Three-Finger Brown") Lucchese, the boss of one of New York's five Mafia families.

John ("Johnny Duke") De Noia, the proprietor, then a man about forty, six feet tall and weighing some two hundred pounds, with black hair and a clean-shaven, pockmarked face. His was the task of running the tavern, handling the staff, and making certain security arrangements were ironclad from bar to kitchen—a task he performed with great efficiency.

Richard Bennet and Peter LaPlaca, two of Johnny Duke's top assistants. Bennet, sometimes known as Dick Bennett, had been a narcotics suspect in New York and was a known bookmaker; in years to come, he was to exercise increasing authority in Duke's and to be identified by witnesses as the man who handled many important details for Joe Adonis. LaPlaca served as bodyguard and chauffeur for Willie Moretti.

Willie Moretti and his darker, more silent shadow, his brother, Salvatore ("Solly") Moretti. The Moretti brothers were to be almost daily habitues of Duke's for the next ten years, their function the fixes for the Combination's varied operations.

Anthony ("Greenie" or "Tony Greeno") Guarini and Arthur Longano, both trusted subalterns of Joe Adonis and the managers of gambling casinos he soon established in the Bergen County paradise.

One name was conspicuously absent from this 1941 narcotics bureau memorandum—that of Joe Adonis. Though many of his henchmen were at the new headquarters, the boss himself was temporarily absent, wrestling with the threat of the Murder Inc. probe in Brooklyn. With the last fatal plunge of Abe Reles, however, the dark clouds broke and faded away, and 1942 dawned in a sunburst of prosperity that was to last for ten years. The war

boom was on. Manufacturers and executives of every sort
—and many of their employees—were rewarded for doing
their patriotic duty with a flood of cash that exceeded their
wildest dreams of avarice. Pigeons by the thousands were
ripe for the plucking, and there was no more masterful
plucker of pigeons than Joe A. . . . .

Once freed of the Murder Inc. threat, Joe Adonis took
command of the underworld government that operated
from the crime capital in Duke's; and there, for more than
ten years, he and his crime cabinet held what can only be
described as miniature weekly Apalachins, attended by
some of the most powerful figures in the American underworld.

It has been the general assumption of the public—and
at times of much of law enforcement—that criminal enterprises are *ad hoc* adventures that run more or less on their
own, with minimal supervision by individual racketeers.
Logic, if used, reduces such assumptions to absurdity.
Multi-million-dollar rackets, running in defiance of the
law, are genuinely big business; and, since they are illegal,
since they necessitate an infinity of subterfuge and the
most complex protective arrangements, they require even
more managerial direction and control than comparable
legitimate businesses. Just as General Motors could not
function without a headquarters staff, a board of directors
and a hierarchy of lesser executives, so the commerce of
the underworld cannot be conducted without expert organization and control. This managerial role was performed on a daily basis by Joe Adonis and his crime directorate in Duke's.

District Attorney Hogan's office in New York, by tailing mobsters who "went over the bridge" to Jersey,
through information gleaned from informants and by legalized New York State wiretapping, obtained a clear per-
spective of the operation in Duke's as it was running in the
early 1950s. Joe Adonis was the autocrat at the council
table. At his right hand sat his favorite enforcer, Albert
Anastasia. Also on this board of control were Willie and

Solly Moretti, past masters of the fix. And finally there was the cadaver-thin, doleful-visaged shadow figure, Anthony ("Tony Bender") Strollo, racket czar of the Lower Manhattan and New Jersey docks, owner of Greenwich Village nightclubs, a licensed real estate agent, a man who at the time had never made the headlines but had been long known to narcotics agents as the "chief lieutenant" of Vito Genovese. This was the board of directors known in the underworld as the Big Five, and their decisions packed all the authority of the most ruthless dictatorship.

Hogan's listening and watching agents later recalled in anecdotal form an incident that illustrated perhaps more vividly than any other the awesome scope of Joe Adonis's power.

It happened on a bright spring day. The ponies were running at Aqueduct, and a New York mobster who considered himself quite a bigshot had entrancing plans. He had lined up a Broadway showgirl to party with him at the races, a dinner, and then at a little pattycake afterwards. The sun was shining, and all was well with the world.

But over in Duke's the outlook was not so bright. There were problems. Joe Adonis swung into action, and telephone call chased telephone call from Cliffside 6-1799. The legions of the underworld were being summoned for the business of the day. Illustrative of the kind of nerve center Duke's was in such times of crisis was a compilation made later by New York Investigations Commissioner James H. Sheils. He found that in one ten-month period, from May 1948 to February 1949, the startling total of 6,191 telephone calls had been made from Duke's to just fifty-nine mob-connected phones in New York City.

One of those phones belonged to the big shot who had had such delightful plans for this particular spring day. When the summons came from Duke's, he scrapped everything, hopped into his Cadillac and sped over the George Washington Bridge to the tavern. It was obvious from later developments that he had the mistaken idea that Joe A. had summoned him to an individual summit meeting.

When he walked through the door of the tavern, his ego plummeted into his socks. The bar was jammed with the strongarms of the mob; and the big shot saw at once that he had not been summoned to a tete-à-tete of masterminds —*he* was just one of an army. He put the best front possible on the deflating situation, announcing himself with a flourish to a flunky. Then he found a vacant niche and consoled himself with a drink. One drink led to another— and another.

Time passed. The door of the inner sanctum swung open and shut. Others among the waiting strongarms were summoned and departed on their missions. But the big shot was ignored.

That evening, Hogan's men heard him moaning over his fractured ego as he bleated the story of his ruined day to a confidant.

"Imagine Joe A. treating *me* like that!" he rumbled in an aggrieved, whiskey bass. "I get this call, I give up everything, I dash over there—and then I don't even get in, I don't even get to see him! All I got is a big head."

It was no consolation that most of those who had been ordered to report for duty hadn't been admitted to the presence either. When Joe A. had a mission to be performed, he called out all the troops like a good field marshal wanting to make certain that, whatever emergency should arise, he would have on hand the battalions to cope with it. It was a cavalier way to operate, but it was typical of Joe Adonis.

"There probably never has been a more complete autocrat," said Assistant District Attorney Andrew J. Seidler, one of Hogan's aides in the Duke's investigation. "He was wholly indifferent to the convenience or sensibilities of his underlings. It was nothing to him to call out two or three times the number of men he could possibly use in one day—as he frequently did—just to make certain that, *if* he did need some special talent, the right man would be handy and *he* wouldn't have to be kept waiting."

Such was the man who dominated what was probably the most powerful daily-functioning crime cabinet in the history of the American underworld. The secluded council room in Duke's became a focal point for mobsters across the nation. Time and again, in testimony before the Kefauver committee and other investigative bodies, major racket bosses acknowledged that they had "dined" in Duke's. Willie Moretti tried to excuse his constant presence there by explaining that the food and atmosphere were so excellent—"like Lindy's on Broadway." Tony Bender Strollo, more frank and more revealing, claimed the privilege of the Fifth Amendment against self-incrimination in refusing to say whether he had ever been in the place. When counsel for the Senate Crime Committee asked him in amazement how it could possibly incriminate him just to admit he had been in a restaurant, Strollo replied: "I fear it might." No better epitaph could be written for Duke's.

The Federal Bureau of Narcotics, which began watching the shady tavern in 1941, never relaxed its vigilance, and over the years, in report after report, its agents spelled out the role of Duke's as a nerve center for Mafia chiefs and their allies. Tuesday was the regular meeting day for consultations between Joe Adonis and his directorate, and the regional monarchs of crime. Regularly, each week on this day, about twenty criminal overlords and their top henchmen would gather for a business luncheon. They would arrive between noon and one P.M. "The big men drive their cars into a large garage which is two doors north on the same side of Palisades Avenue," the bureau noted in one confidential memo. "The rest park in the general vicinity."

Over drinks and food, the delegates would discuss their problems. Sometimes these discussions lasted until four P.M. About this hour, sometimes earlier if the issues were simple, the guests would disband, and Joe Adonis and his crime cabinet would be left to implement the decisions taken.

The national significance of this underworld headquarters was emphasized by the stature of the gang rulers who attended some of these Tuesday conclaves. This was a time in the late 1940s and early '50s when the national commission of the Syndicate was dominated by the so-called Bix Six. Two, Jake Guzik and Tony Accardo, were the heirs of Al Capone and represented the Chicago mob; the other four came from the East, then the dominant wing of the combine, and all without exception were identified by investigators as habitués of Duke's. Joe Adonis, of course, was one of the four reigning Eastern powers. The others, who were spotted going in and out of Duke's during the major Tuesday strategy sessions, were:

Frank Costello, known to the underworld as The Boss or The Prime Minister, a power behind the political scene in New York, the target of much quiet New York surveillance, and a frequent traveler across the bridge to the freer air of Jersey, where the law didn't seem to care.

Meyer Lansky, the former partner of Bugsy Siegel in the infamous Bugs and Meyer mob, a man who increasingly handled investments in gambling enterprises for gang interests across the nation. He teamed with Costello and Adonis in multi-million-dollar gambling rackets at Saratoga and Miami; and in Florida he was the financial link between the Eastern Costello-Adonis axis and the Midwestern gangs who were cut in for their share of the loot in this "open" territory.

Abner ("Longie") Zwillman, the ruthless Newark bootleg king of the Prohibition era, who had invested a fortune in legal enterprises, but who remained primarily a gangster with a secretive hand in lucrative rackets. He had established a reputation of not having guessed wrong on a New Jersey election in twenty years and of having had, on occasion, a persuasive voice in the selection of the State's Attorney General.

In addition to these reigning powers of the day, there

were many second-echelon hoods who were formidable in their own right and were, in some instances, heirs of the future. Two of the most noteworthy were Vincent ("Jimmy Blue Eyes") Alo, a dock and gambling figure sometimes known as Costello's "right power," and Gerardo ("Jerry") Catena, who had close ties to Zwillman, Costello, and Genovese, and who eventually was to share with Tommy Eboli the rulership of the Genovese Mafia family.

These were the men and this their operating powerhouse in Duke's—the crime center that directed expanding rackets that produced a flood of dollars rivaling the golden take of Prohibition. . . .

Fiorello LaGuardia was correct in thinking he had chased many "tin-horns," as he called them, over the bridge to Jersey; but he was wrong if he believed that he had put the slightest dent in mob operations in New York. He was a personal and political inconvenience, nothing more. The nation's largest metropolis, prosperous from the wartime boom, represented a gambling gold mine, and the city's Mafia families, operating through Duke's, made sophisticated arrangements to tap it by remote control.

A telephone network was set up that threaded Bergen County. Householders were offered fifty dollars a week just to let some quiet, unobtrusive little man enter their homes and tie up their phones for a few hours each day. The visitor usually worked such a rented phone between noon and six P.M.; but on nights when there were prize-fights or basketball games, he would stay on the line until about 9:30 P.M., then depart. The fifty-dollar-a-week windfall just for letting some stranger have the use of your phone for a few hours a day proved irresistible to homeowners with a mortgage to pay off, and in time some 2,600 telephones throughout Bergen County were rented on this basis.

These phones were used, of course, to handle the betting play from New York. There, despite the LaGuardia crackdown, bookies still operated, either collecting bets themselves and phoning them in or having their clients dial certain New Jersey numbers. The Knapp Commission in 1971 showed that the New York Police Department was so deeply corrupted that many of its members were directly involved in the narcotics traffic. But the N.Y.P.D. had been just as worm-eaten with corruption thirty years earlier. Underworld runners and bookies grumbled at the time that the only real effect of the LaGuardia crackdown was to give crooked police an excuse for demanding heavier bribes. The argument went that police had to take much larger risks to protect their "friends"—and so they had to be compensated in more rewarding fashion.

Ironically, then, despite the best efforts of LaGuardia and one of the toughest police commissioners New York had had, the late Lewis P. Valentine, the rackets went right on operating, no more disturbed than a camper in the wilds who has brushed off a few gnats. The huge betting play from the horses, prizefights, baseball and football games, college and professional basketball, continued to flow into the coffers of the mob. One official estimate placed the total play—money that was bet and rebet—as high as *four billion dollars a year*. One New Jersey State Senator charged on the floor of the legislature that the crime syndicate was making a gross profit of *$1 million a day* from its New Jersey rackets. Grandiose as such figures are, there was enough hard factual evidence to show that the flow of gambling cash through underworld conduits reached truly staggering proportions.

In addition to the telephone network that recorded the daily gambling play, the Syndicate had established in Bergen County a layoff headquarters that handled the top-level action from all forty-eight states in the nation. The layoff is a vital process at the heart of the bookmaking operation. It is the underworld's form of gambling insurance. Say, for example, that a local book becomes overloaded with bets on a longshot in the third at Aqueduct; if the nag wins and the book has to pay off all his lucky clients, he can be ruined. To avoid such disaster, he bets himself on the longshot with a larger book, balancing his accounts, as it were. If the larger book with whom he lays off is similarly overloaded, the process is repeated through a top-level "layoff" clearing house.

This operation in New Jersey was masterminded by Frank Erickson, a bald, roly-poly, cherubic-faced master of mathematics who became the Syndicate's wizard of the layoff. The magnitude of Erickson's operation may be gleaned from some of his bank accounts that were uncovered in later investigations. On December 31, 1940 Erickson opened an account in the National Bank of New York. Deposits were soon amounting to as much as $100,000 a day, and on a single day, August 10, 1943, they climbed to $152,532.80. This one New Jersey bank account—and there were other accounts handling Erickson cash during the same period—showed total deposits of $2,860,667.98 between the opening date of December 31, 1940 and June 3, 1943, an average of more than $1 million a year.

Other bank accounts disclosed a little more about the tip of the iceberg. In 1945 New York investigators traced three "dummy" Erickson accounts in another New Jersey bank. These showed deposits of $6,683,362.20 in a little more than four years. These four accounts, then—and there were probably others—showed deposits that totaled more than $9.5 million in about four years' time. And this represented just the top-level play, the bets that were so risky they had to be funneled through the complicated layoff system. There was never any way of obtaining comparable records on the far larger, day-by-day sucker play that posed no threat to the solvency of smaller books, but the mechanics of the trade say that this must have represented incredible sums, dwarfing even Erickson's incredible millions. And this was not all. Bookmaking was not by any means the Syndicate's only source of gambling revenue.

There was also casino gambling, and this became the special, personal province of Joe Adonis, aided by the

Moretti brothers and by such major lieutenants as Anthony Guarini and Arthur Longano. Beginning sometime in 1942 and continuing for ten years, Joe Adonis splattered the northern New Jersey countryside with a string of gambling casinos, miniature Monte Carlos in which the nightly play ran into millions of dollars.

His technique was sophisticated and deceptive. He would take over an abandoned factory, an old barn, or a Quonset hut in the countryside. The exterior would be left untouched, its drabness acting as a protective camouflage. But no expense would be spared to redo the interior, creating a decor and atmosphere that would have done credit to the Stork or El Morocco. Sometimes as much as $150,000 would be spent on splendiferous faceliftings whose opulence was intended to lure the high-rollers to their doom. Furnishings were of the costliest materials, paintings by good artists decorated the walls, rugs were ankle deep. The food was always exemplary, the service flawless. Waitresses and cigarette girls were as curvaceous and scantily clad as any to be found in a Broadway chorus line. Croupiers and stick men wore full dress. Glamour, the spice and thrill of a secret rendezvous with fortune, the climactic gamble at the tables—all of this Joe A. provided for the customers who poured in an unending stream across the bridge from Manhattan.

A whole fleet of chauffeured Cadillacs brought the sheep to the shearing. A phone call from a swank Park Avenue apartment or one of the more prestigious New York hotels was all that was needed to trigger the evening's adventure. One of the drivers in the limousine fleet —"luggers," they were called—would roll up to the door and pick up the high-roller and his wad, returning him in the gray of dawn much lighter in the pocket. All of this was happening in wartime when gasoline rationing curbed the travel of ordinary mortals, but naturally such a technicality could not be permitted to interfere with the business of the underworld. There was always plenty of gasoline to fuel the gambling motorcade that streamed nightly over

the George Washington Bridge in such tailgating proces-
sions that agents of the Office of Defense Transportation
became suspicious.

When such nosy operatives caused trouble, the local law,
to save face, would have to pretend to act. What followed
was a charade enacted by two agreeable and cooperat-
ing partners. As an informant later told a federal narcotics
agent, Joe Adonis always received a tip that an "inspection" was about to be made by the law. It was then
that the summonses went out from Duke's, and handy-
men, truckers, and helpers pitched in with feverish energy.
Adonis's blueprint called for a flossy gambling house to be
dismantled and moved in an hour. This meant that the
crap tables, roulette wheels, birdcages, *chemin de fer*—all
the devices for a frenzied evening of risk and loss—had to
be carted out and loaded on waiting trucks. The costly
rugs, paintings, furnishings had to be transported, too, for
the object was to leave nothing but bare boards for the
law. When such operations went off smoothly—and Joe
Adonis saw to it that they always did—the outside helpers
who had been called in to assist in the vanishing act would
report to Duke's the following day to be paid off. They
were always happy if they found Willie or Solly Moretti on
the premises, for the Morettis were lavish with their tips.
But if Guarini or one of the lesser bosses was the paymas-
ter for the day, all a man could expect for exerting himself
beyond the call of duty was his stipulated fee.

Such lightning-fast changes of scene—it was almost
standard practice for Joe Adonis to gut a threatened casino one night and be in full operation somewhere else the
next—could be accomplished only through a smoothly
functioning executive staff. The ramifications of illegal
operations of this magnitude were almost infinite. Real estate deals had to be negotiated for gambling sites and business offices; contractors and decorators had to be hired;
protection arrangements ratified; large staffs, ranging from
strongarms and spotters on the doors to cigarette girls and
croupiers, chefs and waitresses and kitchen help, had to be

organized and paid, their withholding taxes accounted for; friendly truckers must always be on standby alert to transfer menaced equipment at a moment's notice; and warehouses must be available to hide and store the gambling paraphernalia until it could be used again. A number of dummy corporations were set up to handle the routine details of paying bills and salaries and accounting for withholding taxes due the federal government. These fronts all had innocuous names that gave no hint of their real purpose—the G & R Trading Company, the B & T Trading Company, the General Trading Company, the PAL Trading Company, to name just a few.

A business that could spawn such satellite companies had to be rolling in millions—and this business definitely was. Two of the Federal Bureau of Narcotics' best agents, George White and Ross B. Ellis, monitored the activities in Duke's in 1945. Their information was funneled to Garland B. Williams, the bureau's district supervisor in New York. Typical was Ellis's report on an Adonis gambling game being run in West Paterson, N.J., just over the Passaic County line. A staff of fifty well-paid employees was required to keep the operation going. The investment was large, but so were the profits.

Summarizing Ellis's information, Supervisor Williams wrote:

"It is conservatively estimated that the average nightly 'play' over the three crap tables, four roulette wheels, and three *chemin de fer* tables is considerably in excess of one million dollars. The house 'take' from this play is unknown. . . ."

The bureau subsequently estimated that Joe Adonis and Willie Moretti were reaping a gross profit of *$100,000 a week* from the play in this one establishment in West Paterson. And they had other games going at the same time.

Bookmaking millions, layoff millions, casino gambling millions—the loot pyramided in astounding mountains of cash whose true total will never be known. The Mafia chieftains of the New York area were wallowing in the green; and across the nation the picture was much the same. It was the best of times, and a golden stream poured night and day into the pockets of the underworld.

8.

The Mafia, Coast to Coast

The entire nation was now up for grabs. Abe Reles had told Burton Turkus: "We are out to get America by the pocketbook . . . the whole Syndicate." It was no idle boast. In the boom times that followed America's revving up for war in the late 1930s, the Mafia chieftains of New York and their allies stretched their talons from coast to coast, from north to south. Louisiana became virtually a principality of the Syndicate; Florida was host, playland, and gold mine for most of the major mobs in the nation; California, with its glamorous movie studios and enormous wealth, was given a post-graduate course in extortion and gambling, Mafia style; and, finally, miracle of miracles, the Syndicate discovered the perfect paradise—Las Vegas, where gambling was perfectly legal and some of the most vicious thugs in the country could operate within the provisions of the law. What an oyster loaded with pearls this was for the underworld! Racket money financed the most lavishly appointed hotels and casinos along The Strip, and racketeers and their front men found it delightfully simple to rook the rubes on the one hand and, on the other, to fleece the state and federal governments by skimming millions off the top of their take before they reported that take for tax purposes.

A pioneering and omnipresent force in this expansion of mob influence into far-distant reaches of the nation was the man who had succeeded Lucky Luciano as the most powerful Mafia chieftain in New York. Frank Costello, born Francesco Castiglia and raised amid the steaming stews of New York's Lower East Side, had become a conservatively clad pinstripe-suited millionaire who lived in a lavish penthouse on New York's Central Park West, had a summer estate in exclusive Sands Point, L.I., and was an habitué of the Waldorf-Astoria Hotel and the Copacabana nightclub.

He was of medium height, strongly built, with a short neck and broad shoulders. His black hair was brushed straight back from a narrow forehead, and there were deep creases about his thin, mobile lips. He had a long sharp nose that gave him a Cyrano de Bergerac profile, and he spoke in a hoarse, raspy voice that he strove to modulate as a gentleman should. His sharp intelligence had made him a respected figure in the Mafia ever since the early days when he had counseled Joe ("The Boss") Masseria, and it showed at times in the striking phrases that popped to his lips in moments of inspiration. Once, discussing his boyhood trials with the law in the East Side hovel where he was raised, he simply shrugged his shoulders and commented: "Tough times make monkeys eat red pepper."

When Fiorello LaGuardia began his crusade against the tin-horns, Costello and his partner, Philip ("Dandy Phil") Kastel, had a lock on the slot machine racket in New York. They had an exclusive franchise to buy the machines from the Mills Novelty Company, of Chicago, the largest slot-machine manufacturer in the nation, and they had flooded the city with the so-called "one-armed bandits." The machines were placed in speakeasies, cigar, stationery and candy stores throughout the five boroughs; and in some locations, if the machines were placed on a counter above the reach of small neighborhood school children, ladders were thoughtfully provided so that the tots could climb up and contribute their nickels to the Costello-Kastel welfare fund.

Most of the one-armed bandits simply gulped the five-cent pieces; but some swallowed dimes, quarters and half-dollars—and a few, in the swankier joints, had an exclusive taste for silver cartwheels. At the height of their operation, Costello and Kastel had 5,186 slot machines, and their take was enormous. A nickel machine in a good location could take in as much as twenty dollars a day; the higher-priced ones, of course, returned much more. With some five thousand machines gulping money, it was estimated that Costello and Kastel were enjoying a gross return of some $100,000 a day.

Then LaGuardia began to swing his ax. Since each machine cost about $100, the idea of having more than five thousand of them smashed to bits was enough to make the sensitive soul of any Mafioso shudder. Obviously, protective measures were in order. Costello and Kastel spirited some forty-five hundred of their machines out of the city before LaGuardia's wreckers could get at them, and they began to hunt for a more salubrious climate in which to operate. Their search took them to New Orleans and Louisiana—and Carlos Marcello. . . .

Carlos Marcello, still a power in Louisiana, was born Calorso Minicari in Tunis, North Africa, on February 6, 1910. His parents were Sicilian, and they brought him to New Orleans, site of the first Mafia scandal in America, when he was only eight months old. When he was nineteen, he began to build a police record that would become almost as long as John Dillinger's. Only, like Willie Moretti, he soon learned not just how to circumvent the law, but to use the law for his own personal benefit.

Marcello's most unfortunate experience was an early one, a 1930 conviction for assault and robbery, for which he was sentenced to serve nine to fourteen years in state prison. He put in less than four-and-a-half years and had been at liberty barely four months when he was arrested again for assault, beating, and wounding with intent to murder a member of the New Orleans Police Department. All of these charges flew out the window, and Carlos Marcello wasn't even inconvenienced by parole authorities, perhaps the first indication that he had achieved some mysterious status. Ratification of such suspicions came quickly and in highly tangible form. On July 25, 1935 Governor O. K. Allen, a stooge of the all-powerful Huey Long, granted Marcello a full pardon on that old assault and robbery rap for which he had been so inconsiderately sent to prison.

It was, doubtless, only a coincidence that, just at this precise moment in history, Costello and Kastel were inundating Louisiana with their slot machines; only a coincidence that Marcello became their partner in widespread gambling operations. The law at times continued to annoy him. He was arrested for selling marijuana, case dismissed; he was sent briefly to Atlanta penitentiary for another marijuana sale. He was charged with beating up a newspaper photographer in front of the Gretna Green Court House under the very nose of the sheriff, but the case faded away. He was threatened with deportation by U.S. Immigration agents as early as October, 1940—and they haven't succeeded in deporting him yet.

While the law was making such futile gestures, the Costello-Kastel-Marcello combine turned all Louisiana into a money-making fief for the Syndicate. Horserace wirerooms flourished openly. Marcello's companies cornered the jukebox and pinball market, with deputy sheriffs sometimes making this sales pitch: "Put in *our* machines or we'll close your handbook." And then there was casino gambling. Marcello went into partnership with Costello and Kastel in The Beverly Club, one of the most lavish nightclubs and gambling casinos in the nation. It did a roaring multi-million-dollar annual business; and Marcello, bankrolled by his share of this river of cash, expanded in 1948, setting up the New Southport Club in Jefferson Parish, a casino whose operation was patterned after the famous Beverly.

The Kefauver probe in 1951, with its attendant nation-wide publicity, put a crimp in some of these operations. The lid was put on temporarily for appearance's sake—but only temporarily. Aaron Kohn, a former FBI agent who headed the Metropolitan Crime Commission in New Orleans, kept close tabs on the activities of the Costello-Kastel-Marcello triumvirate and reported that The Beverly Club, after undergoing elaborate redecoration, was open and running again in 1959 on as grand a scale as ever.

According to Kohn when he testified before the McClellan Committee in 1963, nothing had changed in Louisiana despite Kefauver, despite the relentless exposure of the rackets by his commission, despite some courageous exposé journalism by the New Orleans *States*. He ticked off the names of a whole string of gambling casinos, some of which hadn't even closed their doors for Kefauver: the Chesterfield Club, the Keyhole Club, Lambert's Owl Club. There was not much mystery about the means by which such magic was accomplished. The secret lay as always in the close, corruptive alliance of the mob and politics. One court case was especially illustrative.

In January, 1955, Horace Perez, a notorious gambler and an associate of Marcello, went on trial for bribery. State Police Major-Inspector Aaron Edgecombe had constructed an airtight case. He introduced into evidence several thousand dollars that, he said, Perez had paid him to protect gambling in Marcello's special preserve, Jefferson Parish, the area to the west and south of New Orleans. The physical evidence was backed up by recordings Edgecombe had made of conversations with Perez. These were played for the jury. The evidence was overwhelming, and Perez was convicted. He and an associate were later convicted of a similar bribery attempt in Orleans Parish. At this juncture, politics stepped in. The late Governor Earl Long, brother of the more famous Huey, pardoned both Perez and his assistant, and, after the pardon, the courts ruled that the graft money had to be returned to the once-convicted bribers.

With this kind of immunity, with millions of dollars pouring in from a variety of illegal enterprises, Carlos Marcello branched out into the world of legitimate business. He had millions of dollars invested in real estate, bars, restaurants, nightclubs, oil wells, motels, a quick freeze and storage company, and a sea shrimp company operating trawlers in the Gulf of Mexico.

A few transactions, selected at random among many, are sufficient to indicate the scope of his enterprises and his truly enormous wealth. In 1958 he and his brothers and sisters sold a 183-acre tract in Gretna for a penny less than $1 million. In the same year, Marcello's attorney and business partners appeared as major stockholders of record for the million-dollar-plus Town & Country Motel, which had just opened in Rossier City. Marcello also had a substantial interest in the Holiday Inn Motel in Jefferson Parish, purchased for $1.8 million.

The influence wielded by the one-time punk turned bloated millionaire was demonstrated time and again by the snake-eyed charm he exerted over tax assessors. These considerate gentlemen were never tough in evaluating the holdings of Carlos Marcello. Marcello's home in Marrero, Louisiana, advertised for sale in 1959 for $125,000, was assessed for $8,000. The New Southport Club, the gambling casino for which he had paid $160,000, was assessed for $7,200. The Town & Country Motel in Jefferson Parish, offered for sale by Marcello in 1959 for more than $1 million, was valued on the tax rolls at a mere $17,500.

Such was Mafia magic under the Costello-Kastel-Marcello regime in Louisiana. Florida was not much different. . . .

The penetration of Florida on a large scale stemmed from the collaboration of the Big Three of eastern gambling and eastern rackets: Joe Adonis, Meyer Lansky and Frank Costello. Their partnership first became visible in the early 1940s in the operation of the Piping Rock Casino in Saratoga Springs, N.Y. Piping Rock was a high-class, fashionable restaurant catering to the fast racetrack crowd and the gambling millionaires of business and society who annually descend upon Saratoga for the August racing meet.

The restaurant was connected to the gambling casino by a door that led into a narrow passageway. Two strong-arm men, former New York City policemen, were always stationed just inside this connecting door, and with them were three "spotters" whose job was to clear the bettors. One of the "spotters" was an expert on the Saratoga gambling crowd; the second knew the Florida and out-of-state playboys; the third was the expert on New York City's high-rollers.

During the 1941 and 1942 racing seasons, the whole operation was under the direct supervision of Joe Adonis, who sat night after night at a table just inside the door of the gambling casino, playing gin rummy while he watched the customers file past and kept an eye on the action at the tables. His role and his ties to Costello and Lansky were documented in a series of hearings held by the New York State Liquor Authority in 1944 when it weighed the issue of renewing the liquor license of a restaurant with which such suspect gentlemen were connected. *The New York Times* devoted considerable space to the disclosures, especially to the testimony of Costello, who had an ingeniously casual explanation about the manner in which he became involved. He testified:

> There is a Joe Stein which is a good friend of mine. I have known him for years, which I consider very honorable. He came to me and he gave me this proposition—that he had a lease on a casino in Saratoga called Piping Rock and would I undertake running it?
>
> I told him I wasn't interested, didn't have no time for it. A few days later he came to me and he says he had some people interested, but they won't take a hundred percent of it. I say, "What have you left?" He says thirty.
>
> I said, "Well, I will have thirty percent under one condition. I will finance my thirty percent, but you will

have to look after my interests, because I will probably never be up there." Being I trust the man, I gave him the money, and I have a thirty percent interest.

There was no hint in these remarks by the trusting Frank Costello that the vague "some people" who held the remaining seventy per cent interest in Piping Rock were brother moguls of the Syndicate whom he knew perfectly well, or that the principal caretaker of his own interest was Joe Adonis, with whom he regularly traded ideas on the plush greens of the Pomonok Country Club or in that shadowy back cavern in Duke's.

Adonis himself, some years later, was more frank about his role. In an interview he gave to Edward T. Folliard, a reporter for the *Washington Post*, he described himself as a big businessman whose "big business" was gambling. He compared himself to a financial titan in Wall Street. The Wall Streeter, he said, furnishes capital for legitimate enterprises; he supplied the capital to set up gambling casinos. The motive in both cases was the same—profit.

Of course, Joe A. explained, he had to be extremely careful in making such investments. He had to decide three vital questions. What was the community like? What were the prospects of action—that is, patronage or business? And what about the law? This last issue was basic to everything. Joe Adonis, as he explained to Folliard, never wanted to operate where the law took a blue-nosed attitude about gambling; and he preferred to set up his casinos in areas where, if some eager-beaver investigator did become obnoxious, a gambling arrest would be treated as a mere misdemeanor, not a more serious felony.

From every standpoint, Florida was ideal. It was certainly not a blue-nosed state. A powerful Mafioso, Santo Trafficante Sr., had been operating from his base in Tampa for years and controlled the wide-open bookmaking and gambling activities along the Gulf coast, linking up in some enterprises with the Marcello ring in neighboring Louisiana. Anthony ("Little Augie Pisano") Carfano, when Brooklyn became too hot for him as the result of an indiscreet hijacking in the early 1930s, had found Miami an ideal refuge in the sun. He had purchased a hotel there, had developed his own gambling preserve and had demonstrated again that this was a friendly land, indeed. And so now, with the wartime boom putting ridiculous amounts of money into pockets under foolish heads, Meyer Lansky went south to establish another mecca for the gambling partnership.

Leaving Miami to Little Augie, he concentrated on the Broward County area just to the north of the city. The setup was similar to that at Saratoga. The great Gulfstream Park racetrack was located here, and Lansky operated on the business principles that had proved so valid in New York. Gambling addicts, not content with dropping a wad at the races—or, if they had won, feeling that luck was with them—would want to find a convenient establishment where they could dine in style and gamble away the night.

To accommodate them, Lansky supervised the purchase of the Colonial Inn, just south of Gulfstream Park. Like Piping Rock, the Inn was a classy restaurant and casino, the kind known in the trade as "a carpet joint." As in Saratoga, the law cast its protective arm around the establishment. An obliging sheriff supplied armed deputies to guard the casino and to protect the armored cars that carried the spoils of an evening's play to the banks.

The result was a veritable gold mine. District Attorney Hogan in New York later seized the financial records of Frank Erickson, the bookie king, and also obtained the files of the accountant who had handled Joe Adonis's financial affairs. These documents illustrated two major points: the manner in which different mob interests collaborated in territories that the Syndicate had decreed to be "open," and the staggering amount of swag a single operation like the Colonial Inn put into the pockets of its gangster proprietors.

The records showed that Mert Wertheimer, boss of the Detroit mob, had a one-third interest in the Colonial Inn. Meyer Lansky held sixteen percent; Joe Adonis, fifteen percent. Other partners included: Meyer's brother, Jake Lansky; Costello's right-hand man, Vincent ("Jimmy Blue Eyes") Alo; and, of course, Frank Erickson.

As for profits, the seized records showed that in a single year ending October 31, 1946 the Colonial Inn had netted $685,538.76—a juicy bit of pie to be split up among its mob owners. This, of course, was not all. Adonis also had the Greenacres Club in Hollywood, north of Miami, and there were other lesser gambling joints splattered around the winter playland of the nation. Putting it all together, officials estimated that the mob was probably cleaning up some $20 million a year from its Florida rackets. . . .

And then there were California and Las Vegas, Bugsy Siegel and Virginia Hill.

It was in 1937 that the national commission of the Syndicate, or the Combination as it was sometimes called, decided to send Bugsy west. Like Meyer Lansky, his partner in the Bug and Meyer mob, Bugsy was Jewish and so no *capo* Mafioso; but both he and Lansky had been favorites of Lucky Luciano when executions were needed, and their status in the ethnic-melded underworld of the new gangsterism was high. California had its own powerful *capo* Mafioso in Jack I. Dragna, but the members of the national commission evidently felt that the possibilities of the movieland gold coast were being only imperfectly exploited. And so Bugsy was sent west as the agent of the Syndicate, with the Mafia bosses of New York and Chicago solidly behind him.

Handsome, hot-tempered and vicious, Bugsy Siegel was also an insatiable stud. He and Hollywood seemed meant for each other. He loved the bedroom as much as he loved murder; and, with his looks, most girls were willing. But if one proved obstinate, Bugsy was fully capable of enjoying a little rape. After his first taste of Hollywood, he is said to have wisecracked to Meyer Lansky: "There are no virgins there, but it's virgin territory for us."

Soon Bugsy Siegel became the gangster chic and lover boy of Hollywood. He ensconced himself in a $200,000,

35-room Holmby Hill palace, complete with swimming pool. He hobnobbed with the stars. George Raft, tough guy of the movies, became a friend and companion. Jean Harlow was said to have found him irresistible. Ditto Wendy Barrie, who accompanied Bugsy on several of his trips to the East, apparently under the delusion that someday she was to marry him.

Bugsy had not gone west, however, just to enjoy the stars and starlets of Hollywood; he had business to attend to for the Syndicate. And business meant gambling and extortion.

In 1940, during the Murder Inc. probe, Burton Turkus went to California, following the trail of a Syndicate murder that Bugsy had arranged with his associates back East. Turkus got a warrant and invaded Siegel's Holmby Hill retreat. There he discovered a couple of guns tucked away in a wall safe and, more important than the guns, a fascinating set of account books.

These showed that Bugsy, almost from the moment he landed in Hollywood, had been systematically shaking down many top film idols. Neatly recorded were "loans" running into four and five figures. None had ever been repaid. One lever Bugsy used to pry such favors out of movie stars was his hold over the movie extras' union. He would simply point out to a star that, unless he or she made a sizable contribution to "the union," the extras would walk off the lot and boycott any picture in which the star was to appear. No extras, no picture—and no future for the star. The logic of Bugsy's reasoning was irrefutable; and, in one year, Turkus found, these mysterious movieland "loans" to Bugsy totaled $400,000.

Bankrolled so handsomely, aided by Dragna and Mickey Cohen, Bugsy pressed the expansion of the Syndicate's enterprises on all fronts. An offshore fleet of gambling vessels transferred casino hijinks to the high seas. Horse-race betting was expanded, and Bugsy warred for control of the racing-wire service in the state. During this struggle, he extended his activities into Arizona and Nevada—and so discovered a new and better gambling gusher for the mob.

Gambling had been legalized in Nevada in 1931, but the big shots of the underworld had been slow to recognize the enormous potentiality of a haven that made the illegal legal. Siegel, backgrounded as he was by association with Meyer Lansky and Joe Adonis, took one good hard look around him in 1942 and almost whooped for joy. He was as elated by his discovery of Nevada as Christopher Columbus had been at the thought he had found the fabulous East Indies. Bugsy bought into the Golden Nugget and the Frontier Club, two of Las Vegas' busier joints; and as he began to reap the rewards of these financial enterprises, a grandiose vision came to him. He would build a fabulous hotel, dedicated to twenty-four-hour gambling, right on the three-mile Strip that separates McCarran Airport from Las Vegas. He would call it the Flamingo.

Vast though his own resources were, Bugsy didn't have the cash for such a venture. But the Syndicate did. He couldn't wait to tell Meyer Lansky and the others what a gold mine he had found for them all. The evidence is that they listened and got the point, for Bugsy returned to Nevada with the financial support of top-level mob bosses in cities like New York, Chicago and Cleveland.

Del Webb, the contractor who was later to become part-owner of the New York Yankees baseball team, was hired to turn Bugsy's dream into reality. That dream now began to be Bugsy's undoing. His imagination kept soaring; the size and appointments of his palace of chance became ever larger and more costly. The Flamingo became a bottomless maw into which Bugsy poured some $1 million of his own money and some $5 million of other persons'— dark, hard-featured men who would expect not only their money back, but a solid return on their investments.

An anecdote related years afterwards by a man who was an adviser to Bugsy during the building of the Flamingo gives an insight into the brash hood's struggle to raise ever more cash. Millions had been poured into the gaudy project, and still the end was not in sight. Regretfully, the adviser broke the news to Bugsy: more money would be needed, thousands more. Bugsy nodded casually, like a man who has just been told by his wife that he had better get his shirts from the cleaners, and soon afterwards he departed on one of his periodic trips back East.

When he returned, he walked into the adviser's office, lugging two heavy satchels. He grunted with the effort as he swung first one satchel, then the other, up to the top of the adviser's desk.

"What's this?" the man asked.

"Money," said Bugsy. "You said we needed more. Here it is. Let me know if it's not enough."

The satchels were bulging with $400,000 in cash.

And so Bugsy got his Flamingo—and at the same time Virginia Hill. . . .

Virginia Hill was the leggy, bosomy, chestnut-haired glamour girl of the Syndicate. She had the features of a Hollywood starlet—and the temper and vocabulary of a stevedore. She wore mink like a lady—and she could sock harder than some prizefighters. She was a poor little barefoot girl from Georgia, and she had worked her way up through the ranks of the mob so successfully that she kept a wardrobe of seventy-five to a hundred expensive dresses, which she always discarded after a couple of wearings. Her extravagant tastes led her to take hoydenish delight in throwing $7,500 champagne parties on the whim of the moment. She was a riddle of conflicting complexes, but she wasn't a very hard riddle to read. Most men had to take only one look at Virginia Hill to know the reason for her success in life. As Longie Zwillman told the Kefauver committee with ungallant candor, "She didn't look as if she would be hard to know." She had wide, voluptuous lips and smoky gray-green eyes, seductive behind half-hooded lids. Any way you look at her, she spelled sex— and had ever since she began to acquire and discard husbands at the rather tender age of fifteen.

Her talents were not unique, but her artistry was far from inconsiderable. She had invaded Chicago at the time of the 1934 World's Fair, and before long there wasn't a major mobster who wasn't panting to stuff her handbag with bills. Her philosophy of life seemed to be wrapped up in a favorite saying. "A good girl isn't necessarily a nice girl," she'd tell the boys—and the boys could take it from there.

Virginia's climb upwards through the bedrooms of the Syndicate began with a mousy, inconspicuous, and worshipful little man named Joe Epstein, a bookie, an accountant and the income-tax expert of the Capone mob. Joe gave Virginia a leg up, and it wasn't long before she was pitching curves at some of the mightiest sluggers in the rackets.

She got to know them all, and they all got to know Virginia. She was the party girl, the star of every big mob blowout. On her calling list were Charlie Fischetti and his younger, handsomer, more suave brother, Joe; Tony Accardo, Murray ("The Camel") Humphreys, and Frank Nitti—all of the Capone dynasty; Tony Ginzo from Kansas City; Carlos Marcello from New Orleans; and Frank Costello and Joe Adonis.

The suspicion existed for years—the Kefauver committee was certain of it but couldn't prove it—that Virginia Hill was more than just the sex symbol of gangdom. She was also the cash-and-carry girl, a mink-clad female treasure chest. When fortunes in cash had to be ferried from the Midwest to the East to square the balance sheet of the Syndicate, playful Virginia was the courier who did the ferrying. She seemed to be constantly traveling back and forth, riding trains almost as often as the train crews that handled them.

Virginia got into the cash-and-carry trade, so the story goes, by proving her reliability with money as the layoff girl for Joe Epstein. Joe had decided that, when he had a dangerous wave of wagering on certain longshots, it was simpler to have little Virginia bet a wad at the track to knock the odds down and balance his books than it was to go through the more complicated underworld layoff system. Joe entrusted Virginia with his credit card to place the bets, a demonstration of his faith in her; for if Miss Hill had ever decided to go on a spree, the result would have been havoc. Virginia, who had a sharp mind under those chestnut tresses, knew better. She might toss her own money around like confetti, but she was scrupulously honest where Joe Epstein was concerned. And so she passed the qualifying test for a cash-and-carry girl.

Soon she was practically on a commuter's schedule between Chicago and New York. She rode the Twentieth Century Limited, an extra-fare train; she always had a bedroom to herself; and she always seemed to be carrying an extra, especially heavy purse. When she was asked about these trips by Kefauver aides in private questioning, Virginia gave them her hooded, gray-eyed stare, shrugged her shapely shoulders and quipped: "Maybe I just liked to ride on the trains."

This train-riding to the East brought Virginia into the orbit of Joe Adonis. Both were always quite reticent about the nature of their relationship. Joe A. in fact, was so close-mouthed he wouldn't even admit to the Kefauver committee that he had ever known the lady. The lady herself wasn't quite *that* bashful. She was a little coy, a trait not usually associated with Virginia Hill, but she was much more frank than Joe A.

She was on one of her regular trips to New York sometime in 1942, as she recalled it, and one evening she was perched at the bar in the Madison Hotel, enjoying liquid refreshment like a lady, when a cafe-society playboy who had been hovering around brought over a stocky, darkly handsome, extremely well-dressed gentleman of quiet voice and manners.

"Virginia," said Cafe Playboy, "this is Mr. Adams."

Innocent Virginia was quite taken with "Mr. Adams." She sighed and her distinctive gray-green eyes grew soft as she recalled for Kefauver probers years later just the way it had been. Of course, she explained, she had no idea at the time who "Mr. Adams" really was. How could she? He was just so nice and so charming that the shy little soul of Virginia was captivated almost at once; in practically no time at all, she discovered that they made a striking twosome on the town. They had, Virginia said, about half a dozen dates before she even realized that the suave and soft-spoken "Mr. Adams" was really Joe Adonis, one of the ruling powers of the mob. This discovery, it seems, didn't trouble Virginia; she kept right on seeing that kindly gentleman she had known as "Mr. Adams," but it was all just in good fun, you know.

The fun lasted for a long time. When Virginia was smitten with the movie craze and went to Hollywood in an effort to break into pictures, Joe A. became the commuter, making frequent "business trips" to the West Coast. He was such a constant visitor, indeed, that Hollywood gossip columnists noted he had been seen strolling hand-in-hand with Virginia on Sunset Strip or dining with her in a quiet, softly lighted corner of the Trocadero.

The idyll of Miss and Mr. Syndicate came to a grinding halt after Virginia and Bugsy Siegel met. Sparks flew. Electricity crackled. Virginia soon became Bugsy's girl.

They were well-matched in many ways, both physically attractive, ruthless and unscrupulous, with volcanic and unpredictable tempers. Bugsy's viciousness and wild rages, his reveling in the act of murder, became the stuff of legend. Vain of his movie-star looks, the swaggering hood tried to ape the gentleman through his costly and flashy wardrobe, just as Virginia aped the fine lady with her constantly replenished closetful of fine dresses.

Bugsy wore broad, snap-brimmed hats; pinstriped suits; specially tailored overcoats with fur-lined collars; handcrafted shoes with pointed toes agleam; handmade silk shirts and shorts, both decorated with his monogram. He was so vain he was combing his wavy hair every five minutes; and when it began to thin out on top with the years, he splattered it with every lotion known to man in the futile hope of growing a new crop.

Virginia and Bugsy were constantly traveling back and forth between California and Mexico (they liked Acapulco), both to play in the sun and make the arrangements needed to keep the narcotics pipeline open to the States. Eventually, they were secretly married south of the border, and legend has it that Virginia would have been content to retire on Bugsy's racket millions and seek out the secluded penthouse somewhere. But by this time Bugsy had lost all touch with reality, carried away his vision of the glorious Flamingo—and then, too, Bugsy's sexual appetite being what it was, there were always other women.

As the Flamingo neared completion, Bugsy found it handy to have three other girl friends established in apartments within easy reach. This drove the tempestuous Miss Syndicate up the wall. She was insanely jealous, especially of Wendy Barrie, who on one occasion, and quite prematurely, had announced her engagement to Bugsy. One night, finding Miss Barrie on the premises, Virginia swung a haymaker that almost dislocated the jaw of her actress-rival. Bugsy, whose temper erupted like Vesuvius in action, swung a right cross at Virginia, screaming, "You ain't no lady."

Miss Syndicate fled to her penthouse suite, where she promptly gulped a handful of sleeping pills. Dick Chappell, hotel manager of the Flamingo, later recalled for Ed Reid and Ovid Demaris what happened next. He was alerted to the crisis by the sight of Bugsy leaning from his window and screaming, "She's killed herself."

They bundled the unconscious Miss Syndicate into Bugsy's car; and Chappell, driving, pressed the accelerator almost to the floor, roaring at eighty-miles-an-hour-plus down The Strip. All the time, Bugsy was pounding him on the back, cursing in an unending streak. "Goddam stupid bitch. Why did she have to do that? Bitch, bastard, go on, hurry. Step on it."

They got Virginia to the hospital in time to save her life on that occasion; but, in the dark days ahead, she was to keep on popping pills in the attempted-suicide routine until finally, years later, she succeeded.

The Flamingo was not yet completed, despite all the millions spent on it, when Bugsy decided it was finished enough for the grand opening. The theater, casino, lounge, and restaurant were as lavish as they would ever be, and so Bugsy scheduled the event that was to launch a new gambling era in Las Vegas. The date he picked was December 26, 1946. Bugsy in evening dress, glamorous Virginia on his arm, threw open the doors of his "fabulous Flamingo" and prepared to revel in his greatest triumph.

He had planned lavishly as always. Entertainment featured major stars. Jimmy Durante topped the headliners. Also on hand were Tommy Wonder, Baby Rosemarie, the Tunetoppers, Eddie Jackson and Xavier Cugat's band. Specially chartered Constellations were to bring a galaxy of Hollywood stars whose presence could be guaranteed to create a headline splash that would catch the eyes of rubes and high-rollers across the nation.

Bugsy Siegel had planned grandly, but now everything went wrong. Bad weather grounded the Constellations in Los Angeles. Only a few Hollywood stars—George Raft, Charles Coburn, George Sanders, and Vivian Blaine among them—showed up. The crowd was sparse, the gambling tepid. The casino went into the red the first night.

A spotter for the Syndicate phoned the word back to Meyer Lanksy in Florida: "It's a washout."

And a washout it was. The Flamingo stayed open for a mere two weeks. In that time, it dropped another $100,000.

Bugsy Siegel's prophetic vision, it seemed, had turned into a costly mirage; and all the way across the nation, from the West Coast to the Midwest and the East, there were those hard-featured men—his multi-millionaire underworld backers—who did not like it one little bit. The man had failed them with their money and at their expense—and that, for Bugsy Siegel, could be a very costly failure, indeed.

9.

Lucky Luciano Rides Again

The face of the postwar Mafia was changed by two major events: the springing of Lucky Luciano from what had been a virtual life-sentence in prison and the return of Vito Genovese from his years-long exile in Italy. Luciano's release coincided significantly with the sudden mushrooming of the international narcotics traffic and the vast new wave of American addiction that resulted; Genovese's return to America signaled the eventual end of the rule of order that had marked the years of Luciano-Costello-Adonis dominance, and the Mafia was to be ripped apart by bloody feuds that have lasted to the present day.

The pivotal event, the one that was to have the most profound impact on American life, was the freeing of Luciano and the letting loose of his evil genius to work its way on the world. Here undoubtedly was the greatest executive talent the American underworld had ever produced; his ruthlessly efficient elimination of the Moustache Petes in the nationwide murder-coup that had remade the Mafia overnight had demonstrated that. Yet, in the immediate aftermath of World War II, a determined effort was made to portray Luciano as a great American patriot whose invaluable services to his country justified his premature release.

In the mystery that now unfolded—and there remains to this day no other word for it—the role of Thomas E. Dewey was a most ambivalent one. Dewey's greatest service to his country had been performed in the days when, as a dynamic young prosecutor, he had smashed at underworld combines and their vast corruptive power. This was, and remains, one of the greatest menaces to American society, for it gives the worst and most vicious rats in the nation subversive influence over the democratic process and undermines the faith of the American people in the honesty of their officials and the viability of their government. Young Dewey, the demon of the courtroom, had exposed and fought this evil with a brilliance and a courage that excited national admiration; but after he was bitten by the Presidential bug and became the Republican governor of New York, he suddenly lost all passion and commitment.

Statewide political campaigns, let alone Presidential campaigns, require huge and increasing sums of money, running into many millions of dollars; and in New York, New Jersey and many other states of the nation, a tacit partnership has been forged between political parties needing vast amounts of cash and the underworld with its enormous reservoirs of cash to give. Willie Moretti in New Jersey told rackets-buster Nelson F. Stamler on one occasion: "I always operated strictly pari-mutuel"—his way of saying that he always paid off the political powers. The rate of payoff, Stamler was told, ran as high as sixty cents on every racket dollar.

Similarly, in New York, Thomas E. Dewey as governor presided over a Republican regime that pretended to be unaware of the wide-open gambling at Saratoga Springs in the very heartland of upstate Republicanism. Dewey, as a young prosecutor, had denounced Joe Adonis as the Public Enemy No. 1 of Brooklyn; Dewey, as governor, appeared to be unaware that this same Public Eenemy No. 1 was running the wide-open gambling casinos at Piping Rock and the Arrowhead Inn.

This anomalous situation was exposed by the Kefauver

committee in a sideswiping, half-hearted peek into the
New York situation in 1951. The committee established
that the New York State Police had investigated the wide-
open Saratoga gambling in August, 1947, and had found
six casinos running full blast. The police identified Joe
Adonis and members of the Detroit mob as the partners in
the gambling casino at the Arrowhead Inn. Superintendent
of State Police John A. Gaffney testified that, when he received the report, he commented: "This looks like a sizable operation." Then he pigeonholed the damning document.

Asked to explain this curious lack of zeal, the superintendent alibied that state police weren't supposed to raid
over the heads of local authorities except by special re-
quest or order of the governor. But, in this instance, New
York had a governor who had been a famous rackets-buster. Surely Superintendent Gaffney must have notified *him*
of the horrendous situation his detectives had uncovered?
No, Gaffney said, he hadn't. He felt, he testified, that the
governor and the governor's staff must have known all
about it since "it's been going on for twenty-five years to
my knowledge." Senator Kefauver asked: "In other
words, you just knew you weren't supposed to do anything
about it?" The badgered superintendent agreed; he went
further. He said that he had felt, if he had called attention
to the Saratoga gambling, that he might have found himself "out on the sidewalk."

And so, though newspapers like *The New York Times,*
which certainly has a considerable readership in official
circles, had publicized mob control of Saratoga gambling
as early as 1944, no official action was taken to cast a pall
over the sunny world of Joe Adonis, Meyer Lansky, and
company.

It is against this ambivalent background of official per-
missiveness that one has to assess the astonishing release
of Lucky Luciano from New York state prisons on February 2, 1946. Governor Dewey, who, as a young rackets
buster, had packed Luciano away, was the same man who,

as governor, commuted his long sentence with the agreement that he would be deported to his native Italy.

The rationale for what appeared to be a startling about-face was that Lucky Luciano, in prison, had performed such invaluable wartime services that, in other circumstances, he might have been deserving of the Congressional Medal of Honor. Later, when the Kefauver committee tried to determine precisely what it was that Luciano had done, the trail became murkier and murkier. What appears from the sketchy and embarrassed official record is essentially this:

In 1942, Naval Intelligence was greatly concerned about the possibility of sabotage and espionage along the sprawling New York waterfront. The great French liner *Normandie,* converted to a troopship capable of carrying an entire division, had burned and sunk at her Manhattan pier in a mysterious disaster; German submarines seemed to be supplied with uncannily accurate information about sailing dates of convoys bound for England. Navy Intelligence felt a counterforce was needed along the waterfront, and it was suggested that perhaps the underworld dock mobs could help. Some of the more scrupulous officers at Navy Headquarters at 90 Church Stree reacted with horror, but wartime exigencies overrode all ethical sensibilities.

The late Cmdr. Charles Haffenden (USNR) was placed in charge of Operation Underworld Counterespionage. Haffenden contacted District Attorney Hogan, and Hogan assigned Murray Gurfein, then in charge of his rackets bureau, to work with the navy. With Gurfein's help, an approach was made to Joseph ("Socks") Lanza, czar of extortion in the huge Fulton Fish Market and the Lower East Side docks. Lanza was then under indictment and about to go to trial, and Gurfein made it clear to him he could expect no deal. "Socks" decided to cooperate anyway, but shortly afterwards he told Haffenden "certain elements" wouldn't help unless they got the word from Charlie Lucky.

This brought Moses Polakoff, Luciano's attorney, into

the act. Polakoff discussed the matter with Meyer Lansky, who always had Luciano's ear, and Lansky reported back that he had broached the subject to the imprisoned boss. Luciano was willing to be patriotic, the word was, but he wanted some consideration in return. He was unhappy in Dannemora, a prison in the farthest reaches of upstate New York; he felt he would be much more comfortable in Great Meadow Prison, just north of Albany, known as the "country club" of New York State penal institutions. This was a small favor, and his transfer was obligingly arranged.

There followed a fantastic series of pilgrimages from New York to Albany. Polakoff and "Socks" Lanza made the first trip, explaining the proposition to Charlie Lucky. Polakoff said later that Luciano appeared surprised, but agreed to do whatever he could to help. As a result, during the next three years, Polakoff made some two dozen similar visits to Great Meadow, ten with Meyer Lansky, three or four with Lanza before "Socks" himself was sent to prison, nine with Mike Lescari, one with Costello, one with Willie Moretti, and one with Mike Miranda. Polakoff always insisted that he had no idea what was discussed during these prison conferences held under the aegis of Navy Intelligence; he always sat off to one side, and besides everybody was jabbering away in Italian.

It strains credulity to imagine that these officially arranged conferences between major bosses and the Mafia's mastermind were devoted exclusively to Charlie Lucky's patriotic duty and that racket problems were never mentioned. But, according to the official *mea culpa* later, the meetings were helpful. Luciano is supposed to have sent out word to the boys—to Joe Adonis ruling the crime cabinet in Duke's; to Albert Anastasia, whose brother, Tough Tony, ruled an impressive stretch of Brooklyn piers; and to Vincent Mangano, general overlord of the Brooklyn docks. Just what the word was, no one could say. There was, however, virtually no sabotage in the vital port of New York during the remainder of the war. Did Lucky Luciano's magic wand accomplish this miracle, or should the credit go to the FBI, whose nationwide protection of vital industries was almost perfect throughout the war? There was no evidence, and one is left to chose between Charlie Lucky and the FBI.

There was one other strand to the official version that Lucky Luciano had been one of the nation's foremost patriots. When American forces invaded Sicily in the summer of 1943, an American fighter plane with a yellow flag displaying the black letter "L" on its belly flew low over the town of Villalba and dropped a packet containing a smaller replica of the flag near the church. This yellow "L" flag was passed along to Don Calogero Vizzini, ruler of the Sicilian Mafia; and when American tanks rumbled upon the scene, the soldiers found the countryside swarming with Sicilians eager to assist in the free world's crusade against the hated dictator, Benito Mussolini. The American military was so impressed by the knowledge, efficiency, and good will of these anti-Mussolini "patriots" that, according to Norman Lewis in *The Honored Society,* they armed the Mafiosi who had survived Cesare Mori's purge and turned the machinery of local government over to Don Calo—and, of course, the Mafia.

Such was the shadowy official account for whose veracity and details no official on any level would put his reputation on the line. Even if one grants that Lucky Luciano made some notable contributions to the war effort, the question remains: Did his actions justify release from prison after serving only nine and a half years of his thirty to fifty-year sentence? There were many who didn't think so. One of these was Supreme Court Justice Philip J. McCook, who had sentenced Luciano. In 1943, George Wolf, a lawyer who represented both Costello and Luciano, argued before Justice McCook that Luciano's patriotic endeavors entitled him to a reduced sentence of ten years, an action that would have made him automatically eligible for parole. But Justice McCook ruled that it would be wrong to liberate the most powerful Mafioso in the nation when many of his henchmen were serving longer sentences for comparatively trivial offenses.

Balked in this first attempt, the Mafia wasn't discouraged. Mafiosi are always convinced that there is a way, if one can but find it, to get anything one wants out of the law. In Luciano's case, they decided upon an end-run around the obstruction represented by Justice McCook; on V-E day, Luciano's astute mouthpieces, Polakoff and Wolf, applied to the New York State Parole Board for clemency, again citing Luciano's high patriotism and his remarkable, though unspecified, contributions to the Allied cause.

Now some strange things began to happen. New York gossip columnists noted rumors in underworld circles that large sums were being amassed to finance Charlie Lucky's expensive tussle with the law. One columnist reported that $100,000 had been raised for "legal expenses." Across the nation, minions of the mob were moaning in pain. Out in St. Louis, Paul Meskil, a reporter with a flair for knowing what goes on in the underworld, found all of his mob acquaintances wearing faces hounddog sad. "They're breakin' our backs to kick in to get this big sonofabitch out of jail in the East," victims of the special assessment complained.

Underworld scuttlebutt has long insisted that, by such cross-continental effort, some $250,000 was raised to defray Charlie Lucky's "legal expenses." Whether this sizable fund had anything to do with the outcome, no man can say; but it should perhaps be noted that Socks Lanza, whose patriotism by all accounts had equaled Charlie Lucky's, did not receive equal consideration. He served out his seven-and-a-half to fifteen-year term.

Charlie Lucky was luckier. The New York State Parole Board recommended that his sentence be commuted. Noting that he had never bothered to become a naturalized citizen, the board suggested he be shipped directly back to his native Italy. Governor Dewey went along with both suggestions, and prison gates opened for the so appropriately named Charlie Lucky.

There followed a scene which was one of the most brazen public expressions of Mafia power and contempt for

the law in American history. On February 9, 1946, just a
week after Dewey had acted, Luciano was taken from
Ellis Island and escorted by immigration officials to Pier 7
at the Bush Terminal in Brooklyn, in the heart of Anastasia country. There he was placed aboard the frowzy little
Liberty ship *Laura Keene* for the voyage back to his homeland.

Immigration officials had invited reporters to a shipboard
press conference with Luciano, and the newspaper fraternity of New York turned out en masse for the anticipated
face-to-face confrontation with the overlord of the city's
rackets. Newsmen and photographers, all with properly issued passes, were accompanied by Harry Ratzke, the Immigration Bureau's assistant superintendent of security.
But, as the group approached the pier entrance, their way
was barred by a line of fifty tough-looking Anastasia dock
wallopers, equipped with ugly, sharp-pointed bailing
hooks.

When Luciano arrived at 2:30 P.M. he was greeted
with an outburst of cheering, but when reporters tried to
follow him aboard ship, they found their way blocked.

"Nobody goes on the pier because somebody might get
hoited," one of Anastasia's stooges announced. "We gotta
watch out for lawsuits. Somebody might trip over something."

Ratzke snapped: "That's ridiculous." And he told the
newsmen: "Follow me."

But it quickly became apparent that official rank counted for nothing here.

"Where d'ya think you're going', chum?" challenged the
tough, runty-looking boss of the dock wallopers.

"I'm from the Bureau of Immigration, and I'm taking
these boys to see Luciano," Ratzke told him.

"I don't give a damn where you're from," came the answer. "You ain't got no right to take nobody on this pier."

The stevedores closed in around Ratzke, toying idly
with their bailing hooks. Ratzke got the idea. Meekly he
asked if it would be all right if *he* went aboard ship and
saw Mr. Luciano. This permission was granted, but the re-

porters and photographers had to back off under the threat of being thrown bodily into the water. Ratzke was gone only a few minutes, then he returned to announce the obvious: Luciano had said to hell with the goddamned press; he wasn't seeing anybody.

"I want you fellows to know it wasn't the Bureau of Immigration that kept you off the boat," Ratzke told reporters lamely.

It quickly became obvious that an authority greater than that of this arm of the U.S. Government was in control of events on the pier. Mob chiefs and their allies appeared and were passed through the bailing-hook, stevedore screen to give Lucky Luciano a farewell shipboard party that should have buoyed his spirits halfway across the Atlantic. They brought hampers crammed with wines and liquors, lobster and caviar. Frank Costello came, and Joe Adonis, and Albert Anastasia. Mike Lescari, an associate of Longie Zwillman, an old boyhood friend of Lucky's and one of the consultants at Great Meadow, was also there. So were Meyer Lansky and a half-dozen politicians, including a former judge. When at last the revelry ended and the *Laura Keene* pulled away from the pier, the stevedore honor guard sent Lucky on his way with a rousing cheer. One bull voice bellowed over all the rest: "Keep the old chin up, Boss. You'll be back in the driver's seat soon."

It was a prophetic remark . . .

If the Brooklyn dock scene did not give Governor Dewey cause to wonder about the wisdom of his action in letting Lucky Luciano loose upon the world, the events of the next few months must have caused some private doubt and anguish. For the deported Luciano did not just stay quietly in Italy. Before the end of 1946, he was back in Cuba, just ninety miles from American shores, and he was installed in imperial grandeur in a lavish penthouse atop one of Havana's gaudiest hotels. The pilgrimages that now began were in themselves a testament to his status in the underworld.

Frank Sinatra, idol of teen-aged fans and star of Broadway and Hollywood, was one of those who flew down to Havana to visit Charlie Lucky. Much later, on August 3, 1962, a special nineteen-page report prepared for Attorney Robert F. Kennedy would spell out Sinatra's ties with some ten of the best-known gangsters in the country during the 1950s and 1960s. A year later, in 1963, one of these friends—Sam Giancana, the powerful Chicago Mafioso—was to cause Sinatra all kinds of trouble. The Nevada State Gaming Control Board took a dim view of Sinatra's association with Giancana and Sinatra's playing host to the mobster at his Cal-Neva Lodge. The Board started legal action to revoke Sinatra's gaming license; and so pressured, the singer agreed to sell his Nevada gambling interests, reportedly valued at some $3.5 million. In all of the federal reports on Sinatra, however, no incident is quite so titillating as the account of his reunion with Charlie Lucky in Havana.

According to the Federal Bureau of Narcotics, Charlie Lucky celebrated the event by throwing a classic party that roared full tilt into the early morning hours. As ill fortune would have it, the great star's arrival in Havana had been duly noted in the press, and the next day a group of Girl Scouts appeared at the hotel to see their idol. The eager girls, with a nun as chaperone, were herded into an elevator and delivered to the penthouse. The door stood ajar. The visitors timidly ventured in, by some mischance unannounced. What met their innocent young eyes was a scene of chaos. Bottles littered the floor; lingerie was draped from the wall brackets; and bodies in various degrees of nudity were scattered wherever they had fallen. A white-faced nun herded her charges back into the elevator and reported the disaster to her mother superior. The mother superior forwarded the incredible account to her bishop, and for a moment it seemed that the scandal might erupt in glaring headlines in the press. At this juncture, the Federal Bureau of Narcotics stepped in. The bureau didn't want Charlie Lucky to know that it was aware he was in

Havana and had him under surveillance there. And so it pulled all the wires it knew how to pull, the news was suppressed—and Luciano remained for a time in ignorance of the watch that was being kept on his activities.

Those activities were pivotal. The entire hierarchy of the Combination was traveling to Havana for consultations with Luciano, who remained, despite his long years in prison, the acknowledged mastermind of the American underworld. The crime cabinet from Duke's was represented by its most powerful members, Joe Adonis, Albert Anastasia and Willie Moretti. The names of other consultants read like a blue book of the Mafia and the Combination: Frank Costello, Charlie Fischetti, Vito Genovese, Tony Accardo, Joe Profaci, Phil Kastel, Meyer Lansky, Vince Mangano, Little Augie Pisano, Mike Miranda, Joe Bonanno, Joe Magliocco, Tommy Lucchese, Carlos Marcello.

The major item on the agenda, as events were to make clear, was the question of what to do about Bugsy Siegel. This handsome, psychopathic hood, who once bragged to Del Webb that he personally had killed twelve men, had gone off the reservation. Not only were mob rulers unhappy about the millions of dollars they had plunged into the quicksand of the Flamingo, but Bugsy, desperate for the cash needed to keep his gaudy dream alive, was double-crossing the Chicago mob by keeping the rich rewards of its horserace wire service for himself. One of his assignments when he had been sent West as the representative of the Combination had been to capture the territory for the Chicago wire; and in his ruthless way, Bugsy had accomplished his purpose. Then, his wits addled by his obsession with the Flamingo, he had hijacked the proceeds, as it were, to help finance his incredibly costly venture in the Nevada desert. He had committed the unforgivable offense.

The decision reached under Luciano's leadership was made explosively clear on the night of June 20, 1947. Bugsy had opened the Flamingo again, and for the first time its casino was showing a healthy profit. It appeared that Bugsy had turned dreamland corner and was making it back into the world of solid, profitable reality. His brazen defiance of his underworld partners apparently had been shoved into the back of his mind; he may even have believed he had gotten away with it. The only apparent shadow on his life at the moment was the rupture of his relationship with Virginia Hill. The tempestuous pair had quarreled again violently, and Virginia had packed up her trunkloads of finery and taken off for Paris.

Bugsy, in her absence, was staying in the pink Moorish mansion in Beverly Hills that he had maintained for her. On the night of June 20, he had dined out with Allen Smiley, one of his closest pals. They returned home, and Bugsy settled himself with the *Los Angeles Times* on a chintz-covered loveseat in front of a picture window. Smiley was sitting on the other end of the couch when, as he later said, "all of a sudden there was a hell of a racket, shots and everything, and glass breaking."

Smiley dove for the floor; and when he looked up, he saw that Bugsy Siegel was decidedly dead. A sharpshooter outside the window had opened up on the one-time partner of the Bug and Meyer mob with a full clip of steel-jacketed slugs, fired from a carbine. Bugsy's handsome face had been literally torn apart by slugs that had smashed his nose, tore out his eyes, ripped his cheeks apart, and shattered vertebrae at the back of his neck.

He had hardly hit the floor dead before, out in Las Vegas, a delegation of strangers walked into the Flamingo and took charge of operations. The new proprietors were Little Moey Sedway, Morris Rosen and Gus Greenbaum, who was to assume actual management of the hotel for the next seven years. They were accompanied by a representative of the Eastern mob—Joseph ("Doc") Stracher, a Newark gangster with a long record who had been associated with such eminents of the Duke's coterie as Meyer Lanksy, Joe Adonis, Longie Zwillman, and Willie Moretti. Stracher, in close association with Meyer Lansky, was to become one of the major powers behind some of the fanciest hotels and gambling casinos along The Strip.

The Bugsy Siegel execution, carried out with the ruthless efficiency that was a Luciano trademark, was a historic first. It was the first time in nearly fifteen years that the reigning powers of the national commission had met and condemned one of their fellow moguls to death. In its way, it was a departure point, the beginning of new waves of violence that have wracked the underworld ever since.

Lucky Luciano now became an acute political embarrassment. His presence in Havana and the assassination of Siegel on his orders were such sensational events that they could not be forever ignored. Items began to creep into the American press and news magazines, and the late columnist Robert Ruark, in a series of scathing columns, focused on Luciano's dark presence just off American shores and asked the indignant question: How come? He got no satisfactory answers; and when he began to probe into Governor Dewey's role in releasing Luciano, some of his columns were killed. So much heat had been generated, however, that even the dictatorial regime of Fulgencio Batista, with whom Meyer Lansky was especially friendly, felt compelled to wash its hands of the troublesome Charlie Lucky and deport him back to Italy.

If nothing else, the Havana sojourn and penthouse conferences with top powers of the national crime syndicate had demonstrated that, in freeing Luciano, Governor Dewey had released from the prison bottle an evil genie whose potential for harm was infinite. The Federal Bureau of Narcotics, monitoring Luciano's activities in Italy and his contacts in the United States, became convinced that he was the brains, the organizing genius, behind the suddenly mushrooming international narcotics traffic. "We *know* this; we know it absolutely, beyond question," one of the highest ranking executives of the bureau declared upon one occasion.

There was no question that narcotics addiction was spreading across the nation in an unprecedented wave. In the early 1950s pushers began invading the playgrounds of New York's grammar schools and hooking youngsters not yet in their teens, the first shocking development in what was to become a massive national addiction problem. The old East Side 107th Street mob, composed of many former Luciano subordinates, was one of the major importers and suppliers of heroin, and the connection that the narcotics bureau made between Luciano and the suddenly increased Mafia narcotics traffic made the mystery of his prison release a more sensitive issue than ever.

Governor Dewey issued explanations that did not fully explain. He argued that Luciano's supposed wartime patriotism had been one reason for his release, but not the "compelling" one. It had been customary, he said, to free felons who could be deported, and he cited records to show that his three predecessors had commuted the sentences of fifty-seven such aliens, including eighteen murderers. A point that the governor ignored was that there was only one Luciano, only one man as he himself had said in his earlier career who rated the designation as "the overlord" of vice and crime. This ancient history was seemingly forgotten now. Taking their cue from the governor, Republican press agents tried to convince the public that Dewey had acted wisely and thriftily by shipping Luciano back to Italy, thus sparing the state the cost of housing, feeding and guarding him.

None of this propaganda was convincing enough to remove from itself the obvious stigma of propaganda. More was needed; and so, in the closing days of his administration, Dewey had one of his aides conduct an exhaustive investigation into the whole Luciano affair. Testimony was taken for weeks. The object was transparently twofold: first, to show that Luciano had performed such invaluable wartime services that his release from prison was an appropriate reward; second, to stigmatize the narcotics bureau's Luciano-narcotics equation as a myth propagated by the bureau for its own purposes. One witness who was questioned in the secret inquiry said later: "I have testified in court in many cases. I have been cross-examined by some of the best lawyers in the business, but I want to tell you that I have never been treated as roughly as I was in these hearings. It was as if I were a murderer on the stand." In the end this effort of self-justification failed in its double purpose, and the record of the private hearings never was publicly disclosed. Indeed, after Governor Dewey left Albany, taking with him several truckloads of records, no trace of the hearing transcript could be found. Subordinates of the incoming Democratic governor, Averell Harriman, were informed of the mystery of the investigation that was but wasn't, and their researches in the remaining files drew a blank.

Unaffected by all of this, Lucky Luciano continued to function on a broad international scale. Though it was never publicized, Charlie Lucky apparently slipped back into the United States to preside at what the Federal Bureau of Narcotics considered one of the most important meetings of Mafia chieftains ever held. The account comes from one of the former high executives of the bureau, based upon what is considered reliable information from inside the mob.

The grand council conclave, according to this account, was held in the Plantation Yacht Harbor, not far from Miami, in 1952. Thirteen of the men who attended were later identified for the bureau. They included Mafia powers who were strategically placed in regard to the narcotics traffic. Chief among them was Vito Genovese, soon to become the American "boss of bosses" and a man who was ultimately to be convicted and sent to prison in one of the largest narcotics cases the federal bureau ever broke. Also prominent at the conference were Vincent Mangano, the veteran Brooklyn Mafioso and waterfront power, and Vinnie Rao, a veteran mobster who was the consigliere of the Lucchese family.

Italian police supposedly had been keeping a close watch on Lucky Luciano's movements, but the Italian police were at times notoriously less than perfect. According to informants whom the narcotics bureau believed to be reliable, Luciano succeeded in giving his Italian watchdogs the slip and smuggled himself back into this country for brief consultation with major Mafiosi. The purpose that justified the risk, according to the bureau's information, was the perfection of arrangements for an increased narcotics traffic. New sources for heroin and more perfect arrangements for smuggling the drug into American ports were principal items on the agenda. The whole chain of heroin processing, smuggling and distribution was reportedly overhauled during these discussions in Plantation Yacht Harbor.

It may have been pure coincidence, though the narcotics bureau remained skeptical, but it was approximately at this very point in time that narcotics addiction in cities across the land took off in a new spiral, spreading until it became one of the major national problems of today.

10.

Vito Genovese

Vito Genovese rose from pimp to multimillionaire to companion of Il Duce and boss of bosses. The matador of the bedroom, he liked to beat up his women, sometimes in front of a party full of guests—just one indication of the ingrained violence in his treacherous nature. He was in essence a cheap, vicious and violent thug, and he scrapped the Luciano-Costello blueprint for a rule of order, reinstituting the ancient system of unrestrained murder carried out at the whim of any boss powerful enough and wily enough to accomplish it.

This was the real Vito Genovese; but, at least in the closing years of his career, there was another and, to many, a more believable Genovese. This was the aging, gray-haired man, his eyes often hidden behind dark glasses, who lived alone in a small white cottage in Atlantic Highlands, N.J.; cooked his own Italian dishes, raked the leaves in his yard, and patted neighborhood children on the head in the best godfatherly tradition. So convincing was the act that police and neighbors in that bayshore New Jersey area found it simply impossible to believe that this quiet, unassuming man was the authentic terror of American gangdom. But the record is documented beyond

163

cavil, and it is written in blood—the blood of brother mobsters and the blood of the innocent.

Vito Genovese was born in Rosiglino, near Naples, on November 27, 1897. His father, Phillipo Genovese, a hard-working small contractor in Queens, brought the boy to this country when he was fifteen. Even at that early age, Vito had all the instincts of a bum. Hard work and calloused hands were not for him; his goal was the fast and easy fortune, acquired any way it could be had. His father, in disgust, sent him to live with relatives in Mulberry Street in the heart of Little Italy section of New York's Lower East Side. Here his boyhood pals were the hoodlums who rose step-by-step with him to become major Mafiosi—Mike Miranda, Anthony ("Tony Bender") Strollo and Lucky Luciano.

Vito began making the police blotter when he was nineteen. He was arrested for carrying a gun and was sent to jail for sixty days. After that the charges came tripping on each other's heels, but nothing much ever happened to any of them. Almost every time the young Vito Genovese and the law crossed paths, Vito was carrying a gun. He was charged variously with felonious assault, vehicular homicide, burglary, homicide, counterfeiting. But he was now a member of the Mafia; when charges were filed against him, witnesses were suddenly afflicted with amnesia—and Vito Genovese, time and again, strode out of court, snapping his fingers at the law.

In the gang wars of the early 1930s Genovese became underboss of what had been the Masseria family, second in rank only to Lucky Luciano. Luciano entrusted him with the care of one of his East Side brothels, just three blocks from New York police headquarters; and here Genovese kept a stable of twelve beautiful girls whose major task in life was to romp between the sheets with a select clientele of important politicians and high police brass. Genovese himself "went upstairs" to sample the wares almost as frequently as the customers.

Lust and violence were twin strands of his character, and the two were never better illustrated than in the way he accomplished his second wedding. His first wife, whom he had married in 1926, died of tuberculosis in 1931; and in less than a year Genovese's roving eye was enchanted by the brunette beauty of his fourth cousin, Anna Petillo, 22, twelve years younger than Vito. There was only one obstacle to the happy consummation of Vito's desires; Anna already had a husband.

This unfortunate individual was Gerardo Vernotico, 25, a carpenter; and what happened to him was what happened to almost anybody who possessed something that Vito Genovese wanted. Vernotico was found strangled on the roof of a six-story building at 124 Thompson Street in the Greenwich Village section of New York, his arms and legs bound, a sash-cord serving as a garrotte around his neck. Nearby, similarly strangled, lay a second victim, Antonio Lonzo. Police theorized that he had been where he shouldn't have been and had seen more than he should have seen—and that death had been the reward for this lack of circumspection.

Just twelve days after this bloody deed, Genovese got what he wanted: he married the bereaved brunette widow in a ceremony in the Municipal Building with Anthony Strollo and his fiancée as witnesses.

By 1934 Vito Genovese had graduated from his role as pimp and procurer to status as boss of the Italian lottery. He quickly discovered that gambling was a more rewarding racket than prostitution, for the incredible take from the daily numbers play soon had him rolling in millions of dollars. Even so, his greed as insatiable as his lust, he could not resist the opportunity to fleece a sucker.

A small-time Brooklyn hoodlum, Ferdinand ("The Shadow") Boccia, steered the wealthy victim to a crooked card game run by Genovese and his associates. When the game was over, Boccia's pigeon had contributed $116,000 to the growing Genovese fortune. Boccia, as the steerer, naturally expected his just reward, and he informed Genovese that he valued his services at $35,000. Foolish crook, he should have known that Genovese never parted with such a sum once it was in his grasping hands. Vito told Boccia to just be patient; he needed the money for a big deal he was swinging.

Patience was not Boccia's long suit. He became irritated at the stall and decided in an irrational moment to take at gunpoint some of the green that he felt should rightfully be his. With a fellow hood, he strode into a garage used by Tony Strollo as a liquor drop, held up Strollo at gunpoint, and heisted $5,800. Few men have signed their own death warrants so cheaply.

Genovese's executioners caught up with Boccia while he was sitting at another card game in the restaurant run by his uncle in the Williamsburg section of Brooklyn— and that was the end of The Shadow. Ernest ("The Hawk") Rupolo began to talk about his inside knowledge of the murder plot; the law began to hone in on Genovese; and Don Vitone, as he was called respectfully in the Mafia, decided it would be healthier for him in Italy.

Genovese, when he fled abroad, had no reason to fear the anti-Mafia wrath of Il Duce. He and Anna in the previous year, 1933, had made a pilgrimage back to the homeland and had been well received. On that occasion, Genovese had carried a letter of introduction to Achille Pisani, secretary of the Fascist Party; and he had found Pisani and the Fascist hierarchy as easy to know as the politicians of New York. He had simply unfolded his ample bankroll and had wined, dined, and wenched the officials he had wanted to cultivate. This successful wooing of the powerful seemed to demonstrate, as Bill O'Dwyer was later to tell the Kefauver committee, that it doesn't matter who a man is, businessman, or racketeer—his pocketbook is always attractive.

Thus, when the Boccia unpleasantness made it advisable for Don Vitone to make a second trip to Italy, it was like returning to visit old friends. Just to make certain of his welcome, according to his wife, Anna, he took along with him a little kitty—some $750,000 in cash. Anna was left behind to keep the lottery wheels spinning, and she did this most efficiently, operating from a plush apartment at 29 Washington Square West in Manhattan, just one floor above the quarters occupied by Eleanor Roosevelt, wife of the President of the United States.

During the eight years of Don Vitone's self-imposed exile in Italy, Anna (until war interfered) made frequent trips abroad to visit her husband, always insuring a warm welcome by bringing with her on each trip some $100,000 in cash. With his private exchequer thus replenished, Vito Genovese swaggered his way through the court circles of Il Duce. He became on the one hand the chief of Italy's Camorra, blood twin of the Mafia; and on the other, a benefactor of Fascism. He contributed $250,000 to the construction of the Nola municipal building; and Mussolini expressed his gratitude for such a sterling contribution to the cause by conferring upon Don Vitone the title of *commendatore,* the highest civilian award in Italy.

This paradoxical love affair between the powerful Mafioso and the dictator who had sworn death to the Mafia lasted right up to the moment of Italy's collapse in World War II. For Mussolini, the disaster spelled death; for the agile Don Vitone, it meant simply new opportunity. Like a big jungle cat, Don Vitone leaped from one side of the fence to the other; and when American forces came up the Italian boot, they found this patriotic American waiting to receive them with open arms.

In the tick of a watch, metaphorically speaking, Vito Genovese became the indispensable man to the American military. They rated him so highly that officer after officer signed testimonials to his value and his virtue. He was, one wrote, "absolutely honest" and "devoted to his adopted home, the U.S.A." A major for whom Genovese served as an interpreter deposed: "He would accept no pay; paid his own expenses; worked day and night and rendered most valuable assistance to the Allied Military Government." Another major, whom Genovese also served as an interpreter, signed a testimonial saying he regarded Genovese "as trustworthy, loyal and dependable" and "most helpful" to the cause of the United States.

These glowing tributes became an acute embarrassment to the military brass when it was discovered that the "absolutely honest" and "trustworthy" Don Vitone had been robbing the army blind while working "day and night" at his own expense, ostensibly to assist it. Orange C. Dickey, an agent for the Army's Criminal Intelligence Division, conducted an investigation of widespread black market activities in the Foggia-Naples area. Wheat, sugar, and olive oil were being stolen from army depots by the ton; army trucks were being used to spirit the cargoes right out of the depots; and then the emptied trucks would be taken to a truck-graveyard near Nola, where they would be burned. The password for this operation, Dickey discovered, was three words: "Genovese sent us."

After an investigation that lasted more than two months, Dickey felt that he had developed an ironclad case against Don Vitone and made the pinch. Almost the instant that he did, he found himself suddenly unpopular. The military brass had absolutely no enthusiasm for pressing charges against their invaluable interpreter and Man Friday. Dickey, however, as a matter of routine, had notified the FBI of his accomplishment, and the FBI turned up the fact that Don Vitone was wanted back in the States for that old Boccia murder. The army breathed a great, gusty sigh of relief, and Dickey was assigned to take his troublesome prisoner back to America.

Despite his demonstrated patriotism for his adopted land, Vito Genovese seemed most reluctant to return. Dickey later testified before the McClellan committee about some of the inducements that were dangled before his eyes:

"At various times, I was offered many things. At one point, I was offered a quarter of a million dollars to let this fellow out of jail. On one occasion, when I was offered another sum of money, I had with me an officer by the name of Lieutenant Dillon."

Dickey refused all such bribe offers and turned Genovese over to the Kings County District Attorney's office in Brooklyn. The event seemed to say that, except for his own honor and self-respect, Dickey should have closed his eyes and taken the money.

Rupolo was scheduled to testify against Genovese, but under New York law the testimony of an accomplice is not sufficient; there must be corroboration of his story by some independent, outside source. In the Boccia case, such a witness was available. He was Peter LaTempa, a cigar store salesman, who had not himself been involved in the plot, but had happened to be present when some of the details were discussed. LaTempa, in fear of his life, was placed for safekeeping in the Brooklyn city jail.

There on January 15, 1945, the fate that had overtaken Abe Reles overtook LaTempa. LaTempa suffered from gallstones and had obtained a prescription for some pain-killing tablets. On this January morning, he asked for some of his medicine. A glass of water, with the tablets presumably dissolved in it, was given him. LaTempa drank the potion—and, in minutes, he was dead. The city toxicologist later reported that he had been given a dosage potent enough "to kill eight horses." With the indispensable witness removed from the scene, the law was hamstrung; and on June 11, 1946 Vito Genovese walked out of prison a free man—and a new, disturbing, primal force in the American underworld.

This triumph over the law propelled Vito Genovese back onto the American underworld scene as a man who had demonstrated his power in the manner Mafiosi most respect. Honors were due him; and so, just thirteen days after his release from prison, the chieftains of the clans rallied to do him homage. The party was held in a small private banquet room in the Hotel Diplomat in midtown Manhattan; and, though the mobsters themselves weren't aware of it, the FBI had had an advance tip and had wired the premises for sound.

Genovese was welcomed back into the world of the American Mafia, as protocol prescribed, by the eldest Mafia chieftain present. This happened to be Santo Volpe, the Pittston, Pennsylvania, Mafioso who went by the so-briquet, King of the Night. Volpe embraced Genovese and led him to the leather-upholstered chair, the seat of honor, at the head of the long rectangular banquet table. One by one, major Mafioso came forward and paid their respects to the man who had hobnobbed with one of the world's most powerful dictators and had just added to his stature by doing a classic, Mafia-style jobbing of the American law.

Despite the conviviality, Vito Genovese was not happy. When he had left America, he had ranked right behind Lucky Luciano as a power in the underworld; when he returned, he found himself displaced by the new structure that had ruled so efficiently in his absence. Frank Costello was "The Boss" or "The Prime Minister," the secret power behind Tammany Hall. Joe Adonis ran the affairs of crime from Duke's, flanked by Albert Anastasia and the Morettis. There was no room for Vito Genovese, who felt he should have inherited the mantle of Luciano—and Vito decidedly didn't like the situation.

Joseph Valachi later testified for the McClellan committee about the extent of Don Vitone's unhappiness.

> Well, when he came back, he was mumbling and grumbling and he was giving hell to Tony Bender, as "You allow these people to sew up everything and tie up everything," but Tony told him, well, he told him to make the worst of things, so that is what I have been doing. Well, he said, "I didn't tell you to get chased out of Duke's. ". . . Yes, he felt that Moretti, Albert and Frank—and I don't remember whether Joe Adonis was included in this, but he felt that they had everything sewed up.

Genovese kept grousing. He had power, but the channels were blocked off that would have given that power full play. In 1949, the mob threw a big bash at the Copacabana, Frank Costello's favorite stamping ground; and when Vito Genovese appeared, he was treated with such marked and servile respect that New York detectives concluded he was, as of that moment, the single most powerful figure in the American underworld. It became the fashion to refer to him as "the kingmaker," a kind of Mafia elder statesman; and, though this designation was not completely accurate, it did reflect both the degree of his power and the anomaly of his position. He was such a menacing figure that the Costello-Adonis dynasty treated him warily and with respect, but as long as Joe Adonis commanded the troops from his power base in Duke's there was not too much Vito Genovese could do to right the wrong that he felt fate had done him.

He could only live and enjoy. . . .

The scale was royal, Bacchanalian. According to Anna Genovese, in testimony she gave in a separation suit in Freehold, N.J., in 1952, her husband lived in a fashion Louis XIV might have envied. He spent money as lavishly; he had as many women; and when she protested about the women, he simply belted her with his powerful fists, both in public and in private.

This carnival of high jinks and domestic fisticuffs began, Anna testified, right after Genovese thumbed his nose at the law on the Boccia murder charge. He moved his family from the Washington Square apartment to a mansion on the Skyline Drive at Atlantic Highlands, N.J., a place with a panoramic view over New York harbor with the spires of lower Manhattan in the background.

According to Anna, the mansion cost Genovese $75,000; and he spent another $100,000 on renovations and $250,000 for bric-a-brac and furnishings. There were two marble fireplaces and a few life-sized statues imported from Italy, a cream-lacquered grand piano, and two five-foot Oriental vases of the costly Imari pattern. Anna told the Monmouth County Court what life with Don Vitone was like in these words:

> We lived very high. We traveled to the best places with a personal maid and chauffeur. We were entertained by very big people . . . money was no object.
> Our living room was a forty feet long. The dining room was exactly the same size as the living room. Our bedroom was twenty-five feet long.

A marble staircase led from the living room to the dining room. A very beautiful nude marble statue was at the foot of the staircase. One wall in the living room took an artist six months to paint. He depicted the whole outside of the house—the grounds, the water, the yacht basin— everything.

The furniture in the bedroom was imported Chinese teakwood. The bed had a swan back made of lucite. All of our furniture was made to order.

We had twenty-four-carat gold and platinum dishes. Our silverware was the best money could buy.

We had parties every weekend. Twenty-five to thirty persons always showed up. Vito insisted that I buy the best champagne—sometimes we even hired entertainers from New York City. We never spent less than five hundred dollars on a party . . . Vito liked company.

The personal wardrobes of the lord and lady of the mansion comported with the grandeur of this life style. Anna was swathed in assorted furs—a $4,500 mink coat, a $1,500 Persian lamb coat, a $2,500 ermine coat, an $850 broadtail coat, and mink stoles costing $1,200 and $800. She had more evening gowns than housedresses. There were always, she said, "at least thirty gowns in the closet," and "I paid anywhere from $350 to $900 a gown." Her husband arrayed himself in equally expensive garb. "He never paid less than $250 for a suit," the estranged Anna told the court. "He pays $350 for coats, $35 for shirts and $60 for shoes."

Back in the late 1940s, those were mighty fancy prices and proof enough that the Genoveses had eliminated one of the most common causes of domestic friction, financial worries. But the house on the heights was not a happy one; there was discord. It stemmed from Vito's passion for bedroom frolics. According to Anna, he liked nothing better than to induce her best girl friends to adventure with him beneath the sheets, tributes to his virility that he liked to relive with Anna in exacting detail. Anna put up with such indignities until 1948 when affairs built to a crisis. Don Vitone became so enchanted with the performances of one of his mistresses that he began to talk of shedding Anna and marrying the girl.

Recalling the manner in which her own first husband had been shed, Anna became a worried woman. She tried to reason with Vito, she said. She argued that he had had other women before and that this marrying mood would pass, "but he wouldn't listen to anything. He would punch me and slap me and use terrible language. He would tell me he was going to find a way to get rid of me; that he would either put me in an insane asylum or have me killed."

At one party, she said, Genovese knocked out two of her front teeth. When one of the women guests tried to intervene, he slugged her, too. Frank Costello tried to mediate the unseemly discord on one occasion, Anna said, but even Costello, the master diplomat and politician of the mob, couldn't do anything with Don Vitone. No one could. Finally, Anna became convinced that her husband might really kill her; and so, in desperation, she filed suit for separation, asking $350 a week alimony. She did even more. She actually took the stand and testified against her husband, exposing him as a man who made *a million dollars a year* out of the Italian lottery—thus breaking the rule of *omertà* with a vengeance; an unprecedented act for a Mafia wife whose lips above all others must remain sealed. The women of the mob never talk, if they know what is good for them, an axiom that was perhaps best illustrated by the showboating but innocuous performance of hard-boiled Virginia Hill before the Kefauver committee.

The Kefauver probe, the sensation of its day, was only a partial success. It gave the average American his first real peek into the nether depths that had come to dominate so much of legitimate society, with the worst and most vicious bums in the nation acquiring a pervasive power. The influence of the pimps and loan sharks, the gamblers and narcotics peddlers and murderers had reached such proportions that one of the best New York detectives of his time had expressed the reality to me years earlier in this pithy sentence: "The underworld runs the world only the people don't know it."

The Kefauver exposure was costly to many of the mob figures who starred involuntarily in the television extravaganza that aroused the nation; but despite the public backlash, despite official pressure and threats of future prosecution, the law of *omertà* prevailed over the law of the land. Lips remained sealed, and the big breakthrough that would have revealed the vital secrets never came.

Typical of performances that sometimes used a lot of words to tell nothing was the act of tempestuous Virginia Hill, the Miss Syndicate of mobdom. Virginia swept into the hearing room in New York's Federal Courthouse on Foley Square wearing a wide-bimmed hat and a platinum mink stole that practically swept the floor. She opened with a volley of curses and closed the same way. These expressions of her inner sweetness were triggered by the annoying presence of photographers and reporters. She swore at the cameramen like a top sergeant as they kept popping their flashbulbs and instructed the committee: "Make them stop doing that. I'll throw something in a minute."

The committee was convinced that Virginia could expose the inner secrets of the Syndicate if she would, and they pressured her on her most vulnerable point, her extravagant scale of living that far exceeded anything that would have been possible according to her income tax returns. Miss Syndicate had once purchased a New York nightclub so that she could throw her own parties in her own spot; she had blown $11,251 in just five weeks in Sun Valley, Idaho; she was in the habit of tipping bartenders $4.50 for a fifty-cent drink; she tossed away $7,500 on a one-night, champagne-party binge in Hollywood. Yet she had never reported an income of more than $23,780, the high-water-mark return she had filed in 1946. How come?

Virginia explained that it all had been quite simple. Her

success formula contained two parts: first, men; second, horses. The men gave her money, and the horses won. She spoke gratefully of both. Of the horses: "I won it on the horses. I'm just lucky, I guess." Of the men: "Well, fellows would give me things. I would go out with them—like lots of girls did—and they would give me presents. . . . The fellows gave those parties for me. I would not spend my money for those parties. There were always plenty of fellows who wanted to give parties for me."

That was all there was to it, Virginia said, with her best actress's imitation of wide-eyed innocence. She hadn't the faintest idea about crime. She had always gone out of the room when the boys talked business; she had just closed her pretty ears. She confessed that she was plenty miffed at federal narcotics agents. Those suspicious gentlemen had annoyed her by following her all across the country on the theory that, on trips back and forth to Mexico, she might have been a narcotics courier. Ridiculous, Virginia snorted. She knew nothing about narcotics; she knew nothing about crime; she knew nothing about anything.

The strain of this long nonexplanation obviously frazzled the lady's nerves, for as she stormed out of the hearing room, she let off steam in characteristic fashion. Reporters and photographers streamed after her, hoping for a final moment of drama, and they weren't completely disappointed. At the elevator bank, Miss Syndicate whirled and planted a gloved right fist squarely on the jaw of slim Marjorie Farnsworth, a reporter for the *New York Journal-American*. Out on the street, heading for a cab, the mob's glamour girl treated reporters to a sample of her invective. After a string of expressive if not very original epithets, she finished off the photographers with an unforgettable exit line: "You goddam bastards! I hope an atom bomb falls on all of you!"

It was quite a performance, even for Virginia Hill. Yet it was mild compared to an incident that took place in the questioning of Miss Syndicate in private session. Senator

Tobey had become curious. He wondered how one girl, even one so bounteously packaged as Virginia, had come to know *every* mob emperor across the land.

"Young lady," the senator asked, "what makes you the favorite of the underworld?"

"Senator," Virginia replied, not batting an eyelash, "I'm the best goddamned cocksucker in the world!"

It was great fun and games, but it was also serious business. Internal Revenue hit Virginia with an $80,000 tax claim, and she decamped to Europe, there to spend the rest of her life out of the reach of Uncle Sam. Frank Costello, whose fingers twitched nervously before the television cameras and whose voice rasped as he told the senators precisely nothing, found himself enmeshed in so many legal difficulties that it was almost impossible for him to function as the boss of New York's criminal empire. Ultimately, he went to prison on a five-year, income-tax-evasion sentence. An equally important casualty, a by-product of the Kefauver threat, was the disruption of the crime cabinet that had sat for so long in Duke's.

For this, District Attorney Hogan's office in New York deserves the primary credit. In 1948 Hogan's aides began to probe a flagrant Park Avenue charity gambling party that had been run by some of Joe Adonis's New Jersey henchmen. The investigation led to the discovery of Joe A.'s favorite cash-and-carry messenger, multiple-chinned Max Stark. Stark, Hogan discovered, made daily trips from New Jersey to the Canal Street branch of the Merchants Bank of New York. Sometimes he lugged in suitcases containing as much as $90,000; it was a poor day, indeed, when he appeared with a mere $50,000.

These were sweat-stained, crumpled bills that had been fleeced from suckers in the previous night's agony in Joe Adonis's Bergen County gambling traps. The stained money had to be counted, bill by bill, and crisp, new, unsullied currency (payoffs, when there are such, are always made in such crackling new bills, one of the gimmicks of the trade) had to be counted out and given to Stark, a transaction that tied up the services of a bookkeeper and teller all day long. The normal activity of the bank was sometimes disrupted in this effort to process Max Stark's daily mountain of cash, but the Merchants Bank had to be nice to Stark. After all, he owned ten per cent of its stock.

Hogan's inquiry—conducted by his chief assistant, Vincent A. G. O'Connor and Assistant DA Andrew Seidler—documented from bank records that Joe A.'s Jersey gambling halls were doing a $13.5 million annual business. Actually, since this figure was based on just the one Max Stark bank account in New York and since Stark had other accounts beyond the reach of New York law, Hogan's aides felt confident they had uncovered an underworld gold mine with a cash flow of some $15 million to $20 million annually, and they called Bergen County "the richest preserve of the Syndicate east of the Mississippi River."

Those disclosures were picked up by Kefauver and given a headline whirl. Kefauver did little else with them, but he did threaten to hold full-scale hearings on the New Jersey rackets unless the state acted. So pressured, the state sent rackets-buster Nelson Stamler into Bergen County to clean up. Hogan's evidence was made available to Stamler; and, almost before the mob knew what had happened, Joe Adonis and Solly Moretti, together with some of their lesser henchmen, were packed away in state prison in Trenton. The underworld legions that had operated for so long out of Duke's had lost their commander; the crime cabinet was disrupted; and Duke's, its purpose gone, soon closed its doors.

No developments could have pleased Vito Genovese more. The Costello-Adonis coalition which had forced him into the background had become so prominent it had been thoroughly zapped in the Kefauver exposé. All the time, Vito Genovese (worth some $30 million, federal agents calculated) had been so far behind the front lines of action that he remained inconspicuous and was passed over with hardly a glance. With the kings of the old order dethroned, most of them, the crown was waiting for a new ruler strong enough and ruthless enough to seize it.

Don Vitone had already been laying the groundwork. A full two years before Kefauver, he had started a whispering campaign against the most vulnerable member of the Costello-Adonis axis—wisecracking Willie Moretti. The tactic he used was a carbon-copy of the elaborate apologia he and Luciano had invented decades earlier to justify the unauthorized slaying of Maranzano: poor Willie had become a menace to the interests of all and so would have to go.

The rumor Genovese spread so industriously among his followers was that Willie, like Al Capone, had contracted syphilis. This, Genovese claimed, had resulted in a weakening of the brain cells; thus Willie would babble dangerously about the most precious secrets. This propaganda in Vito Genovese's hand was a double-edged weapon; it was used to tarnish the reputation of Frank Costello for allegedly protecting Willie at the risk of all. Costello, so the story went, had sent Willie out to California to hole up for a time until his babbling tongue quieted down, but was this really the proper way for a boss to act? Didn't his followers deserve more permanent protection?

One prop in this subtle Genovese campaign to undermine the ruling dynasty rested upon Willie's supposedly damaging admissions before the Kefauver group when he was questioned on December 13, 1950. The canard was spread so industriously that many so-called experts bought it completely, and it still crops up at times in articles and books about the Mafia. But anyone who takes the trouble to read the Kefauver transcript is forced to conclude that Willie Moretti exhibited no signs of softening of the brain. Quite the contrary. The following exchange between Willie and Rudolph Halley, the committee counsel, was typical. Halley had been questioning Willie about his associations with Luciano and Capone. Weren't they racketeers? he asked. Then it went like this:

MORETTI: Well, I don't know if you would call it rackets.

HALLEY: How would you put it?

MORETTI: Jeez, everything is a racket today. (Laughter in the courtroom.)

HALLEY: Well, what do you mean by that?

MORETTI: Everybody has a racket of their own.

HALLEY: Are these [the] people you are thinking of when you are talking about the mob?

MORETTI: Well, the newspapers call them the mob. I don't know whether they are right or wrong. If they would be right, everybody would be in jail; is that right?

HALLEY: Is that what you mean when you say the mob, these fellows that you meet at the racetrack and the gambling places?

MORETTI: People are mobs that makes six percent more on the dollar than anybody else.

Titters swept the hearing room. Halley, it was obvious, was hitting only foul balls and getting nowhere. John Selser, an attorney who had represented the Morettis and probably knew Willie as well as anyone, told a New Jersey Legislative Committee much later that he, too, had been willing to accept the story that Moretti's mind had been affected until he read the Kefauver testimony. Then he concluded, he said, that Willie was "mentally capable—more so than the examiners."

Since mobsters are not the most avid readers of official transcripts, the actual record of the Kefauver hearings lost out in credibility to Genovese's version of it. It became an accepted article of faith that Willie had become dangerous to everyone and that, if he were to be given a violent shove into the world beyond, it would be, as Joe Valachi put it, "a deed of mercy" that even Willie, in his right mind, would have appreciated.

Willie, of course, had not been consulted and given a chance to cast his vote on this proposition when he drove to Cliffside Park, N.J., on the morning of October 4, 1951. Duke's having closed, he and Albert Anastasia had fallen into the habit of meeting at another rendezvous in the same block, Joe's Elbow Room, at 793 Palisades Avenue. Willie's chauffeur let him out in front of the restaurant, then parked the new, cream-colored Packard convertible down the street.

As Willie started toward the door of the restaurant, a man who had come out to the sidewalk, apparently looking for him, shook hands effusively and followed Willie to a table where three other men were waiting. They all shook hands and began to talk in Italian. The conversational flow was interrupted when one of the men asked the waitress, Mrs. Dorothy Novack, to bring them menus. Mrs. Novack obliged and then went through a swinging door to the kitchen to get silverware. She was hardly out of sight when the most infernal racket broke out in the dining room behind her.

When the startled waitress and the kitchen help peered fearfully through the swinging door, the restaurant was deserted except for Willie Moretti. The four "friends" who had welcomed him so effusively had disappeared and had left behind them Willie's recumbent form.

The fifty-seven-year-old wisecracker and fixer of the mob lay on his back, his feet stretched toward the door, legs apart, the toes of his polished shoes pointed up. His red tie had been half-twisted around his neck as if somebody had tried to throttle him. One hand was clutched at his chest like that of a man trying to rid himself of some smothering pressure; his other arm was outstretched, flung wide across the floor. Two pools of blood were spreading around his shattered head. And almost directly above him was a gaudy sign reading: "Chicken in the Rough— $1.50."

Vito Genovese's execution squad had fired the first of the guns of October. Their reverberations had wiped out the rule of order, and soon murder would pile upon murder.

11.

Costello, Anastasia, and Apalachin

Frank Costello wormed his way out of federal prison in March, 1957, after serving only eleven months of his five-year-income-tax evasion sentence. His legal brain trust sprang him on a technicality, and The Boss returned to his former Manhattan haunts.

The law was still making bee-buzzing noises about deporting him on the ground he had falsified his criminal record when he obtained his naturalization papers, but The Boss treated this threat with the contempt that the futile future would show it deserved. He evidently considered himself practically in the clear and ready to resume his underworld throne. Disillusionment came swiftly.

According to what is considered solid underworld information, the boys threw a party for The Boss in one of the city's fancier bistros. All of the ranking Mafiosi of the city showed up to do him honor; but, if Costello had envisioned the affair as a second coronation party, he was soon undeceived. His fellow chieftains made it clear to him that they weren't welcoming him back to power; they had simply turned out to pay their respects to him for past services—and to bid him a polite farewell.

The warning was implicit: yield to the dictates of the new order—or else. The evidence would seem to indicate that Costello was not willing to surrender power so meekly.

On the night of May 2, 1957, Costello and his wife went out on the town. They had dinner with some friends, then went nightclubbing. About eleven P.M. Costello recalled that he had to get back to his apartment to receive an expected telephone call from one of his lawyers, Edward Bennett Williams, of Washington, D.C. With a partying companion, Philip Kennedy, he hailed a cab and was driven to the Majestic Apartments at 115 Central Park West at the corner of 71st Street. As the cab pulled up in front of the door, a large black Cadillac stopped behind it, and a fat, flabby-looking man in a dark suit, with a hat pulled down over his forehead, got out and shuffled to the main entrance of the apartment building.

Costello left his cab and hurried to the door that a doorman held open for him. He entered a foyer that was separated from the lobby of the apartment house by a glass partition. Crossing the foyer in rapid strides, Costello passed the pudgy man in the dark coat and hat without giving him a glance. As he did, the pudgy one moved. His hand came out of his coat pocket. It held a gun.

"This is for you, Frank," he cried.

With the words, he fired a shot pointblank at Costello's head.

The result would seem to say that, if one is going to kill, one shouldn't announce the intention first. The words, "This is for you, Frank," alerted Costello just enough to save his life. The Boss started to turn his head as he heard the voice behind him, and this slight movement made all the difference between life and death. A .38 caliber slug slashed along the right side of his head, ripping his scalp just behind the ear. The fat gunman, evidently thinking he had accomplished his mission, whirled around the instant he had fired the shot, waddled out to the waiting Cadillac and sped away into the night.

Costello was taken to a hospital to have his dented skull

patched up, and while this was being done, New York detectives thoughtfully examined the contents of his jacket pocket. They found some eight hundred dollars in cash and a cryptic note showing that Costello was still being bankrolled by large gambling revenues. "Gross Casino Win as of 4-26-57—$651,284," the note read. The total was broken down this way: "Casino win less markers (that is I.O.U.'s)—$434,695. Slot wins—$62,844. Markers—$153,745."

Great reams of bilge have been written about the glamour of Las Vegas's night spots, and Nevada's efforts to make certain that the city's gambling casinos are run only by the most estimable gentlemen and in the most honest fashion. The truth is that Las Vegas, ever since the days of Bugsy Siegel, has provided a legitimate front for many of the most ruthless, bloodthirsty hoods in America; and the note found in Frank Costello's pocket was just one proof of this.

The Nevada Gaming Control Board subsequently showed that the figures on Costello's note matched item for item the officially reported gambling revenue for the first twenty-four days' operation of the new plush Tropicana Hotel. Dandy Phil Kastel, the lifelong gambling partner of Costello, had been one of the original backers of the Tropicana; and the note in Costello's pocket, though Costello blandly protested he had no idea what the thing meant or how it got there, was evidence that the gang boss had a major financial stake in the welfare of the new casino.

The shooting of Frank Costello, though it failed of its major purpose, was a sensational headline event. Here was the man who had been one of the authentic powers of the Mafia, one of the brains of the Syndicate, for the past quarter century. The mere fact that some hood would be brash enough to attempt his assassination was in itself dramatic evidence of a major upheaval in the New York underworld.

The powers behind this bloody turmoil left no doubt

about their intent. I was the medium they chose for a public announcement of their purpose. Why this should have
been so, I have no idea. In 1953, as a crime expert for the
New York *World-Telegram and Sun,* I had written a series
of articles on the Bergen County rackets and the suzerainty of Joe Adonis. Perhaps this was remembered; perhaps
someone reasoned that my crime articles would be read by
those for whom the message was intended. In any event,
only two hours after the firing of the bullet that creased
Costello's skull, a tough-talking caller tried to reach me by
telephone at the office, and not getting me at that hour,
left a message. Its burden: the Costello shooting was only
a sample of what was to come. Its justification: Costello
had been shot because the old regime had been too ruthless in dealing with its followers.

"They stepped on some good guys' toes," the caller
said. "All I can say is that, if Albert or Freddie steps in,
they'll get it too."

The reference to "Freddie" puzzled authorities, but no
one had any doubt who was meant by "Albert." That
could be only Albert Anastasia.

Frank Costello, wearing the scar of his close brush with
death, was a reasonable man and heeded the warning; Albert Anastasia had never been noted for the quality sometimes called sweet reasonableness.

Costello retired into the shadows, becoming lovable
"Uncle Frank," a man of past stature and diminished
power. He took out a health insurance policy by adhering
rigidly to the code of *omertà.* Authorities had identified
the overconfident gunman who had thought one shot was
sufficient as Vincent ("The Chin") Gigante, a hulking
Greenwich Village character, sometime chauffeur and full-
time hanger-on of Anthony ("Tony Bender") Strollo, the
longtime lieutenant and underboss of Vito Genovese. Gigante was on the lam for several weeks during which, according to much physical evidence, he must have gone on
a drastic reducing diet in the hope of eliminating his fat
man's waddle and confusing eyewitnesses. Eventually he

returned, went on trial—and was acquitted. The acquittal resulted primarily from "Uncle Frank's" amazing inability to recall a single detail about the man who had tried to blow his brains out at such close range.

Such discretion was foreign to the nature of Albert Anastasia, the headstrong, vicious maverick who ordered murder at the blink of an eyelash. Joseph Valachi described him as "the mad hatter" because he "killed right and left for nothing." Valachi illustrated his point by citing the Arnold Schuster case. Schuster, a young former Coast Guardsman and a crime buff, had happened to recognize a mousy little man who was changing a car battery on a Brooklyn street as Willie ("The Actor") Sutton, the most notorious bank robber of his day. Schuster tipped police; Sutton was arrested; and Schuster became the hero of the moment. According to Valachi, Anastasia watched Schuster on television, taking his kudos, and the old Murder Inc. boss sprang up in a towering rage, screaming, "I can't stand squealers."

Now it must be emphasized that there was no connection between Sutton and Anastastia. Willie the Actor was a loner, having no relationship to the Mafia; but the former Lord High Executioner of Murder Inc. decreed the death of the man who had turned Willie in. The mission was performed by one of Anastasia's gunmen, known as "Chappie;" and when the law began later to pick up the trail, "Chappie" simply vanished from the face of the earth—a typical Mafia tactic to break the chain of evidence that might lead to the top by eliminating the "button man" who has simply followed orders and, by following them, has become a potential danger because he knows too much.

Such, then, was Albert Anastasia. Frank Costello might step aside more or less graciously, recognizing the underworld power that was arrayed against him, but not Big Al. He wasn't going to be shoved by anybody, and he tangled head-on in his willful, violent fashion with the most powerful figures in the crime syndicate.

His first offense, according to later underworld information, was to "open the books" for membership in his Mafia family. By Luciano's decree, new members had not been inducted into the brotherhood since the mid-1930s; and a whole new generation of ambitious and avaricious young hoods, who had faithfully carried out such chores as murder, were clamoring for their reward as full-scale "button men" in one of the Mafia families. Anastasia, it was reported, began to sell such memberships in his family for $40,000 apiece.

He coupled this offense by clashing with Meyer Lanksy and Santo Trafficante Jr. Lansky, as the financial brain for mobs across the country, had established a gambling preserve in Cuba that was returning almost as many millions as Las Vegas. Anastasia tried to bulldoze his way into the picture, insisting that he be given control of one of the largest casinos in Batista-land. Lansky and Trafficante were not the kind of men to tolerate such a holdup.

Affairs had reached this dangerous impasse when, on the morning of October 25, 1957, it became obvious that the telephone caller who had tried to contact me after the Costello shooting had been no crackpot. It was around 10:15 A.M. on this quiet October Friday that Big Al walked into the barbershop of the Park-Sheraton Hotel at Seventh Avenue and 55th Street. He seated himself in chair No. 4 and told the barber, Joseph Bocchino, that he wanted "the works." He wasn't long in getting them.

Bocchino had hardly covered the Lord High Executioner's face with lather when two men, one stout and sallow, the other thin and dark, strode in from the lobby, scarves wrapped around the lower portion of their faces. They walked right up behind chair No. 4 and drew two guns, one a .38, the other a .32. At pointblank range, they opened fire on the back of Albert Anastasia's unsuspecting head.

The first shots struck with such impact that Anastasia was literally blown out of the chair. His legs kicked out in front of him and broke off the footrest. Propelled erect by the bullets, he slammed into the counter laden with shaving and hair lotions, spun as another shot hit him and crashed face down on the barbershop floor. His killers stood over him pumping bullets into his back; then, their morning's work finished, they strode swiftly out and made for the nearest subway.

"The old order changeth," one of District Attorney Hogan's assistants commented succinctly.

He had hardly spoken when, only two hours after Anastasia's rubout, I received another telephone call that emphasized the theme of change. The message was tough, fast and to the point.

"You remember I called you last spring right after Costello was shot, and you printed a warning we issued to Anastasia not to butt in?" the caller asked.

"Yes," I said.

"Well, we're giving another warning now. This time we're telling Frankie—and I don't mean Costello—not to interfere. And we're not fooling."

"Who do you mean by Frankie?" I asked.

"Frankie C., but it's not Costello," the caller said. And before I could ask another question, he slammed down the phone.

The riddle of this second warning revolved about the question Who was Frankie C.? A couple of possibilities suggested themselves. Frank Carbo had long been known as the underworld's commissioner of boxing, the rigger of crooked prizefights. It could be he. Or it could be—and the underworld grapevine later insisted it was intended to be—Frank Casino, a Long Island gambling power with close ties to Costello and the old top-line leadership.

Just one thing was clear at the moment: new forces were taking over in the New York underworld, and as the caller had told me, they were "not fooling."

In retrospect, it can be seen that the slaying of Albert Anastasia was an event of such pivotal importance that its repercussions, continuing to the present day, have changed the face and life-style of the New York Mafia. Its significance was fourfold:

* It proclaimed as had the earlier shooting of Costello

the end of the rule of order and the licensing of unauthorized murder as an instrument of change.

* It catapulted into the big-time a hitherto little-
known, obscure lieutenant of Big Al's—Carlo Gambino,
now generally considered the most powerful Mafioso in
New York if not in the nation.

* It triggered one of the most ferocious gangland feuds
of modern times, the Gallo-Profaci war of the 1960s, a
conflict whose last bloody spasm was the slaying of Crazy
Joe Gallo in April, 1972.

* And it led directly to the Apalachin conference and
the exposure of the inter-state, cross-continental ties of the
Mafia and its allies—one of the worst disasters from a
headline, public-relations standpoint that organized crime
has ever suffered.

The catalyst of such upheavals was Vito Genovese.
When Don Vitone decided the world was too small to contain both Anastasia and himself, he resorted to the kind of
Byzantine planning that is virtually standard operating
procedure in the Mafia. His script was a rerun of the one by
which, whole decades earlier, he and Lucky Luciano had
vaulted to power over the body of their beloved boss, Joe
("The Boss") Masseria.

To kill a Mafioso wielding the immense and dreaded
power of an Albert Anastasia, it is virtually essential to insure his betrayal by the man he trusts most, the one whose
job it is to guarantee his life. Carlo Gambino stood in this
close relationship to Big Al. He was Anastasia's underboss, the commander of the Lord High Executioner's
bodyguards. To execute the executioner with neatness and
dispatch, without a bloody free-for-all, it was necessary to
make certain that his protectors were somewhere else and
looking the other way at the vital moment. And so Vito
Genovese, according to underworld informants, held a private tête-à-tête with Gambino. He pointed out that Don
Carlo's reward for a bit of momentary blindness would be
truly magnificent. Vito would see to it that he became the
boss of Anastasia's leaderless family.

What man was ever offered a finer bargain? Naturally,

Lieutenant Joseph Petrosino, New York City Police Department. In the early 1900s, he launched the first determined campaign in this country against the Mafia with his special Italian squad.

NEW YORK DAILY NEWS

Cesare Mori was Prefect of Police in Mussolini's all-out war against the Mafia in Sicily. Mori fought the Mafia the way a general fights a war; under him, some 2,000 Mafiosi were tried, convicted, and sentenced.

UPI

Johnny Torrio (*center*) united the warring gangs of Chicago and brought Capone west. Torrio hated violence and never touched a gun, but paid well when killing was required.

Al Capone (*left*) and his lawyer, awaiting a verdict for evading payment of U.S. income tax—the usual charge brought against major Mafia bosses, since their security was so tight nothing else would stick.

The famous St. Valentine's Day Massacre: seven men were killed in this gang shooting on Chicago's North Side. By such methods, Capone persuaded rival mobs out of business and grabbed supreme power.
WIDE WORLD PHOTOS

Meyer Lansky, a one-time partner of Bugsy Siegel, is one of the survivors and the crime syndicate's financial wizard and prime international money mover.

NEW YORK DAILY NEWS

Joe Adonis. No racket that would turn a profit was too small for Joe Adonis. He was known as the gentleman of the Mob and one of the new order of businessmen–gangsters. UPI

This man was killed by four bullets in front of several passersby, in another gangland shooting. UPI

Abe Reles (*left*) and lawyer. By 1940, Abe Reles and his murder goons, under the orders of Albert Anastasia and Joe Adonis, had committed an estimated 1,000 killings from coast to coast.   NEW YORK DAILY NEWS

The body of Abe ("Kid Twist") Reles, being carried to the police van after he fell—or was pushed—from the special "squealers' suite" on the sixth floor of a Coney Island hotel.

WIDE WORLD PHOTOS

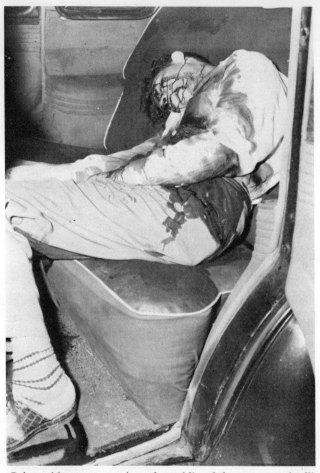

Grim evidence to convince the public of the power and will of the Mafia: an unidentified man riddled with bullets in New York City. UPI

Joe ("The Boss") Masseria had escaped assassination so many times that the legend grew that he could run faster and dodge quicker than any bullet could fly. Joe the Boss ruled a family that was to produce a succession of the most powerful Mafia chiefs in the nation: Lucky Luciano, Vito Genovese, Frank Costello, Joe Adonis, Albert Anastasia, Carlo Gambino.
NEW YORK DAILY NEWS

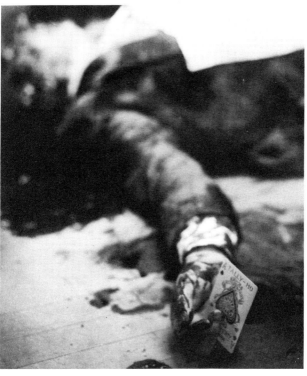

Joe the Boss was killed in a quiet restaurant; Luciano made the arrangements and stepped into the men's room.   UPI

Bugsy Siegel (*left*) shares a word with a good friend, George Raft, screen star. Bugsy, handsome, hot-tempered, and vicious, was lover boy of Hollywood. . . . Jean Harlow was said to have found him irresistible. His business was gambling and extortion in California, until he discovered greener pastures in Nevada.

UPI

Virginia Hill was the leggy, bosomy, chestnut-haired glamour girl of the Syndicate for which she functioned as cash-and-carry girl throughout the country. She was secretly married to Bugsy Siegel during the final days of the Flamingo. She is shown here after testifying at the Kefauver Crime hearings in 1951.   UPI

A coroner's assistant covers the bullet-riddled body of Bugsy Siegel, slain in 1947 by five of nine bullets fired through a window. **UPI**

Charles ("Lucky") Luciano, another of the businessmen–
gangsters, was architect of the international narcotics traffic and ran one of the largest prostitution rings in the New
York area. He became the top Mafioso after arranging
Masseria's murder.   UPI

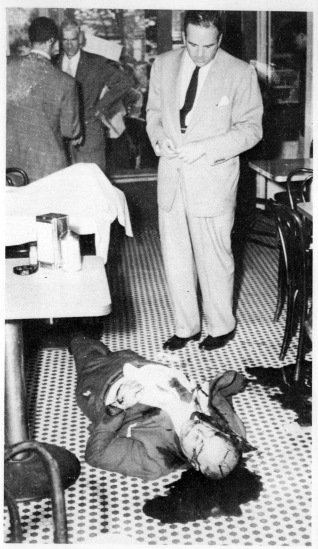

Racketeer Willie Moretti, wisecracker and fixer for the Mob, was killed at Joe's Restaurant in Cliffside Park, New Jersey. Genovese had spread a nasty rumor.... UPI

Frank Costello, blood on his suit and bandage on his head, went to the police when someone tried to kill him, but the bullet only creased his scalp. He had succeeded Luciano in 1936, and he became the secret power behind Tammany Hall.

UPI

Costello, "The Boss" or "The Prime Minister," being transferred from one jail to another, having served one term for
income-tax evasion. He was known to the police as the
gambling czar, but they couldn't catch him in action.   UPI

Albert Anastasia (*left*) and lawyer. Anastasia was known as "The Mad Hatter" because he killed indiscriminately. He was commander of the goon squads of Murder Inc.   UPI

Don Vitone Genovese decided the world was too small to contain both Anastasia and himself; the first shots struck with such impact that Anastasia was literally blown out of the barber's chair. WIDE WORLD PHOTOS

Don Carlo accepted such a generous offer—and so Anastasia's protection simply wasn't there on that fine October morning when he needed it most.

Once Gambino agreed to play the role that Charlie Lucky had enacted so many years earlier, it became necessary to get the right triggermen for the deed. Genovese's own murder crew, with Tony Bender Strollo as its field boss, was fully capable of doing the job, but the link to the man who was determined to become the new "boss of bosses" might have been too direct. A more devious technique was needed, and so Genovese and Gambino broached their proposition to Joseph Profaci, the veteran Brooklyn Mafioso who had always had at his command some of the deadliest torpedoes in the underworld.

Profaci, who had his own ties with Lansky and Trafficante and who had no love for "the mad hatter" of the underworld, agreed to undertake the contract and passed the chore along to the then-loyal Gallo wing of his family. The Gallos assigned two of their most reliable operatives to do the actual blasting: Joseph ("Joe Jelly") Gioelli, the top Gallo enforcer, and Ralph Mafrici, a thin sadistic man who liked to use the knife but was proficient with a revolver when occasion demanded.

The ramifications of the murder plot were filled in much later for District Attorney Hogan by an informer as knowledgeable on his own level as Valachi. He was Sidney Slater, a member of the Gallo mob. According to Slater, he was in a nightclub a couple of nights after the Anastasia killing when Joey Gallo came in with Mafrici, Joe Jelly and two other mob members. They had some drinks and the talk naturally got around to the violent fate that had overtaken Big Al in the Park-Sheraton barbershop. Joey Gallo laughed ghoulishly and said, "From now on, Sidney, you can just call the five of us the Barbershop Quintet."

That told Slater all he needed to know.

The elimination of Albert Anastasia created a void. The new rule of murder rampant created a problem. Both were compelling reasons for the historic rally of the Mafia at

Apalachin, N.Y., on November 14, 1957, only three weeks after Big Al's death.

According to Joseph Valachi, Vito Genovese called the Apalachin parley. He had planned originally to have "the meet" in Chicago, but Steve Maggadino, the powerful Mafia boss of the Buffalo-Toronto area, talked him out of it. Maggadino's logic appeared sound at the moment. According to informants of the Federal Bureau of Narcotics, Mafia rulers had met the previous year in the hilltop mansion of Joseph Barbara, and they hadn't been disturbed; the law hadn't been aware. This time, thanks to Sergeant Edgar L. Croswell, of the New York State Police, it was to be different; and, according to Valachi, "Vito never stopped beefing about that. . . ."

Considerable information has been obtained about the agenda for the Apalachin conference, not just from Valachi but from other informants whose stories have been cross-checked with his by the narcotics bureau. One major purpose was to hear Genovese's explanation of the unauthorized Costello-Anastasia shootings. Don Vitone needed to justify himself before his fellow Mafiosi and to be confirmed in his rule. The conclave was scheduled as a virtual replay of the 1931 grand council session in Chicago at which Luciano and Genovese had defended themselves for the execution of Maranzano, and the technique was the same—the blackening of the reputation of the departed to exonerate the living for their deeds.

Anastasia's reputation was black enough as it was, but there was no lack of helpers willing to paint it blacker yet if need be. Valachi recalled with contempt the turncoat eagerness of Vincent ("Jimmy Jerome") Squillante, the pint-sized hoodlum who dominated the garbage collection racket. Long one of Anastasia's closest followers, Squillante reportedly was with Big Al in the Park-Sheraton barbershop on the day of his murder. Some say he was seated in the next barber chair and that, when the shots began to pop, he crouched down out of sight. Hardly had the powder smoke cleared, according to Valachi, before Squillante came running, practically panting in his eagerness to inform on his departed patron. Valachi testified:

> Jimmy Squillante requested, "If you want me to say more, more things he has done, call on me." In other words, Albert made Squillante. He made him even a godson. In other words, Squillante was getting all the recognition for being with Albert. Now that he was dead he was kicking that he was willing to testify against him. They told him, "All right, if we need you, we will call you." Lots of remarks were passed about it. In other words, the punk, now he is looking to hang him.

With this kind of help, Genovese couldn't lose, and it seems certain that one accomplishment at Apalachin was the ratification of Anastasia's murder as justified and the recognition of Genovese as the new power in the New York Mafia. A second issue on which agreement apparently was reached concerned the Mafia's role in the narcotics traffic.

This was becoming an ever more hazardous business. The Federal Bureau of Narcotics, with a relentless drive in this country and with skilled agents working undercover in both Sicily and Italy, had broken a whole series of important cases. The bureau's success posed one threat; public opinion, another. The very persons who saw nothing wrong with betting with a bookie or playing the numbers or borrowing from a loan shark—all activities that bankrolled the underworld and gave it the money to engage in large-scale narcotics trafficking—became aroused when pushers invaded school yards and initiated teen-aged kids into the euphoria of the needle. A backlash of public sentiment had impelled both state and federal governments to pass new laws imposing far more drastic penalties for narcotics violations.

Assessing all this, the Mafia at Apalachin decided it was time to withdraw discreetly into the shadows. The Mafia had no intention of giving up the traffic entirely; the monetary rewards were too huge for such Spartan self-sacrifice. But Mafia members were not to involve themselves in the hazardous street-pushing end of the operation; this was banned outright. "They even set a date, the end of fiscal 1958, for their members to close out their stocks and clean up pending deals," said one highly placed narcotics expert. "After that . . . they were going to fade practically out of sight. They were going to 'franchise' Puerto Rican groups to handle the drug traffic for them. This meant that the Mafia, with its overseas contacts and sources of supply, would still be supplying the junk, but it wouldn't be taking the risk involved in the actual trafficking; and it would be almost impossible to get evidence against it."

The Mafiosi had other important matters to discuss, but these were never reached. In the midst of the deliberations, the delegates became aware that Sergeant Croswell and fellow state troopers were throwing up a roadblock across the road leading from Barbara's hilltop mansion.

Croswell had been keeping a keen detective's eye on Barbara for several years. The Mafioso had twice beaten what Croswell considered ironclad murder cases, and the detective had become convinced that Barbara was a much more important figure in the sinister brotherhood than was generally believed. His diligence in keeping an eye on activities at Barbara's $150,000 mansion finally paid off in mid-November, 1957, when he learned that Barbara was ordering vast quantities of meat and making a large number of motel reservations in the area. From this, Croswell deduced, correctly, that a huge rally of the clan was imminent.

The instant he began to set up his roadblock, a number of the Mafiosi abandoned their consultations in Barbara's home, jumped into their Cadillacs and Chrysler Imperials, and tried to flee. Croswell and his troopers stopped them one by one as they came down the road and held them for questioning. The roundup netted fifty-eight of the most powerful Mafia chieftains in the nation, and Croswell found that they were all loaded with the kind of pocket cash that was testament to their prosperity. When the sum was totaled, it came to more than $300,000.

The identities of the Barbara fugitives showed how important was the high council meeting that had been broken up by Croswell. Vito Genovese had led the charge down Barbara's driveway to the roadblock. Following him came such powers as these: Joseph Profaci, the Brooklyn don who had attended the first known Mafia grand council session in Cleveland in 1928; Carlo Gambino, the rising new Mafioso; Joseph Bonanno, ruler of the smallest of New York's five Mafia families and the godfather (sponsor) of Joseph Valachi when he was inducted into membership; Mike Miranda, one of Genovese's toughest lieutenants and a man who had spent some time in exile in Italy with the boss during the war; Gerardo ("Jerry") Catena, one of the habitués of Duke's and soon to become chief of the Jersey wing of the Genovese empire; and flashy Big John Ormento, boss of the 107th Street mob and one of the most important figures in the narcotics traffic.

An analysis of the origins of those corralled in the roundup showed that delegates had come to the obscure New York town of Apalachin from New York City, Cuba, Florida, Italy, California and various way stations. When asked to explain their presence in Barbara's mansion, all gave the same ingenious but transparent excuse. They were all, they said, good friends of Joseph Barbara Sr., who had recently suffered a heart attack; and they had all just happened to come on the same day to visit their poor, sick friend and see how he was doing. Barbara was, indeed, ill and was soon to die of his heart ailment; but the idea that his physical condition could have set off a telepathic alarm that had brought some of the toughest hoods of the nation to Apalachin at the same instant must certainly rank as one of the more fanciful tales of the times.

When news of the Apalachin roundup broke, it made headlines across the nation. Despite the Murder Inc. revelations of 1940, despite the Kefauver report of 1951, despite the scandalous North Jersey operation and much else, there had been, incredible as it may seem, heated argument in official circles about the basic question of whether there even was a Mafia. J. Edgar Hoover, the panjandrum of the FBI, had insisted for decades (and was to continue to insist for several years even after Apalachin) that there was no such organization as the Mafia, no such thing as organized or syndicated crime. Hoover, with his enormous prestige, had swayed many and created doubt about a reality that never should have been in doubt; and so, in this respect, Apalachin was important. It was a visible demonstration of a fact of life that could no longer be ignored.

Ironically enough, Sergeant Croswell and his troopers had rounded up only a little more than half of the Apalachin delegates. It is now known from underworld sources that more than one hundred had gathered in Barbara's mansion when Croswell set up his roadblock. Some escaped by fleeing into the neighboring woods, but the majority of those left behind, including leaders of the Chicago syndicate, simply huddled out of sight in Barbara's cellar for several days until the state troopers went away.

Though the headlines and news stories about Apalachin therefore told only half the story, that half was enough to do the Mafia incalculable damage. The now defunct New York *Herald-Tribune* erupted in a roar of editorial outrage, arguing that Apalachin had demonstrated the existence of an "invisible government" of crime so secret and so sinister, possessed of such enormous resources, that it paralleled in its hidden functions the legitimate government of the nation. The *Herald-Tribune* and other papers called for action; and the federal government, heeding the outcry, established for the first time a Special Group on Organized Crime in the U.S. Attorney General's office. The Apalachin delegates were hit with a blizzard of subpoenas and subjected to a variety of prosecutions, trials and harassments. Though many of these failed, Apalachin and its attendant publicity had cost the Mafia dearly.

It had ripped aside the veil of secrecy, had destroyed the most precious Mafia myth—the idea that the Mafia didn't even exist. It had reawakened a law that, for much too long, had been too sluggish and too blind; and only trouble lay ahead.

12.

The Murder Carnival

The era of Vito Genovese was marked by a carnival of murder. Technically, executions were supposed to be carried out, if a major Mafioso was involved, only by decree of the national commission, or, in the case of the lowly "button man," only after a hearing before the powers of his tribal family. But murder now piled upon murder in such swift and gory succession that kangaroo courts would have had to work almost around the clock if hearings were held; and all of the evidence seems to indicate that death sentences now were issued by royal decree.

Some of those who got "dumped" were executed because they had failed or double-crossed the organization and so, in Mafia eyes, deserved their fate; but others were killed, or vanished mysteriously from the world of the living, simply because they knew too much about some of the murders in which the dominant Genovese-Strollo autocracy was implicated. In such circumstances, in the Mafia code, the only safe man is a dead man.

Typical was the exceptionally gory Scalise-Squillante sequence. Frank ("Sceech") Scalise had been for many years the most powerful *Capo* Mafioso in the Bronx. He was on excellent terms with Lucky Luciano, and he never went to Italy without visiting the deported emperor of the rackets. On at least one occasion, he had his picture taken, posing with Charlie Lucky. Scalise, according to the narcotics bureau, was always loaded with talking cash when he went abroad and was always much less heavily burdened when he returned home. But he was always content, for he knew that the heroin for which he had paid would soon follow him across the Atlantic.

"Goddam it," said one of the highest placed narcotics agents at the time, "Luciano was in this traffic; we *know* it. The amounts of money delivered to him by big gangsters in the United States were fabulous. Sccech Scalise and others—they all went to him and dealt with him."

In 1957, however, one of Scalise's heroin deals went awry. Some twenty kilos of heroin were seized, a heavy financial disaster for fellow Mafiosi whom Scalise had brought into the venture. In such circumstances, the originator of the deal is always held responsible if there is some flaw in its execution, and hence Scalise was expected to reimburse his partners. Scalise promised, but didn't pay. Repeated warnings had no effect. And so, about noontime, June 17, 1957, when Scalise stopped at a favorite fruit and vegetable stand at 2380 Arthur Avenue in the Bronx, two young men followed him in, whipped out .38s, and left him dead among the grapes.

According to information that subsequently leaked out, Jimmy Jerome Squillante had been a key go-between in arranging Scalise's murder. One danger in such executions lies in the extremely close family ties among Italians; in the grief of the moment, a bereaved relative is sometimes led to rebel against the deed performed by that larger and more dreadful family, the Mafia. So it was now. Scalise's brother, Joseph, shouted loudly and indiscreetly that he would find out who had killed Sceech and get his revenge. Later, of course, Joseph realized the degree of his indiscretion; and when police questioned him, he adhered faithfully to the code of *omertà*—he knew nothing. He could not be certain, however, that the Mafia was convinced of his steadfastness, and so he departed on a long trip.

Now began a campaign to lure him back. Squillante made the overtures. He passed the word through the underworld grapevine that nobody was sore at Joe for his brother's sins. If Joe would just come home, Jimmy Jerome himself would throw a magnificent party for him just to prove how well he was still regarded by the brotherhood. One federal investigator said:

> Like a fool, Joe Scalise believed it. He came back (this was in September, 1957) and Squillante threw a big party for him at his own house. After the party, they all went to work on Joe Scalise with their knives, and they cut his body up into little, disposable pieces. Then the women of the Mafia took off their party dresses and got down on the floor and scrubbed up the blood.

Squillante, who had been only too happy to perform such services for his Mafia superiors, cast doubt on his own reliability shortly afterwards when he was a witness to the blasting of Anastasia in the Park-Sheraton barbershop. His turncoat eagerness to inform on Big Al carried with it the corollary implication that Jimmy Jerome was not the kind of character in whom the Mafia could repose complete faith in time of crisis. Unfortunately for Squillante, he was now put on the spot in his home Nassau County on Long Island. He was indicted for extortion and scheduled to go to trial on October 20, 1960. He never showed up in court—and for one very good reason. He couldn't. He was dead.

The execution of Squillante was notable for introducing a fiendish new technique in the underworld's Operation Body Disposal. A prominent feature of almost any good-sized auto junkyard is a twelve-foot-high hydraulic press. Two powerful rams, each with a striking power of a million pounds, plunge down into a steel-lined pit, smashing whatever object is in their way. A Cadillac can be placed in the pit, and in ninety seconds it will be hammered into a metal cube 36 inches high, 24 inches long and 24 inches wide. This cube, with a cargo of similar cubes, is then shipped off to a steel mill and plunged into the roaring heat of a blast furnace, where it is melted down to make steel for new cars.

Investigators are positive that Jimmy Jerome Squillante went to his grave in "the crusher." Inveigled out by good friends (it is always those good "friends" in the Mafia who do one in), he was shot and his body placed in a car trunk. Then the car was driven to one of the mob-connected junkyards in the New York area. In seconds it was pounded into just another steel cube, indistinguishable from thousands of other cubes; and there was no chance that the law could ever establish the first prerequisite of a murder case, the body.

"We *know* this is what happened to Squillante, and we suspect it is what has happened to a number of others who have vanished and been merely reported as 'missing,'" one high federal investigator says. . . .

Then there was the case of Anthony ("Little Augie Pisano") Carfano. Little Augie was one of the veteran Mafiosi from the bootleg era of the early '30s, the Brooklyn boss before the days of Joe Adonis. After transferring his operations to Miami, he had faded from the limelight, but he had always maintained close ties with such New York chieftains as Costello, Adonis, and Strollo. The shooting of Costello had outraged Little Augie, just as it had Anastasia, and Little Augie made no secret of his displeasure.

In mid-1957, sometime between the Costello shooting and the Anastasia murder, Vito Genovese called an area meeting of the New York commission in a midtown hotel. His purpose was to explain the past and blueprint the future. Every major mobster in New York heeded the imperial summons, except Little Augie. He pointedly abstained. Genovese was furious and assigned a couple of his "button men" to find Little Augie and hale him into the presence. To Tony Bender Strollo, whom he knew to be a good friend of Little Augie, he raged: "If Augie doesn't come in, you'll be wearing a black tie!"

Augie came, but he made no secret of his feelings. Vito Genovese, a man who could brook no opposition, took offense at Little Augie's obvious coldness and began to act just the way he had in plotting the murder of Willie Moretti. He began to spread stories. Little Augie was weak and not to be trusted, he said; if the law ever caught up with him, he would be certain to break and reveal all the secrets of the brotherhood. This, naturally, was a thought not to be borne. It seemed obvious to Joseph Valachi, listening to the justification that was being put out in advance of the deed, that the skids were being prepared for Little Augie.

Genovese at first assigned a couple of lesser hoods to take care of matters, but they encountered difficulties. "We can't get him alone," they bleated to Don Vitone. "He's always with Bender. Should we kill him, too?"

Tony Bender throughout a long career had been Vito Genovese's most trusted lieutenant, his strong right bower. Vito wasn't ready to part with him—yet.

Having failed to "sneak" Little Augie without Strollo's knowledge, Don Vitone decided he would have to bring his chief lieutenant into the plot. It was a risk, but not much of a one. Tony Bender Strollo's friendship for Little Augie might be quite close, but his fealty to Vito Genovese was more important.

Friday night, September 25, 1959, was Little Augie's night upon the town. He went partying at the Copacabana, where he met Mrs. Janice Drake, the beauty-queen wife of comedian Alan Drake. Little Augie had furthered Alan Drake's nightclub career, and he was considered by the Drakes as a family friend, good old "Uncle Gus." Janice and Uncle Gus had hardly ordered cocktails when, entirely by coincidence, of course, they encountered Tony Bender Strollo, also out for a night on the town. Strollo remarked that he was dining at Marino's restaurant about five blocks away. Wouldn't Augie and Mrs. Drake like to come along? They would—and they did.

Though Little Augie's plans had been indefinite and his meeting with Tony Bender apparently a thing of chance, someone got the word almost the instant Little Augie set foot inside Marino's. A telephone call came for him at the bar from a man whose deep heavy voice, though not his words, was overheard by others. Little Augie chatted with his caller, then went on to dinner. He had arrived at dessert and coffee when a second telephone call came for him. It apparently conveyed exciting news, for when Little Augie returned to the dinner table he was in a fireman's hurry to leave Marino's. He threw down a roll of bills, asking those at the table to settle his tab for him; and then, taking Mrs. Drake on his arm, he walked out into the night.

Some forty-five minutes later, about 10:30 P.M., along a stretch of road not far from New York's LaGuardia Airport, there was an outburst of sound that resembled a series of backfires. Little Augie's big black Cadillac leaped a curb; and when police arrived a few minutes later, they found Little Augie and Janice Drake slumped on the front seat, both dead, their heads drilled with bullets pumped into them from behind.

In the investigation, one striking circumstance was quickly noted by detectives. Tony Bender Strollo and all the major *capos* of the Genovese family, characters like Vinnie Bruno Mauro and Mike Miranda, had been conspicuously upon the town, kicking up their heels in various nightclubs, seen by hundreds, at the hour that murder struck. Their alibis were ironclad, and detectives, defeated before they began, went through the *pro forma* routine of questioning Tony Bender Strollo. The thin, doleful-visaged underboss, who looked at the best of times as if he had just come from a wake, received them politely but with infinite sadness beside the swimming pool behind his New Jersey mansion. It took him some fifteen minutes to tell the detectives how shocked he was at the terrible thing that had happened and to assure them that he had no idea —why, no idea at all—who could have been so inconsiderate as to blast his dear friend into the great beyond.

According to Valachi, the murder of Little Augie Pisano had been quite simply arranged once Tony Bender Strollo put his mind to it. It was obvious, of course, that the telephone calls to Marino's must have come from someone Little Augie trusted completely. This "someone," according to Valachi, was Frank Casino, the loyal Costello henchman who apparently had heeded the warning telephoned to me after the Anastasia assassination. The calls lured Little Augie to the nighttime "business" rendezvous near LaGuardia, and Little Augie did not discover until it was too late that the "business" to be transacted was in the hands of a couple of killers on loan from Vincent ("Jimmy Blue Eyes") Alo's gang of thugs. . . .

Vito Genovese was rampaging through the underworld, a murderous primeval force, knocking off the most powerful Mafiosi who stood in his way or who merely committed the offense of not rendering unto him sufficient homage. His was supreme power, but now, suddenly, he confronted a greater power.

The Apalachin decree against open involvement in narcotics had come too late to help Genovese. In 1957 federal narcotics agents made one of the most important arrests in the history of the bureau. Their prisoner was a small, muscular Puerto Rican named Nelson Cantellops. Charged with selling narcotics on Manhattan's West Side, he was tried, convicted, and sentenced to a four- to five-year term in prison.

Brooding behind bars, Cantellops evidently decided the mob had not done right by him; it had not exerted itself sufficiently to put in the fix. Cantellops became in his own mind a much-wronged man; and so he spilled to narcotics agents the story of his cross-continental career as a narcotics courier, handling shipments of drugs for some of the most powerful Mafiosi in the nation.

He had been introduced to the racket because he owed a gangster $600 that he could not pay. He was told he could square the debt by ferrying ten pounds of heroin valued at $250,000 from Las Vegas to New York. He carried out the mission so successfully that he was soon on a regular shuttle for the mob, making deliveries or picking up incoming shipments in Chicago, Cleveland, Philadelphia, Miami and Los Angeles.

As he became more successful and more trusted, he worked his way up through the ranks of the Mafia until finally his dealings reached the very top. He involved Vincent ("The Chin") Gigante, the Strollo henchman implicated in the Costello shooting; John ("Big John") Ormento, the narcotics kingpin of the 107th Street mob; Natale Evola, one of the powers of the Lucchese family— and finally Vito Genovese himself.

Genovese's involvement, Cantellops testified, came about through a scheme to buy out an East Bronx gambling operation and meld numbers running with narcotics peddling. Ormento was handling the negotiations, Cantellops said, but Genovese, impatient, took a personal hand in the discussion at the end.

"He wanted to know what we decided," Cantellops later testified. "Ormento told him it would cost $150,000 to move into the East Bronx, and said he thought it would be worthwhile. Genovese told him, 'All right, set it up as soon as possible and let me know when I can send the boys in.'"

Cantellops's testimony resulted in the indictment of twenty-four narcotics traffickers, including Vito Genovese, Big John Ormento and Joseph Valachi. Several of those indicted went on the lam, but in the spring of 1959 Genovese and fourteen others were brought to trial in the Federal Courthouse on New York's Foley Square. All were convicted.

Vito Genovese drew a fifteen-year prison sentence. It was to be for him a life sentence; but even in federal prison he was, until he died in 1969, a power to be reckoned with—a man capable of ordering murder from behind bars.

And the New York scene, across which he had slashed his bloody way, was left in turmoil behind him. In his unsanctioned rampages, Vito Genovese had ripped apart the old fabric of commission rule and enthroned again the principle of murder; and it was only logical that, if he could murder his way to the top, others should try it too.

13.

The Wars of Brooklyn

The Gallo brothers were restive and unhappy. They had pulled off one of the underworld coups of the century when they had left Albert Anastasia stone-cold dead on the barbershop floor as a little favor to Joe Profaci and Vito Genovese. Not unnaturally, they expected a reward commensurate with their services. They waited and waited, but no reward came.

Joe Profaci, a chunky square-jawed Mafioso, was one of the tyrants of the clan. In many ways he was an anachronism, a throwback to the days of the Moustache Petes; and he ruled in the modern era in the iron-fisted manner of old, giving little consideration to the sensibilities and desires of his subordinates.

He was not flamboyant. He shunned any cavorting in the nightclubs. He was all business and family, olive oil and rackets on one side; wife and home on the other. Like the old Moustache Petes, he valued most the pure Sicilian bloodline, undiluted by Americanisms, and he regularly gave precedence to followers of Sicilian birth over Brooklyn-born followers who were doing much of the dirty work for him.

His old-fashioned inflexibility was most noticeable in two inviolate rules he imposed on his followers. He insisted that every member of his Mafia family must pay $25 a month in dues into his personal treasury—this long after all other Mafia bosses had abandoned the practice; and he demanded, rather than asked or suggested, that he be given a percentage of every racket that enriched his *capos* and button men. For those who grumbled about the maintenance of such ancient practices in the modern era, Joe Profaci thoughtfully reserved space in a private and secret cemetery he maintained on some New Jersey acres he owned.

After the Gallos had acquitted themselves with such *éclat* in the Anastasia affair, they considered that, as a matter of simple justice, they should be given control of gambling, narcotics and loan-sharking in the East New York section of Brooklyn. There was one hitch: these rackets were the private preserves of some of Joe Profaci's closest friends; and Profaci had no intention of crimping his friends' life-styles to reward the Gallos. Oblivious to the discontent of his prize enforcers, the boss went his own arrogant way and even called upon their expertise to handle another murder item on his agenda.

Frank ("Frankie Shots") Abbatemarco, a policy banker and a member of the Profaci family, had given offense to the boss. Profaci suspected him of the cardinal sin of holding out on the boss's take. Regardless of whether this was true, such a suspicion is never a healthy thing to have instilled in a Mafioso's mind. And so Profaci called in the Gallos and their top enforcer, Joe Jelly, outlining his problem.

Living in precarious unawareness, Abbatemarco went about his usual day-by-day routine; and on November 4, 1959 he stepped out of a Brooklyn bar and was presented with Joe Profaci's greetings—a fusillade of eight shots to the head and body.

The Gallos waited. Surely, this time they would get their reward. But, no, Joe Profaci simply divided up Abbatemarco's business among relatives and friends; the Gallos again were left out in the cold. Their rage at insult added to ingratitude turned them into a ravening wolf pack, and they did the incredible: they defied the boss and the Syndicate.

Leader of the Gallo pack at this time was the oldest of the three brothers, Larry, who in 1961 was in his thirty-third year. After him, a year apart in age, came Crazy Joe and Kid Blast Albert. The Gallos ranked simply as button men in the Profaci family; but their role as the boss's favorite enforcers gave them special status. They had gathered their own followers and were building what amounted to their own regime within the family. Crazy Joe, the most articulate of the three, expressed their philosophy succinctly when he said: "Any man who is strong enough to take something and hold it, he owns it."

Having been shortchanged by Joe Profaci, not once but twice, the Gallos decided in their anger and frustration to see what they could take and hold. They struck on February 27, 1961 when they kidnapped four of Joe Profaci's dearest and closest. They snatched Joseph ("The Fat Man") Magliocco, Profaci's brother-in-law; Frank Profaci, the boss's brother; Sally ("The Sheik") Mussachia, a trusted henchman, and John Scimone, Profaci's bodyguard. They held the four under guard in separate hotel rooms in Manhattan and prepared to parley with Profaci who, unfortunately for them, had escaped the big roundup and sought sanctuary in Miami.

There followed some devious negotiations. The national commission of the Syndicate refused to interfere, holding the dispute was an internal family matter for the Profaci family to solve. Profaci himself agreed to a truce, and the Gallos were given to understand, law enforcement authorities say, that they could operate a variety of rackets with the approval of Profaci and the Syndicate. So they released their prisoners—and were promptly treated to a sophisticated version of the Mafia's favorite tactic, the deadly double-cross.

Joe Jelly, the prize bodyguard of Larry Gallo, was the first to get the word. A beer barrel of a man who walked with a roll, Joe Jelly had a favorite hobby, deep-sea fishing. So, one fine summer day in 1961, a group of close friends, all boys in the rackets, invited him on a little excursion on a cruiser sailing out of Sheepshead Bay. And that was the last the Gallos saw of Joe Jelly.

A few nights later, an unfamiliar car rolled through the streets of Brooklyn's Bath Beach section. As it slowed down near a favorite Joe Jelly hangout in a candy store on Avenue U, the rear door of the car suddenly flew open and a bundle was tossed out. The bundle landed on the sidewalk almost at the feet of some of Joe Jelly's young men. It consisted of Joe Jelly's coat, wrapped around a dead fish.

Before this official obituary notice had been delivered, Larry Gallo also got the news. On the afternoon of Sunday, August 20, 1961, he received a telephone call from John Scimone, the Profaci bodyguard who had been kidnapped and released. Scimone seemed very excited; he had such good news for Larry, he said, that he just couldn't tell him over the telephone. Wouldn't Larry meet him at the Sahara Lounge on Utica Avenue to get the good word and have a drink?

Larry, evidently believing that a peace pact was a peace pact and not yet aware that Joe Jelly had gone deep-sea fishing, went to the rendezvous. Scimone met him, pressed a hundred-dollar bill into his hand as an earnest of things to come, and they had a friendly drink together at the bar. Then Scimone excused himself to go to the men's room a la Charlie Lucky at Joe the Boss's last dinner, and Larry was sitting there, drinking and chatting with the bartender, when he saw, in the mirror over the bar, a rope coming out of the darkness behind him and looping around his neck. Before he could move, a hard knee was thrust into the middle of his back, propelling him against the bar, and two strong hands yanked the rope into a strangling garrotte.

In seconds more Larry Gallo would have been dead, but just at that instant the side door of the lounge swung open and a police sergeant making a routine inspection entered. He saw the bartender calmly polishing his glasses and was about to leave when, beyond the end of the bar, he sighted the protruding legs of Larry Gallo.

"Is that something on the floor?" he asked.

With the question, all hell broke lose. Three figures dashed for the door. One fired a shot that wounded the sergeant's partner, waiting beside their patrol car, and then all three piled into a white Cadillac and fled. That was the real beginning of the Gallo-Profaci war.

The Gallos, outmanned and outgunned, holed up in what became known as The Dormitory, second-floor living quarters running through two connected brick-front buildings at 49-51 President Street. They stocked the place with guns, turning it into a virtual arsenal, and a huge refrigerator in the kitchen bulged with food. The Gallos' father, Umberto, presided over the kitchen, cooking for the twenty-five-man Gallo troop, while out front Larry Gallo handled the details of the war against the Profacis.

Inspector Raymond V. Martin, who made repeated raids on the Gallos' headquarters, came to know Larry Gallo well. Moon-faced, round-eyed, smooth-skinned, Larry Gallo was a human enigma. He had a good housewife's passion for cleanliness. He provided cans in which his gang had to dispose of their cigarette ashes and butts. He decreed that the floors of The Dormitory must be swept daily, and once a week both floors and windows were scrubbed with a strong pine deodorant that made the place reek of the great outdoors.

A moody man, Larry Gallo liked music. He played the violin himself, and he had a large collection of records. When he played the records, he turned up the volume, and the strains of "Aida" or "Il Trovatore" or "Carmen" would float out on the air along the South Brooklyn waterfront, music for the whole neighborhood. Larry disdained jazz and pop and minor classical pieces; for him there was only one kind of music—opera.

When Inspector Martin expressed curiosity about these elevated musical tastes, Larry explained:

Mr. Martin, I ain't goin' to be doin' what I'm doin' for the rest of my life. You may not think so, but life is made for finer things. One day, I'm goin' to retire. I don't want to be like so many fellows I know who retire and they can't do nothin'. When I retire, I'm goin' to be cultured. I'm goin' to sit back and enjoy, enjoy.

In the meantime, guns continued to explode in the streets of Brooklyn, and the score mounted to something like six bodies to two against the Gallos. In addition, Crazy Joe got himself arrested on the extortion rap that was to send him to prison. It was in the midst of this uproar that the incident occurred that made the Gallos, improbable as it might seem, the heroes of the moment, wearing the mantle of Robin Hood.

One day in 1962 they were returning to The Dormitory from a neighborhood luncheonette when they saw smoke curling from the third-floor window of a tenement at 73 President Street. Larry Gallo led the charge upstairs to the apartment of Mrs. Sista Biaz, who had gone out to buy some milk, leaving her six small children unattended. When the Gallos burst into the apartment, they found Evelyn Biaz, 5, with her hair ablaze. Larry stripped off his coat and smothered the fire. Then he and his troop formed a human chain, passing the six Biaz children down the stairs to safety. That done, they smashed out a window and tossed burning mattresses and some burning chairs into the street. By the time firemen arrived, the blaze was out, the children rescued; there was nothing to be done.

"They are good boys, Gold bless them," Mrs. Biaz told the press.

Larry Gallo had labored so heroically that he had to be taken to a hospital for smoke inhalation, but the rest of the troop, rising to the occasion, tossed some money into a hat and began to solicit neighborhood shopkeepers for a fund to help out the Biaz family. Kid Blast, the only Gallo spokesman left on the scene, was a bit doubtful at first about what the public reaction would be. "With our crummy luck, I suppose we'll get arrested for putting out the fire without a license," he said.

But when the television camera crews arrived, Kid Blast blossomed. "Don't try to make heroes of us," he declaimed magnanimously. "We're not heroes. We only done what any red-blooded American boys would do. Do you see any horns here? I got no horns. We're not animals. We're just human beings trying to get along."

It was a good pitch, the forerunner of a public relations gambit that was to be used before too long to embarrass the FBI and the U.S. Justice Department—and it registered amazingly. Inspector Martin was soon deluged with letters from all over the nation, the theme of most of them being that the Gallos were really fine boys at heart and the cruel police had been unfair to them.

"It irks me terrible that these fine boys to my way of thinking can't get a break in life," wrote a woman from Rochester, N.Y. From a parsonage in North Carolina came a letter praising the Gallos for "the great thing" they had done and "the good" in them. It added: "I hope to read more and good things about you in the future. The aged, the blind, mothers such as Mrs. Biaz must need young men like you to read to them, to baby-sit, take them for walks. Be brave and ask the police and fire department if there isn't something they can find for you to do. . . ."

Inspector Martin almost choked at the idea that Larry Gallo, who had come so close to being scragged in the Sahara Lounge, might turn into a baby-sitter. But he got a chuckle out of the most succinct comment he received—a postcard from Houston, Tex., that seemed to sum up the prevailing public reaction. It read: "Gallo, Si! Martin, No!"

The Gallos most certainly had lost the battle with Profaci, but there were some indications that they had won the war. In 1962 the old Mafia boss lay dying of cancer, power slipping slowly from his moribund hands. Heir to his sceptre was his brother-in-law, Joseph ("The Fat Man") Magliocco. Magliocco had labored faithfully in

Profaci's shadow all his life; he had been with Profaci at the Cleveland and Apalachin Mafia conclaves. But he had attracted almost no attention from the law, a plus; and he had less than overwhelming stature in the Mafia, a minus.

The national commission of the Syndicate was worried about the strife in Brooklyn that seemed to be tearing the Profaci family apart, and late in January, 1962, top-level Mafiosi rallied for an Apalachin-by-the-sea in Miami Beach. Lt. Victor Kaufman, of Inspector Martin's Brooklyn South Homicide squad, kept a close watch on the conclave and concluded that the Mafiosi had determined that peace must be made in Brooklyn, whether Profaci liked it or not.

A new underworld figure, hitherto virtually unknown but soon to become one of the most controversial gang chieftains the Mafia has ever produced, now came into the picture. He was Joseph Colombo Sr., who sometimes used the alias Joseph Lefore. To the New York Police Department, he was known as a K.G. (known gambler); a *caporegima* who operated Profaci's floating crap games, and a close associate of the more notorious gamblers, John Frances and Johnny ("Bath Beach") Oddo. He had suffered just three minor arrests and had been fined twice for gambling.

In the Gallo-Profaci war, Colombo had performed the difficult feat of walking a tightrope between the two hostile factions. The Gallos at one point had plotted to kill him, but by luck or guile he avoided the trap. It was fortunate for the Gallos that he did because, when Profaci died and Magliocco briefly succeeded him, Colombo acted in the role of peacemaker and arranged a truce that placated the Gallos by giving them at least a portion of the racket revenues they had sought. It was the first diplomatic accomplishment in Joe Colombo's rise from mob obscurity to status as a Mafia boss. . . .

Murder continued to winnow the ranks of the old rulers, and the man who held a patent on the bloody franchise, even though he was behind bars in Atlanta, was still Vito Genovese.

Tony Bender Strollo, though a contemporary of Costello and Adonis and Genovese, had made himself the standard bearer for a lot of the Young Turks in the Mafia. He had given his quiet support to the Gallos; and, in defiance of the Apalachin decree banning open involvement in narcotics, he had gone along with the rebellious younger gangsters who had not yet made their killing and were resentful of the older bosses, sitting on their moneybags, who had seen fit to ban this most lucrative traffic.

It was Strollo's misfortune that he became deeply involved in a complicated narcotics-smuggling arrangement that backfired. In October, 1960, federal narcotics agents seized a shipment of ten kilos of heroin that had just been smuggled ashore. More important, they arrested the go-betweens in the transaction and were able to follow the trail to three of Strollo's most important henchmen: Vincent ("Vinnie Bruno") Mauro, Frankie ("The Bug") Caruso, and Salvatore Maneri. Also involved was a lesser but highly important figure in later developments, Vito Agueci, whose brother, Albert, had been a member of the ring and had been murdered because he knew too much.

This disaster for which Strollo was held responsible had international repercussions. The narcotics smuggling operation that had failed was traced to the door of Lucky Luciano, and Italian police decided it was time to put the Mafia's mastermind on the grill. They began questioning Charlie Lucky on January 26, 1962, and they listened for hours as he explained he was just a legitimate businessman who had nothing to do with the world of crime. In the light of the Mauro-Caruso-Maneri episode, however, the old refrain didn't sound quite so convincing, and it was evident to Italian detectives that Charlie Lucky was afraid his luck might be running out. He seemed exceptionally tense, nervous, upset.

Finally, he broke off the questioning, pleading that he had to go to the airport to meet a friend, a motion-picture executive named Martin Gosch. Luciano said police could go with him if they wished, but he simply had to meet Gosch. An English-speaking Italian detective, Cesare Resta, accompanied Luciano. While they were waiting for Gosch's plane to land, Luciano fidgeted nervously, acting like a man under intense pressure. When Gosch arrived, Luciano introduced him to Resta, and the three started to walk out of the air terminal. They had taken only a few steps when Luciano staggered, grabbed Gosch by one arm and gasped, "Martin, Martin, Martin." In seconds, he was dead from a heart attack.

These developments made Vito Genovese distinctly unhappy. He confided his disenchantment to friends who visited him in Atlanta. His wishes, according to underworld informants, were channeled back to Tommy Ryan Eboli, one of his most powerful lieutenants in New York. What followed was predictable.

About 10 P.M. on Sunday, April 8, 1962, Tony Bender Strollo told his wife, Edna, that he was going out to buy some cigarettes and that he would be "back in a little while." It was the longest "little while" on record; Tony Bender Strollo, for decades Vito Genovese's strong right arm, vanished as if some junkyard crusher had incarcerated him in a steel cube—as, indeed, perhaps it had.

Inspector Martin's detectives, canvassing their underworld sources, came up with this account of the Strollo murder: a federal investigation of the narcotics traffic had been getting close to Strollo; Tony had created a host of enemies by his roles in the Costello-Anastasia-Pisano affairs; he had made others by backing the Gallos against Profaci; and, finally, he had blundered in his last great narcotics gamble. According to Martin, the underworld version was that the death sentence passed by Vito Genovese from his cell in Atlanta had been cleared with both Joe Adonis and Lucky Luciano in Italy before Luciano's death.

Joe Valachi, who was a cellmate of Genovese in Atlanta, later confirmed Don Vitone's role in the dispatching of his chief lieutenant. Valchi testified:

Vito Genovese told me, that it was the best thing that could have happened to Tony, because Tony couldn't take it "like you and I," and he is talking to me, and so I looked at him, like I snapped back with my head. I thought maybe he was going to tell me he was an informer or something . . . and I said, "What do you mean?"

And he said, "Well, you know he was a sick guy, and he won't be able to take it like you and I." Like he couldn't take time, to put it this way, time in prison or a long prison sentence, and so that is the best thing that could have happened.

Just another of Vito Genovese's "mercy" killings.

And still Don Vitone was not done. According to Valachi, Vito Agueci convinced Genovese that Valachi had been the informer who had brought such disaster on everyone. Don Vitone gave his cellmate the dreaded Sicilian "kiss of death"; Valachi, living in terror, brained a man who he thought had been commissioned to kill him in prison—and discovered, too late, he had killed the wrong person. A cheap thug who had never given a counterfeit nickel for the lives he had helped to take, he was now outraged at the threat to his own; he was filled with a desire for vengeance; and he squealed loud and long about the hidden secrets of the Mafia, breaching the sacred walls of *omertà*—his defection the almost inevitable, final by-product of the ruthless savagery of Vito Genovese. . . .

There was now a growing, gaping void at the top of the New York Mafia. The all-powerful Mafiosi who had ruled the five clans for decades had all gone—or were going. Frank Costello remained inactivated; Joe Adonis, in exile. Dead were Luciano, Anastasia, Profaci, Strollo. Lucchese was ill and would soon die. Genovese was in federal prison, and his Mafia family, formerly the most powerful of the five in New York, was in the divided caretakership of Tommy Ryan Eboli and Jerry Catena. Joseph Magliocco had succeeded Profaci, but he was a weak and indecisive man for a Mafia boss, his tenure shaky and uncertain. The void at the top yawned invitingly for anyone who, in Joe Gallo's words, was strong enough to take and to hold what he took.

One veteran Mafioso thought that he was strong enough. He was Joseph ("Joe Bananas") Bonanno, ruler of the smallest of the five families but still the overlord of a considerable empire. He had expanded his racket fief from Brooklyn all the way to Tucson, Ariz., where he had a home, and he had various enterprises on Long Island, in the Midwest, Canada and the Caribbean. He now conceived the idea, according to authorities, of adding to these scattered interests by a new Night of the Sicilian Vespers. His blueprint called for the disposal in one bloody thrust of Carlo Gambino, the relatively new boss of the Anastasia family; Thomas Lucchese and Stefano Magaddino, the veteran Buffalo Mafioso.

Obviously, Bonanno did not have the resources to pull off such a coup by himself. He would need help and so, according to underworld sources, he turned to his fellow Brooklyn Mafioso, Joseph Magliocco, the new ruler of the lethal Profaci clan. Magliocco, swayed by the more powerful and dynamic Bonanno, went along with the scheme and passed the murder contract to Joe Colombo. It was pointed out to Colombo that rich rewards awaited him if he performed this chore successfully. Colombo pretended to be entranced by the prospect.

What entranced him, however, was not Bonanno's plot, but the opportunity for a delightful double-cross. The rewards, as Colombo estimated them, might be precariously uncertain with Bonanno and Magliocco, far more likely of collection from a grateful Carlo Gambino. And so, authorities say, Colombo went to Gambino and informed him of the fate being plotted for himself and his fellow Mafiosi.

Don Carlo was by now a power on the board of the national commission of the Syndicate, a man with whom it was not safe to trifle. The commission called upon Bonanno to appear before it and explain himself. Bonanno defied the commission; he refused. He was summoned a second time; again he balked. Appreciating that he was in serious difficulty, he tried to name his son, Salvatore ("Bill") Bonanno, the boss of his family on the premise he himself was retiring into the shadows. The commission refused to accede to this kind of nepotism and named its own boss. The hard Bonanno core within the family refused to accept this decision, and the so-called Bonanno War erupted, with bodies once more being dumped in Brooklyn streets.

In the midst of the turmoil, Joe Bananas himself was kidnapped. He had had dinner with his attorney, William Power Maloney, on the evening of October 24, 1964, and he and Maloney were bidding each other good-night in front of Maloney's home at Park Avenue and 36th Street when two hoods popped out of the night. They seized Bonanno, fired a warning shot at Maloney's feet to freeze him in position, and vanished with their captive.

It was generally assumed at the time that Joe Bonanno would not live another twenty-four hours; but, in his case, the national commission under the guidance of Carlo Gambino was not so precipitate. In January, 1965, while the FBI was hunting for Bonanno's bones, top-level Mafiosi held a board meeting in the Capri restaurant in Cedarhurst, L.I. Five members of the national commission attended: Gambino, Lucchese, Salvatore ("Sam Mooney") Giancana, of Chicago, Magaddino, and Angelo Bruno, of Philadelphia. Giancana and Magaddino voted the death penalty, thumbs down; but Carlo Gambino favored a more moderate course.

Shortly after the grand council session, Gambino discussed the situation at a Manhatten luncheon with Sam ("Sam the Plumber") DeCavalcante, boss of a small New Jersey Mafia family. And DeCavalcante, not knowing that the FBI had bugged his office, briefed his underboss, Joe DeSelva, a few days later. It was from this bugged conversation that the FBI learned for the first time that Joe Bonanno was still alive. DeCavalcante said:

> They [the commission] haven't decided yet what to do with Bonanno. We figure we'll take him to Florida . . .

[Bonanno] put Magliocco up to a lot of things. He put him up to hit Carl [Gambino] and Tommy Brown. Now they feel that he poisoned Magliocco. Magliocco didn't die a natural death.

They suspect he used a pill on him. That's what he's noted for.

These few lines of conversation contained a world of information about the internal struggles of the Mafia. Joe Bonanno was, in truth, still alive; and he reappeared in public on May 18, 1966, submissive to a decree of the Syndicate that he retire to his Tucson home and stop causing mischief.

Magliocco, whether he died from natural causes as reported or from a poison pill as DeCavalcante suspected, had departed the scene, leaving a void at the top of the old Profaci family. Carlo Gambino filled it by appointment. Grateful to the man who had saved his life, he anointed Joseph Colombo as the new ruler and even elevated him to Profaci's old seat on the national commission. The brotherhood, from Mafiosi to button men, was stunned by the choice. A measure of the prevailing astonishment was recorded in the DeCavalcante tapes. The Jersey boss and his lieutenant, Frank Majuri, were discussing this new development, and their conversation went like this:

DeCAVALCANTE: Joe Colombo. Where's a guy like that belong in the commission? What experience has he got?
MAJURI: This is ridiculous.

It may have been ridiculous, but Joe Colombo was soon to originate a ploy so daring and so ingenious that even the wiliest Mafiosi would not know what to make of it.

14.

Gambino and Colombo

Carlo Gambino is today the godfather. He is the chairman of the Syndicate's national commission and the most powerful Mafia boss in the nation. He rules the largest family, a clan composed of one thousand "made" members and close associates; and he also dominates the old Profaci family, considered by expert investigators to be the second most powerful in New York. "Joe Colombo's relationship to Gambino was more like that of an underboss than of an equal chieftain," says one veteran investigator with intimate knowledge of the inner workings of the brotherhood.

The man who has thus laid claim to the ancient title of "boss of bosses" is now in his seventies, a frail wisp of his former self. In his more rugged days, he packed some two hundred pounds on his burly five foot seven frame, but the years and an incurable heart ailment have wasted him away to 145 pounds and sharpened his facial features. Old pictures show a round-faced, full-cheeked, brown-eyed hood, with thick black hair combed straight back—a countenance that seems as if it must have belonged to a different man. With the lost poundage, the long nose has sharpened into a parrot's beak; the cheeks are wasted and sunken; and the wide, slashing lips that used to be full

219

have taken on exaggerated dimensions above the nar-
rowed chin and are encased in permanent creases that
produce the effect of a never-ceasing, enigmatic smile.

Benign though his appearance is, the godfather is
murder-tough. Yet, as his role in the Bonanno case
showed, he is no Vito Genovese. His manner even when
he is being his toughest—as, for instance, in shaking down
a restaurant proprietor to pay him for "protection"—is
marked by a soft-voiced gentleness and sympathy. It is as
if, when he is about to hit a man over the head, he wants
to assure him that he is performing the deed most regretfully; and his rule as a Mafia czar is marked by the same
accommodating mildness, a desire to negotiate and settle
the most difficult affairs amicably—a trait, however, that
only a fool would mistake for weakness.

Such is the man who was born on August 24, 1900 in a
suburb of Palermo, Sicily. One of his boyhood pals, born
in the same suburb, was to become known in later life as
Thomas ("Three-Finger Brown") Lucchese. Gambino was
twenty-one when he came to America, entering the country illegally by skipping off an Italian freighter docked in
Norfolk, Virginia.

He was not a stranger in a strange land. He already had
contacts here, both family contacts and Mafia contacts. He
went to work at first for a trucking firm owned by his first
cousins, Peter and Paul Castellano, whose sister, Vincen-
za, he later married. Lucky Luciano brought him into the
Mafia, making him a member of the Masseria clan. During
the gang wars of the 1930s, Gambino remained a relatively inconspicuous soldier in the army, carefully picking his
way, frugally husbanding small racket revenues to build
larger revenues in both illegal and legitimate businesses.

His first big strike came in the days immediately following the repeal of Prohibition. When major mobsters sought
new rackets to replace the doomed bootleg trade,
Gambino quietly bought up their stills until he became the
largest moonshiner in the business. Though liquor was
now legal, taxes on it were high, and fat profits could still
be made by turning raw alcohol into cheap booze.

Gambino cashed in on the opportunity that many others ignored. His chain of stills ran from Brooklyn to the Catskills, from Long Island to the New Jersey pine barrens and on into Pennsylvania and Maryland.

While this activity laid the foundation for Gambino's fortune, it also brought him his only term behind prison bars. Internal Revenue agents finally caught up with him; he was convicted of running a huge, million-gallon still in Pennsylvania; and on May 29, 1939 he was sentenced to serve twenty-two months in prison.

He had hardly been released from Lewisburg Federal Penitentiary when World War II opened up for him new and enchanting vistas for profit. Goods of all kinds were scarce; everything from meat to gasoline was rationed. Accordingly, Gambino and his brother, Paola, set up a ring that did a roaring business in the ration stamp black market. Joseph Valachi later described the racket in these words:

> . . . Him [Carlo] and his brother Paul and Sam Accardi [a New Jersey gangster who has since been deported] made over a million from ration stamps during the war. The stamps came out of the O.P.A.'s [Office of Price Administration's] offices. First Carlo's boys would steal them. Then, when the government started hiding them in banks, Carlo made contact and the O.P.A. men sold him the stamps. He really got rich on that.

Bankrolled by such ill-gotten fortunes, Carlo Gambino penetrated the life of legitimate businesses on a broad scale in the postwar era. His cousins, the Castellanos, became important in the wholesale and retail meat markets. Either through his relatives or front men, Gambino controlled supermarkets, garment factories, pizza parlors, restaurants, bars, nightclubs, vending machine companies, garbage hauling, real estate, and construction firms. His underworld power, especially his strong hold on certain unions, was used to aid and abet his semi-lawful activities.

The most glaring example of this was Gambino's career as a "labor consultant." He even had his own firm, S.G.S.

Associates. The "G" stood for Gambino, and his partners were Henry Saltzstein, a convicted burglar and bookmaker, and a man named George Schiller. From 1955-65, S.G.S. Associates did a roaring business. The word got around in knowledgeable circles that firms hiring S.G.S. never had any labor problems. As a result, the S.G.S. clients came to include Wellington Associates, the real estate concern owning the Chrysler Building and other major properties; Howard Clothes and the Concord Hotel in the Catskills. Investigations by the FBI and two federal grand juries finally exposed Gambino as the "G" in S.G.S., and the labor consulting firm was disbanded.

With the growth of Gambino's power in the underworld, his illegal empire has expanded on a broad front. His rackets now stretch from western Connecticut to the outskirts of Philadelphia, with an offshoot in New Orleans, where he is in partnership with Carlos Marcello. His mob is active in everything that will turn a dishonest fortune—gambling, loan-sharking on an enormous scale, hijacking (especially along the waterfront and at JFK International Airport), labor racketeering, and narcotics.

The gentle-appearing godfather's role in the drug traffic is a hidden and sometimes ambivalent one. With his lifelong love of the shadows, he has never involved himself as openly as Genovese and Strollo; but federal narcotics agents have linked him on occasion to a ploy that has become a favorite of the Mafia. Sicilian aliens, smuggled into this country with the aid of the Mafia, often pay for such help by bringing with them quantities of heroin; and then they become, many of them, new recruits for armies of the brotherhood. Gambino's role in this subterranean traffic was described this way in one federal memo:

> The Gambino brothers (Carlo and Paul) were reported to exercise control of the narcotics smuggling activities between Mafia elements in Palermo, Sicily, and the United States, on behalf of Salvatore Luciano ("Lucky Luciano"). During 1948 both Gambino brothers met with Lucania at the home of their relatives in Palermo.

Investigation conducted by the Bureau of Narcotics, after some thirty odd Sicilian aliens had been smuggled into the United States aboard the *SS Pamorus* at the Port of Philadelphia during May 1948, disclosed that Carlo Gambino was involved in the smuggling of these aliens and that some of the aliens, in turn, had been smuggling substantial quantities of heroin into the United States as payment for being brought into this country.

In recent years, this alien-smuggling, narcotics-smuggling racket has become a major activity of the Mafia, especially across the loosely guarded Canadian border where the powerful Magaddino family of Buffalo and Toronto is strategically placed to further the enterprise.

Though law enforcement agencies all agree that Don Carlo, like almost every Mafioso of stature, has long had his hand in this nefarious traffic, there are times when he likes to play the kindly godfather and protect his own against the ravages he has helped to cause. Paul Meskil, an excellent crime reporter, has recounted the manner in which the godfather "saved" an Italian community in the Fort Greene section of Brooklyn.

The owner of a candy store was selling drugs to school-children. Some of them became mainline addicts. Parents complained to the police, but nothing happened. The candy store proprietor kept right on peddling narcotics. Finally, one distraught mother appealed directly to the godfather.

"My son's on heroin," she told him. "He gets it in a candy store on Myrtle Avenue. The cops can't close this man down and he's ruining a lot of lives."

The very next day, the candy store was closed. The owner had disappeared. And no one in the neighborhood had any idea what could have happened to him.

"God bless that man," said the Brooklyn housewife afterwards, expressing her gratitude to Don Carlo. "He saved the kids in our neighborhood."

The story is not without its deeper meaning. The godfather—the traditional Mafia "man of respect"—often plays the role of benefactor to his people, settling marital disputes, finding jobs for the jobless, performing on occasion services that the law can't or won't perform. For such deeds, he reaps his bountiful mead of credit; he binds the innocent and indebted to him in chains of gratitude and loyalty. Those he has helped in such signal fashion find it difficult to believe, or simply refuse to recognize, that his power to help stems from colossal evil, from pandering to every weakness and vice of man, from undermining broad facets of society, from ruthlessness and brutality and murder.

No Mafioso has ever played this dual role of destroyer and savior with greater aplomb than Carlo Gambino. The godfather throughout his career has shunned the gaudier nightspots in which so many of his kind like to cavort. No womanizer, he was always a devoted husband and father. He has lived for forty years in the neat, two-story brick house at 2230 Ocean Parkway, Brooklyn, in which he raised his family. As prosperity came to him, he indulged in a hundred-thousand dollar waterview ranch house at 34 Club Drive, Massapequa, L.I., where he and his wife would sometimes play host to forty or fifty Mafiosi and their wives at Fourth of July barbecues. Since the death of his wife, however, Gambino hardly ever goes out to his Long Island estate. He lives in "the old house" on Ocean Parkway with his memories, and he putters about the small garden out back where he grows his flowers and tomatoes.

Here he sometimes meets with his underboss, Aniello Dellacroce; here issues his orders; here he rules. The U.S. Immigration Service has tried for years to deport him for entering the country illegally more than forty years ago; but every time the threat becomes serious, the godfather goes into a hospital, suffering from another "heart attack." He is always, at critical moments, just too ill to be shipped abroad or be forced to testify before federal grand juries. He is on the whole a contradictory and bewildering and frustrating figure; but make no mistake about it, he is the most powerful Mafioso in the nation—the man who, with one wave of his thin veined hands, raised Joseph Colombo from obscurity as a mob *capo* to boss of a powerful Mafia family and national prominence.

Joseph Colombo, aside from the role he played in exposing the Bonanno-Magliocco plot, had personal attributes to recommend him when Carlo Gambino elevated him to Mafia boss. The wars of Brooklyn had been attracting too much attention. The headlined Gallo-Profaci bloodletting had been bad for business. A peacemaker was needed, and Colombo in his role as mediator of the Gallo-Profaci *imbroglio* had credibility going for him when he promised to make peace. There was another need. With all of the public attention that had been focused on the Profaci family, it was essential that the new boss be an inconspicuous, low-profile type whom the law could not badger as soon as he ascended the throne. On this count, too, Colombo qualified. The law's dossiers on him were almost nonexistent; and if DeCavalcante and his henchmen found Colombo's sudden prominence "ridiculous," his selection nevertheless had much to recommend it.

Though Colombo would soon be insisting that there was no such thing as the Mafia—it was all a myth made up by law enforcement agencies to traduce honest, hardworking Italian-Americans like himself—his background seemed to give the lie to his protestations. His father, Anthony Colombo, had been a successsful, small-time Brooklyn hood until a misfortune from which he never recovered caught up with him one night in 1938. He was found garroted on the back seat of his car along with his girl friend.

Young Joseph Colombo went to work in a printing plant to support his mother and sister. He enlisted in the Coast Guard in World War II, but he became involved in such difficulties he was sent to a hospital for psychoneurosis treatment and was given a medical discharge. He collected a disability allowance of $11.50 a month.

Returning to Brooklyn, he worked on the piers, then drifted into crime and wound up managing crap games for Profaci. He was clever enough to cover himself with a patina of respectability. He became a licensed real estate agent and worked as a "salesman" out of two Brooklyn firms, Cantalupo and Dart Realty, both of which the Kings County District Attorney's office suspected of being conduits for mob cash. In any event, Colombo's "commissions," said to amount to about $45,000 a year, gave him an ostensibly legitimate source of income of such proportions that it made extremely difficult any prosecution by Internal Revenue, long the nemesis of careless mobsters.

When he assumed command of the Profaci family in 1964, Colombo was only 41, the youngest Mafia boss in the nation. He was short, stocky, dark complexioned, impeccable in dress and manners.

"He's real polished, smooth as silk," said a detective who had all but lived in Colombo's shadow. "If you met him, you would be charmed—you would like him. His whole argument has been that he is a legitimate businessman, but we've tailed him and found him meeting with virtually every important hood in the city."

Such surveillance established that the new Mafioso followed an almost invariable routine. Detectives shadowed him from his home at 1161 86th Street, Brooklyn—a spacious story-and-a-half design, with a small second-floor porch and costly furnishings complete to Italian marble mantelpieces—over to his office at Cantalupo Realty. Most mornings he would leave the real estate office and travel to the Little Italy section of Manhattan's Lower East Side where he would have a cup of morning brew in espresso houses with other mob figures who happened to drop in for a morning pickup.

Virtually everywhere Colombo went in those early days of power, he would be accompanied by his look-alike boydguard, Rocco Miraglia. A detective who had spent many frustrating hours on Colombo's trail said:

It's an amazing thing, but Joe and Rocco are the same height, the same build; they even walk with the same swing to their step. Especially in the winter time, you can't tell them apart from a distance—the same dark overcoats, collars turned up; the same dark fedoras. I know Joe well, but when you see one of them come out of the realty office, I'll say to my partner, "Hey, is that Joe?" And he's likely to say, "No, that's not Joe; that's Rocco." Maybe it turns out it was Joe all the time, but from a distance it's almost impossible to tell them apart. If I was a gangster and I wanted to hit Joe, I'd have to take them both to be sure I got the right man.

All of this tailing and surveillance told authorities much about Joe Colombo's habits—even to the fact that on Friday nights about 6:30 he would often drop into a Chinese restaurant to pick up a couple of boxes of food to take home to the family—but it established little about his activities as a new Mafia boss. Colombo, in this regard, was most circumspect. Known throughout his earlier career as a gambler, he wasn't to be found within leagues of a crap game. He never went to the racetracks. He became a strictly home-to-office-to-home type, frustratingly isolated at the pinnacle of his mob operation. But then, as so often happens if detectives wait and watch long enough, there came the inevitable slip that would swear at all of Colombo's later protestations.

Late on the afternoon of September 22, 1966 police broke up what they called a Little Apalachin in the La Stella Resturant, 102-11 Queens Boulevard, Forest Hills, L.I. The high-level meeting had been called, informants said, to discuss the selection of a successor to Three-Finger Brown Lucchese, who was dying. The diners were all men of decided stature in the underworld: Carlo Gambino; Tommy Ryan Eboli; Santo Trafficante; Carlos Marcello; Mike Miranda—and, of course, that hard-working legitimate real-estate "salesman," Joseph Colombo. . . .

Joe Colombo suddenly scrapped all Mafia traditions and his own lifelong policy of inconspicuousness when he went public in the most public possible way in April, 1970. His son, Joseph Jr., had been arrested by federal authorities on a charge of melting coins into silver ingots (he was later to be acquitted); and Joe Colombo, in a move that left both Mafiosi and federal law enforcement authorities breathless, brashly threw a picket line around New York FBI headquarters on April 30. His pickets carried signs proclaiming that the FBI was persecuting honest Italian-Americans by its campaign against a nonexistent Mafia. Day after day, Colombo led his pickets in the demonstration before FBI headquarters; and day after day, the length of his picket lines grew along with the vociferousness of his denunciations of the bureau and the U.S. Department of Justice. This was such a startling development that, almost overnight, Colombo was being interviewed in the press and appearing on television, wrapped in his new mantle—that of a civil-rights leader.

"According to our information," says one federal investigator, "the older bosses didn't know at first what to think of it. This was contrary to their entire experience, but they weren't certain. It might work, and so they adopted a wait-and-see attitude."

It worked, at first, beyond wildest imagination. Colombo formed the Italian-American Civil Rights League. In the summer of 1970, he held the league's first Unity Day Rally in Columbus Circle—and some fifty thousand persons turned out to join Colombo's civil rights crusade. Politicians began to quake. Colombo, it appeared, was heading a wave of public indignation that could make itself felt at the ballot box. Governor Nelson A. Rockefeller was offered an honorary membership in the league—and accepted.

How had Joseph Colombo, Mafia boss, managed to tap such hidden wellsprings of discontent? Analyses later would seem to indicate that New York's large Italian-American community had developed its own persecution complex; it had begun to feel like a neglected stepchild. Much attention was being focused on other ethnic groups like the Negroes and Puerto Ricans; Italian-Americans felt that, by comparison, they were being treated like second-class citizens. Then along came Colombo, giving vent to their secret frustrations; and almost overnight thousands of honest Italian-Americans, ignoring the quality of the leadership they were being offered, joined his FBI picket lines and swelled the ranks of his civil-rights league.

The results stunned many and seemed to say that, in this society, any kind of a pressure tactic, whether valid or not, gets results. The Justice Department in Washington issued instructions that prejudicial terms like Mafia and Cosa Nostra (Joe Valachi's title for the organization) were no longer to be used. The Ford Motor Company assured the league that its FBI television series would no longer show agents tracking down miscreants belonging to a thing called the Mafia. Alka-Seltzer canceled its prize-winning commercial, "Spicy Meatballs." And when motion-picture producers began to film Mario Puzo's novel, *The Godfather,* Colombo insisted that this account of Mafia intrigue and gore must never mention the Mafia—and Hollywood, too, caved in.

Colombo's league set up storefront headquarters in many sections of Brooklyn, and this, in the words of one investigator, "made it a new ball game." Police could no longer walk in and frisk a suspect as they might have done in the past; now they had to be very careful "about the civil-rights aspect of things." One source says:

> The impression made on our government is one you wouldn't believe. Take Nick Bianco, one of the *capos*— in my book one of the toughest hoods in the family. He was originally a Gallo man during the Profaci war, but he went over to Colombo and remained a Colombo loyalist. Well, you wound up with Nick Bianco having his picture taken with Governor Rockefeller and conferring with Mayor Lindsay in City Hall.
>
> For my money, Colombo did more for the mob than any boss had ever done. He gave them respectability. He claimed 150,000 members for his civil-rights league. Well, I'll give him even more than that. You know Greenpoint? The league's stickers are all over the section. If someone told me the league had 250,000 members, I wouldn't be surprised.

Such were the observable effects of Joe Colombo's hat

trick—by which the Mafia had been made to disappear like a magician's white rabbit. But for every such success there has to be a penalty. Subterranean currents began to work, and the older mob bosses, just as they had feared, began to experience a fallout they did not like.

"The FBI had been keeping track of Colombo and mob activities before he formed his civil-rights league," says one official, "but the FBI's efforts seemed, to gang leaders, at least, to have been greatly intensified after the picketing began. The *capos* and their soldiers found themselves shadowed wherever they went, whatever they did. It became more and more difficult to do business. Finally, even some of the soldiers in Colombo's own family began to rebel because they found they were being so closely watched they couldn't run their rackets as freely as they used to."

Into this nascent unrest, there now popped a catalytic agent that produced a fusion of highly volatile elements— the affair of the black attaché case. . . .

Colombo had been brought to trial for perjury in Manhattan Supreme Court, accused of making false statements when he applied for his real-estate broker's license. On the afternoon of December 10, 1970 he was sitting with his ever-present bodyguard, Rocco Miraglia, in Miraglia's gold Buick station wagon, which had been parked cavalierly in the judges' parking space outside the State Supreme Court. As it happened, FBI agents were looking for Miraglia, who had been indicted for perjury, accused of lying to a Brooklyn Federal grand jury probing organized crime. Spotting Miraglia and Colombo, FBI agents moved in and grabbed Rocco, who was holding the black attaché case.

Colombo began to scream at the top of his lungs: "That's mine, that's mine."

He made a grab for the attaché case, but agents shoved him aside. Since Rocco had the case in his hands, they argued, it must be his, and they hustled away with their prisoner and the prize he was carrying. Colombo's storming and screaming attracted the attention of local patrolmen, and they slapped Miraglia with a $25 ticket for parking illegally in the judges' space.

Denis Dillon, head of the Federal Eastern Strike Force in Brooklyn, later recalled how Colombo accosted him outside his offices, demanding the return of the attaché case and its contents. The case, he insisted, contained only the records of his civil-rights league. FBI agents weren't so convinced. They had had a chance to examine the contents, and they had found long lists of mysterious names—and, opposite them, figures indicating imposing sums of money. Names like "Tony the Gawk," "Frankie the Beast," "John the Wop," and just plain "Carl."

Federal investigators doubted that these gang-sounding aliases applied to innocent civil-rights workers, and they suspected that some of the five-figure amounts listed beside many of the names represented money invested in the loan-sharking enterprises of the Mafia. They told Colombo that, before he could get the attaché case back, he would have to testify before a federal grand jury. He agreed.

He identified "Tony the Gawk" as Tony Angello, now serving twelve years in federal prison for extortion and theft in interstate commerce. "Frankie the Beast" turned out to be Frank Falanga, a long-time associate of Colombo. And "Carl," Colombo admitted, was none other than Carlo Gambino. What did the $30,000 posted after Gambino's name represent? Oh, Colombo explained, that was the sum Gambino had raised by selling tickets to a league civil-rights rally. Aware that Gambino was supposed to be suffering from such a heart ailment that he could not stir from home or honor grand juries with his presence, federal officials were decidedly skeptical about this explanation.

Colombo eventually recovered his papers, but the opportune snatch of the attaché case had far-reaching repercussions. Gambino and the other mobsters whom Colombo had identified had a lot of explaining to do. Many had to appear before a federal grand jury, and they couldn't be

quite certain how much of their account was believed or
what might return to haunt them later.

There were other harassments. Tommy Ryan Eboli,
who, since the death of Vito Genovese, had been sharing
command of the Genovese family with Jerry Catena, was
returning from a trip to Europe. He expected to be treated
like a man of stature and whisked right through customs.
But his name had been on the lists in the black attaché
case; he was taken aside, detained, questioned, every seam
of his baggage examined. Eboli was the very last passenger
to clear customs, an indignity indeed; and, according to informants, he was furious—and blamed Colombo for his
troubles.

Such developments began to build a backlash against
Colombo throughout the ranks of the Mafia. Carlo
Gambino and other mob leaders reached the conclusion
that their original skepticism had been justified; whatever
Colombo's public-relations success with his league, the
price tag on their operations was becoming prohibitive.

The change in the Mafia's attitude toward Colombo and
his public-relations innovation was most strikingly evi-
denced by the withdrawal of support for his second Unity
Day rally in 1971. When the first rally was held in 1970,
all work stopped on the piers so that longshoremen could
attend. Businesses in the Italian sections of Brooklyn and
lower Manhattan closed down for the day. Anthony Scot-
to, son-in-law of the late Tough Tony Anastasio and ruler
of the Brooklyn docks (listed in one federal report as a
Gambino *capo,* a distinction he heatedly denies), was an
honored guest at the first rally but didn't attend the second. His attitude was reflected on the piers where, instead
of closing down, longshoremen kept right on working.
Even many of Colombo's own soldiers didn't take the day
off but continued operating their businesses, legitimate or
otherwise, thus blackballing the second rally.

In addition, there was a revival of Gallo tensions. Colombo had rewarded the maverick clan with the rackets of

East New York, as the Gallos had desired, and all the time
Crazy Joe was in prison, the family had prospered from
revenue derived from a wide variety of sources—vending
machines and jukeboxes, hijacking and shakedowns,
bookmaking and policy, loan-sharking and labor racketeering. Larry Gallo had minded the store, but he had not
had the opportunity to become the cultured gentleman in
retirement and "enjoy, enjoy." He had died of natural
causes shortly before Crazy Joe was released from prison
on parole in 1971.

Unpredictable as ever after his nine years behind bars,
Crazy Joe returned to his President Street haunts and re-
sumed control of the rackets acquired in the Colombo-
engineered peace pact. "He had lost nothing while he was
in prison," one investigator says. And though he made a
great play as the gangster chic of Park Avenue, he was as
tough and arrogant as ever on his native Brooklyn turf.
When Rocco Miraglia came into South Brooklyn to put up
posters advertising the second Unity Day rally, Crazy Joe
ran him right out of the district and personally ripped
down the Unity Day placards.

Such were the behind-the-scenes tensions when Joe Colombo arrived to preside over his second Unity Day Rally
in Columbus Circle on June 28, 1971. The crowd was no-
ticeably smaller than it had been the previous year, but it
was still large and enthusiastic. Colombo smiled, joked,
shook hands, and posed for photographers as he moved
easily through the throng of well-wishers. Then, abruptly
—it was just at 11:45 A.M.—two sharp, staccato sounds
shocked the noisy crowd into momentary silence; and Joe
Colombo was driven into the sidewalk, two bullets in his
brain.

"They've killed Joe! They've killed Joe!" his followers
screamed.

Then there was another sharp burst of gunfire, and a
twenty-five-year-old black, Jerome A. Johnson, of New
Brunswick, N.J., who had gotten close to Colombo, posing
as a photographer, and then had shot him, was killed by

Colombo's bodyguards. Mafia violence had found out Joe Colombo in the midst of a rally dedicated to the proposition that the Mafia doesn't even exist. . . .

Joe Colombo lived. He survived five hours of brain surgery that would have killed a less rugged man. "He's tough," one of his surgeons said. But even Colombo was not tough enough to shake off the terrible effects of the blow that fate had dealt him. He remains paralyzed, unable to talk, unable to command his Mafia legions.

In the weeks and months that have passed since his shooting, the inevitable questions were asked: Who had instigated the attempted assassination? Why?

There were various theories. One was that Carlo Gambino had approved the contract because Colombo's civil-rights antics were hurting mob business. Another pictured Jerome A. Johnson as a loner, a psychiatric misfit who had tried to kill out of some dark inner compulsion of his own. Still a third reconstruction of events—very popular—held that Crazy Joe Gallo had formed an alliance with black convicts while in prison; that Johnson was a recruit of his; that Crazy Joe had learned Colombo had ordered him "hit"—and so he had "hit" Colombo first. In whatever manner rumor and speculation were pieced together, most theories pointed the finger at Crazy Joe Gallo. "Our information is that practically everyone in the Colombo family exclusively blamed Joe Gallo for the shooting," Denis Dillon says.

Joe Gallo went his way undisturbed for nine months after the Colombo shooting until he made that fatal, early-morning visit to Umberto's Clam House. That event naturally revived all the old rumors. According to some reports there had been an "open contract" on Joe for months—that is, he was fair game and anyone who happened to spot him with his guard down was at liberty to take him without the formality of higher authorization. Some detectives insist, however, that they never heard of an "open contract" until the phrases began to appear in the press; mob bosses, they argue, don't leave such matters to chance—they make certain the desired deed is performed by experts, with no likelihood of bungling.

From all that is known of Mafia operations, this makes sense, and because it does, there is another reconstruction of events that seems plausible. It comes from a detective who spent months in 1971 and early 1972 monitoring every movement of Crazy Joe Gallo. He says:

> Three weeks prior to Joe Gallo's getting killed, he, Frank ("Punchy") Illiano and John ("Mooney") Cutrone went out to the San Susan nightclub in Mineola, L.I., in which John Franzese [a powerful *capo* in the Colombo family] is reported to have a hidden interest. Joey is reported to have grabbed the manager and said, "This joint is mine. Get out." In other words, he was cutting himself in.
>
> This was the first sign we had that Crazy Joe was acting up again. Then we come to Easter week, and a lot of things begin to happen. On Easter Sunday night or sometime into Monday morning, there was a safecracking at Ferrara Pastry Shop on Grand Street in Little Italy. [Ferrara's is a famous Italian bakery doing a multimillion-dollar business, a Little Italy landmark since 1892.] It was reported that the safecrackers got $55,000. Now Ferrara's is a legitimate business, but Vinnie Aloi [reportedly the new commander of the Colombo family] is always hanging out around there. It's reported he does a lot of his loan-sharking business in the immediate neighborhood.
>
> O.K. The story about the Ferrara burglary broke on Monday. Tuesday there is a hurry-up meeting at the upstate Saugerties farm of Carmine ("The Snake") Persico. [Persico, now serving a long prison term, heads one of the most powerful and dreaded regimes in the Colombo family.] Vinnie Aloi called the meeting, according to our information, and there were eight guys there.
>
> The very next day, Wednesday, Alphonse Persico, Carmine's brother, and Jerry Angella, his bodyguard, fly to Atlanta to see Carmine in prison. Of course, it may have been just a brotherly visit, but on the other hand. . . .
>
> Well, anyway, on Thursday, we see Gennaro Ciprio on President Street talking to Joey. [Ciprio was a Colombo

bodyguard. He had been on the platform in Columbus Circle when Colombo was shot and nearly went berserk. But he also had some money-making dealings with Gallo, a double tie that could be tolerated as long as just money-making was involved.] We hear during this same week that Joey and Johnny Cutrone have been marked for a hit shortly. At the same time, we notice a change in Joey's pattern. He isn't traveling alone so much. He always has a bodyguard with him, and sometimes he's accompanied by four or five guys in two cars.

Friday morning, Gallo is hit. The way they did it is significant. If the killing had been the result of the Colombo thing, they could have taken him at any time: they wouldn't have had to do it this way. For months, we used to see him driving across the Brooklyn Bridge at night all alone and going down Centre Street; he always followed the same route. All they would have had to do was throw a truck across the road and take him. But, no. They banged him in front of his stepdaughter and his new wife. It shows they meant to disgrace him.

Saturday morning, the day after Gallo is hit, we find the body of Grossman in the trunk of a car, with both eyes shot out. [Richard R. Grossman, 36, was found in the trunk of a car abandoned in a desolate section of Sheepshead Bay, Brooklyn. He had been beaten about the head and face before being killed.] The autopsy showed he had been killed probably on Wednesday, at least two full days before Gallo was hit.

Now we hear Ciprio is carrying a gun. We also learn he had been hanging out in Ferrara's before the burglary. He knew everything about the layout there. Also, there is an association between Grossman and Ciprio. Both were burglars and safemen and had worked together.

Sunday night—that is, early Monday morning, April 10—they bang Ciprio right in front of his sister. [Gennaro Ciprio was caught in a hail of bullets at 2:45 A.M. as he left his restaurant, Gennaro's Feast Specialties at 1744 86th Street, Brooklyn. He had $1,300 cash in his pockets when he was killed.] Again, it's important to remember that they didn't have to do it this way unless there was a special reason. Carmine DiBiase was his godfather. If this all stemmed from the Colombo shooting and Ciprio's association with Gallo, all they would have had to do was to give Carmine the tip, "Hey, tell your nephew to stop going down there to President Street." No, there had to be a stronger reason than that; and the way they did it shows they wanted to disgrace him.

Putting it all together, we believed Grossman and Ciprio went to Gallo and said they could take the safe in Ferrara's, and he gave the okay. That was the straw that broke the camel's back because, from our observation, all of this frantic activity started with the burglary of Ferrara's on Easter weekend.

This detective, one of the best authorities on the Mafia, believes that the "contract" put out on Crazy Joe Gallo was of recent origin, resulting from his maverick cutthroat activities. "There was no animosity when Joey came out of prison," he says. "When the *capos* were asked about him, they'd just shrug and say, 'The guy was in jail for nine years. Leave him alone.'" After the Colombo shooting, the detective says:

We watched Joey going all over town to visit his girl friends, not bothering about protection. . . . If Joey had hit Colombo, you would have had the soldiers of every family after him because the bosses would have been saying to themselves, "Hey, what about us? Are we next?" If the family heads thought he did it, Joey wouldn't have lasted two days.

15.

Black Clouds and the Gold Bug

The Mafia at the close of 1972 was in the worst trouble in its long and bloody history. Misfortunes piled upon it in a seemingly endless chain of disasters.

It was suffering from the loss of top-quality leadership. Repeated exposures and a backlash stemming from them had produced a public less willing to tolerate mayors and judges and congressmen hobnobbing with Mafiosi. Stimulated by the late Robert F. Kennedy when he was Attorney General, state and federal prosecutors had mounted a determined, coordinated attack that led veteran experts on the Mafia like New York's Ralph Salerno to proclaim, "It's a new ball game." An indication that perhaps it was came in October, 1972, when the Mafia, in addition to all its other troubles, was confronted with what may turn out to be the enforcement coup of decades—the successful bugging of a Mafia control post in Brooklyn by the special rackets squad of District Attorney Eugene Gold.

Yet, with all its setbacks, the Mafia is far from dead. There are some twenty-four Mafia families spread across the nation. Their total "made" membership—that is, members inducted into the fraternity by the ancient Mafia blood rite—is only about five thousand. New York re-

239

mains, as always, the hub of this secret criminal power. It is the only city with five active Mafia families. These families represent some 1,700 of the nation's 5,000 "made" members. And they have, like all Mafia families, double or triple that number of associates—that is, members of other ethnic groups who are closely tied to Mafia operations or aspiring young Italian-Americans who carry out the orders of *capos* and button men, hoping to prove that they are worthy of admission to the select and rewarding ranks of the brotherhood.

This is a minute band—the "made" members comprise only about one five-hundredth of one percent of the U.S. population—but it is an organization that has arrogated to itself incredible billions and incredible power. Authorities estimate that the cash flow from various rackets amount to $40 billion a year, with gross profits totaling something more than half of that. This black money, "laundered" by passing through hard-to-trace numbered bank accounts in Latin America and Switzerland, finds its way back into business channels—into ostensibly legitimate operations run by Mafia fronts in the cutthroat, extortionist fashion in which the clan always runs its businesses. In many suburban areas of the nation, it is impossible to get garbage collected or to build a new schoolhouse without dealing at exorbitant prices with Mafia-controlled firms. Through their huge bankrolls and menacing power, these Mafia-held firms have driven out all honest competition.

The riches of Golconda never beckoned more invitingly. It is enough to tempt a saint. And there are not too many saints around. . . .

Mob wars, the attrition of age and relentless prosecutions have winnowed the ranks of the old leadership of the Mafia on both the international and local levels. Joe Adonis, the most prominent Mafioso in residence abroad, died in 1972 of a heart ailment after Italian police, in another of Italy's periodic drives against the Mafia, had pulled him out of his plush Milan apartment and sequestered him in the hills north of Rome. Another who suffered double trouble from a heart ailment and legal harassment was Meyer Lansky, the seventy-one-year-old financial wizard of the Syndicate. He had been one of seven persons indicted by a federal grand jury in Las Vegas, Nevada on charges of skimming $36 million off the top of the gambling take at the Flamingo Hotel between 1960 and 1967. Ignoring federal subpoenas, Lansky had fled to Israel, where for two and a half years his lawyers fought efforts to deport him.

The end of this legal battle came in early November, 1972, when Lansky lost his last appeal, and Israeli authorities ordered him out of the country. There followed a two-day flying odyssey during which Lansky reportedly offered one million dollars to any nation that would grant him sanctuary. But the old boss of the Bugs-and-Meyer mob was now too hot; not even one million dollars could save him. His Braniff International jet liner took him to Argentina, Brazil, Paraguay, Bolivia, Peru, and Panama. Nowhere was he permitted to leave the plane and so, perforce, he had to fly on to Miami where he was delivered into the arms of waiting FBI agents.

Released under $650,000 bail, Lansky promptly went into the hospital for treatment of cardiac insufficiency. He was out again after a week and went into seclusion, facing multiple federal charges for the skimming operation in Las Vegas, income-tax evasion and criminal contempt of court —his fate a symbol of what was happening to veteran Mafiosi on a broad front.

The top command of the New York Mafia families, the most powerful in the nation, has been literally decimated. Carlo Gambino remains the only boss of stature, and even he is in his seventies and in failing health. His Mafia legions, authorities estimate, number some five hundred "made" members and at least an equal number of associates; his "family" is the strongest, the best money-making machine among the five in New York. But what happens when Gambino can no longer direct its activities? It is an uneasy and worrisome question.

Equal in size, but far less powerful, is the old Genovese

family that used to be Number One. It is today much like a rudderless ship. After Genovese's death, his resident caretakers met with misfortune. Jerry Catena is in prison for contempt of a suddenly revivified New Jersey law. And Tommy Ryan Eboli, who shared control with him, was caught in a hail of bullets and slain gangland style about 1 A.M. July 16, 1972 as he left a girl friend's apartment in Brooklyn. This was a murder, authorities believe, that stemmed, not from the Gallo-Colombo feud, but from an internal revolt within the ranks of the Genovese family. The causes are not clear, but the effect was to leave the family for the moment without a powerful, operating chieftain. Control, temporarily at least, is said to be invested in Frank ("Funzi") Tieri, 67, listed in 1964 merely as a button man in one regime of the family. Tieri apparently is having some difficulty establishing clear-cut authority over a group of rebellious Young Turks rallying around another formerly obscure button man, Philip ("Cockeye") Lombardo, who is said now to be "quite highly regarded."

The situation in the strife-riven Profaci-Colombo family has been equally chaotic. One of the most authoritative sources on the Brooklyn mobs rates this as the second most powerful family in New York, with 104 "made" members and some 350 associates. In numbers the family is inferior to the old Genovese mob, but it plays a major role in every racket of the Mafia—hijacking, bookmaking, policy, dice games, loan-sharking on a fantastic scale, and a whole swatch of legitimate businesses ranging from bars and nightclubs to firms in Manhattan's garment center. With Colombo deactivated, control was invested for a time in Joseph ("Joe Yak") Yacovelli, the *consigliere,* or counselor. Yacovelli throughout his career had always treasured his anonymity; and when he was suddenly propelled into the spotlight and summoned before federal grand juries, he did not take kindly to the notoriety. In the spring of 1972, therefore, a change was made, and Vincent Aloi—a *capo* in the organization since 1964 and the

son of the veteran Mafioso, Sebastian ("Buster") Aloi—
was given command of the troop. Vincent Aloi, like Colombo before him, looks and acts the part of a legitimate
businessman. "If you met him at a cocktail party, you
would like him at once," a detective says. "He's smooth,
lots of class. A good family man with three children; goes
to church on Sunday—the whole bit. This is why they
gave him the family. They needed someone with his kind
of image and his ability to handle people." But will Vincent Aloi become another Joe Profaci? It remains to be
seen.

The Bonanno family has suffered more from internal
feuding than any of the others. Hard-core Bonanno followers refused to accept the leadership imposed upon
them by the national commission; indeed, by all accounts,
this leadership was not very impressive. It was changed a
couple of times, apparently in a hunt for the right strong
man who could restore order; and control has now been
entrusted, investigators say, to Natale Evola, a veteran
capo in the Lucchese family who was shifted over to the
Bonanno group. Evola is rated as probably the most capable of the new crop of Mafia bosses.

The Lucchese family from which Evola came is now
under the rule of Carmine ("Mr. Gribs") Tramunti, who
controls a large part of the the numbers racket in East
Harlem and runs one of the major floating crap games in
the city, the so-called "Harlem Game." Tramunti and
Vincent Aloi were both tried and acquitted in Federal
Court in December, 1971, on charges of masterminding a
multimillion-dollar stock swindle in Wall Street—a verdict
that put Aloi in the clear and made him available as the
new boss of the Colombo family. Tramunti, multiple-
chinned and beefy, has power, but it is not the awesome
power of Lucchese, who often dined with mayors, judges
and assistant district attorneys, who bragged that he ran
five garment factories doing a $10 million annual business
and selling one, specially trademarked line to Sears Roe-
buck. "Mr. Gribs" is not so towering a figure; and, in ad-

dition, he has been embarrassed by being enmeshed in the disclosures of the Gold bug.

Years ago, in discussing the crime cabinet that had operated in Duke's under the guidance of Joe Adonis, I asked one of District Attorney Hogan's aides: "Is something like this in operation now?" He replied: "It has to be. I don't know where it is, but something of this kind has to be running somewhere. It's just impossible to manage rackets of such magnitude without a headquarters and an operating staff."

In October, 1972, District Attorney Eugene Gold and his crack rackets-busting staff in Brooklyn disclosed that they had discovered and, for months, they had monitored just such a headquarters. It was located in a blue and gray, two-room trailer parked in an auto junkyard at 5702 Avenue D in the Canarsie section of Brooklyn. The yard was about two hundred by three hundred feet in area. It was surrounded by a twelve-foot high chain link fence, topped by two more feet of barbed wire. At night, it was illuminated by a spotlight and guarded by a watchman and two German shepherd dogs.

The security arrangements, as it turned out, were not anywhere near as perfect as those that had been established by Joe Adonis in Duke's. Joe A.'s screening had been so efficient that investigative agencies had found it impossible to get an agent into his inner sanctum; they had been reduced to learning what they could by more remote surveillance. The Canarsie "summit" headquarters, as Gold called it, proved much more vulnerable.

Gold's detectives began their observation of the trailer during the 1971 Christmas season. They worked from a stand across the street, selling Christmas trees like ordinary Christmas-tree salesmen. Subsequently, by an ingenious bit of detective work whose details have not been disclosed at this writing, they managed to get inside the trailer and install a bug in the ceiling. The device consisted of a silver and copper-colored microphone about six inches long and an inch thick, wired to a transmitter about five or six inches square. The microphone picked up the conversations in this headquarters of crime, and the transmitter sent out the revealing details to be tape-recorded by Gold's listenting detectives.

Gold's men established a lookout post in Nazareth High School, directly across the street from the junkyard, and from this aerie they trained still and motion-picture cameras on the entrance of the trailer. In months-long surveillance, Gold said, his rackets squad compiled this mountain of evidence:

  * 1.6 million feet of tape produced by the electronic bug.

  * 21,600 feet of tape from court-approved wiretapping of the two telephones in the trailer.

  * 36,000 feet of color movies and 54,000 still pictures.

The recorded conversations, Gold said, dealt with almost every crime in the book: narcotics sales, assault and robbery, extortion, hijacking, receiving stolen property, loansharking, counterfeiting, forgery, possession and sale of weapons, official corruption, stolen-auto rings, labor racketeering, insurance frauds, coercion, bookmaking, policy, bootlegging of untaxed cigarettes, prostitution, and liquor violations.

The district attorney promised sensations that would last for months as prosecutors, both state and federal, develop criminal cases based on the evidence disclosed by the Gold bug. The fearful reaction of mob leaders indicated that they felt he might be right.

In the early morning hours of October 16, 1972, the district attorney issued 677 subpoenas—all for persons, he said, who had been identified as having been physically inside the criminal headquarters. A special force of twelve hundred policemen was rounded up to serve the subpoenas under security precautions that were so tight the squads of process-servers had no idea, in most instances, of the magnitude of the case in which they were involved. Such care was necessary, for God's bug had identified

some one hundred policemen—including a lieutenant who
had warned the crime headquarters that its phones were
being tapped—as having had dealings with the staff of the
trailer.

"We have pierced the veil of organized crime, stripping
away the insulation that had hidden and protected many
of the most important people," Gold said.

Two Mafia family bosses—Natale Evola and Carmine
Tramunti—were among those who had been directly implicated by the bug, Gold said, and subpoenas for them
were among the first to be issued.

The trailer headquarters had been under the direct control of Paul Vario, a counselor in the Tramunti family, according to Gold. Police process servers caught up with
Vario as he came out of a bar at 9508 Flatbush Avenue,
Brooklyn, about 4:45 A.M. Vario saw them and started
to run. The policemen gave chase; and, after a four-block
duel of foot leather, they ran down Vario and stuffed the
subpoena in his shirt pocket.

Even more revealing was the reaction of Carmine
("Mr. Gribs") Tramunti. Two policemen staked out before dawn in a car opposite his home at 145-79 Sixth Avenue, Whitestone, Queens. They kept a long vigil opposite
the two-story brick and shingle house until hours after
daylight came. Finally, about 8:45 A.M., Mr. Gribs came
out the front door of his fifty-thousand-dollar home;
yawned, stretched and scratched his beefy midsection.
Then he strode to the curb and climbed into his 1973
Buick Electra.

As he started the motor, the detectives swung their car
across the street and cut him off. They demanded his driver's license and auto registration. Tramunti got out of the
car and took out his wallet. He was so flustered that his
hands shook and he dropped a pack of Pall Mall cigarettes. Detective Kenneth McCabe checked his papers,
then told him: "I've got a subpoena for you."

He handed Tramunti the paper requiring his presence
before a Kings County grand jury. Tramunti obviously
recognized that this meant real trouble. He angrily crum-

pled the yellow sheet into a ball and crammed it into his pants pocket. Then he roared away—in a cloud of exhaust fumes and loud-voiced obscenities.

Index